Joel Dorman Steele

The Story of Rocks

A Fourteen Week Course in Popular Geology

Joel Dorman Steele

The Story of Rocks
A Fourteen Week Course in Popular Geology

ISBN/EAN: 9783744692144

Printed in Europe, USA, Canada, Australia, Japan

Cover: Foto ©Andreas Hilbeck / pixelio.de

More available books at **www.hansebooks.com**

Fourteen Weeks

IN

POPULAR GEOLOGY.

BY

J. DORMAN STEELE, Ph.D.

FELLOW OF THE GEOLOGICAL SOCIETY, LONDON, AND AUTHOR OF THE FOURTEEN-WEEKS SERIES IN PHYSIOLOGY, PHILOSOPHY, CHEMISTRY, AND ASTRONOMY.

"My heart is awed within me, when I think
Of the great miracle which still goes on
In silence round me — the perpetual work
Of Thy creation, finished, yet renewed
Forever." —BRYANT

A. S. BARNES & COMPANY,

NEW YORK AND CHICAGO.

1875.

F. W. G.

TO

MY PUPILS,

WHOSE

NEEDS FIRST SUGGESTED THE PLAN OF THIS SERIES,

AND

IN WHOSE APPRECIATION AND LOVE

I HAVE FOUND MY CONSTANT

SATISFACTION AND REWARD,

This Volume

IS

AFFECTIONATELY INSCRIBED.

PREFACE.

THE present work is based upon the same general plan as the preceding ones of the series. The aim is to make science interesting by omitting the minutiæ which are of value only to the scientific man, and by presenting alone those points of general importance with which every well-informed person wishes to become acquainted. The thing is of more value than the name. A pleasant fact will be recollected long after an unpronounceable term has been forgotten. Therefore, only enough geologic nomenclature is used to make the study systematic, to awaken a love for the order of nature, and to afford a plan around which other knowledge may crystallize.

The author is satisfied from his experience as a teacher that pupils take no interest in the fossils which characterize the various geologic epochs, except the few which are typical, unless they have access to a paleontological cabinet; in that case, they learn the names best by association with the objects. If any attempt is made to name and illustrate the fossils of any group, the limits of a small text-book permit but a scanty selection, which is of little value in the identification of the fossils gathered by a class even within the limits of that group, while to those outside it is useless. Hence a school Geology should give only the general outlines, leaving to the teacher, with a copy of the survey of his own State, and such collections as he may have or can gather, to impart the instruction in local paleontology. The author has sought to develop the following peculiarities: (1) To give the general outlines of each subject, and only enough of the details to interest without burdening the mind; (2) to develop the theories of the science thoroughly, and thus afford a clear idea of the methods of geologic study as a basis for future progress; (3) to give blackboard analyses of each subject for topical recitations; (4) by means of foot-notes to present the pupil with much geologic literature, thus affording the information and culture of an extended range of collateral scientific reading which would otherwise be within the reach of few pupils; (5) to add the benefits of the "question and answer" system to those of the topical method by means of a set of thorough review questions at the close of the book; (6) to lead the pupil to a study of natural objects by treating very fully the stones common in the Drift, and thus giving practical field-work at once; (7) to adapt the book to all sections of our country by means of a clear presentation of the typical New York system, and such modifications in the text or foot-notes as will enable any pupil to make the application to his own State.

It is hoped that this book will render the study of Geology possible to young persons striving after self-education—to men of business, whose leisure allows only a limited acquaintance with books, and to schools where the fresh buoyant spirits of youth are now repelled by cold, formal statements of purely technical truth. The author's most earnest desire is to awaken the thought and quicken the imagination of the pupil; to lead him to trace in nature the hallowing and refining influence of Divine truth, and thus to become one of that happy number who

> "As by some secret gift of soul or eye,
> In every spot beneath the smiling sun
> See where the springs of living water lie."

The author would take this opportunity of thanking the following teachers and friends, who have aided him throughout this entire series with many valuable suggestions, as well as in the reading of manuscripts and proof-sheets: L. S. BURBANK, A. M., Teacher of Nat. Science, High School, Lowell, Mass.; J. J. STEVENSON, Ph. D., Prof. of Geology, West Virginia University; S. G. WILLIAMS, Ph. D., Prin. High School, Cleveland, Ohio; J. W. P. JENKS, A. M., Prin. Middleboro' Acad., Middleboro', Mass.; A. D. SMALL, A. M., Prin. High School, Rockland, Maine; A. P. STONE, A. M., Prin. High School, Portland, Maine; B. S. POTTER, A. M., Prof. of Nat. Science, Illinois Wesleyan University; C. H. CHANDLER, A. M., Prin. Norwood Ladies' Institute, Northampton, Mass., and many others who have kindly furnished the rich fruits of their experience.

The author takes great pleasure, also, in acknowledging his particular obligations to Foster's Mississippi Valley, Winchell's Sketches of Creation, and Agassiz's Geological Sketches. Many of the drawings are copied from nature; the ideal views are taken from Figuier's World before the Deluge. The Scenic Descriptions, which are a peculiar feature of the book, are rhetorical flowers culled from the broad field of geologic literature. The Glossary at the close of the work is based upon standard authorities.

The author would recognize his obligations, in general, to the following authorities:

Manual of Geology	DANA.
Manual of Mineralogy	DANA.
Geological Sketches	AGASSIZ.
Methods of Study	AGASSIZ.
Travels in Brazil	AGASSIZ.
Elements of Geology	HITCHCOCK.
The Mississippi Valley	FOSTER.
Our Planet	DENTON.
Chips and Chapters	PAGE.
Elements of Geology	PAGE.
The Earth's Crust	PAGE.
Past and Present Life	PAGE.
Medals of Creation	MANTELL.
Wonders of Geology	MANTELL.
The World Before the Deluge	FIGUIER.
Elements of Geology	LYELL.
Earth and Man	GUYOT.
Végétation des Diverses Periodes du Monde Primitif	F. UNGER.
Recent and Fossil Shells	WOODWARD.
Man in Genesis and in Geology	THOMPSON.
Acadian Geology	DAWSON.
Old Red Sandstone	HUGH MILLER.
Testimony of the Rocks	HUGH MILLER.
Popular Geology	HUGH MILLER.
State Report of New York	HALL.
State Report of New Jersey	COOK.
State Report of California	WHITNEY.
State Report of Illinois	WORTHEN.
State Report of Pennsylvania	ROGERS.
Manual of Geology	EMMONS.
Elements of Geology	ANSTED.
Siluria (fourth ed., 1867)	MURCHISON.
Sketches of Creation	WINCHELL.

SUGGESTIONS TO TEACHERS.

THE author has followed, in general, the classification given in Dana's Manual of Geology. The teacher will therefore find that book of great value for reference. In the eastern States, Hitchcock's works are of especial service. The geological report of one's own State is essential to furnish local information, and to enable the teacher and pupil to identify the fossils they may gather. Geology can be pursued without a cabinet, and yet a small collection of the most common minerals is almost indispensable, and can easily be obtained for comparison. Fossils are more difficult to secure. The teacher must rely mainly on his own collection and exchanges with friends. Plaster casts of typical genera and species can be purchased of Prof. Henry A. Ward, of Rochester, N. Y. They answer all the purposes of instruction, and in color and form can scarcely be distinguished from the original specimens. Information concerning the cost of small cabinets can be obtained of the publishers of this work. Geological excursions to river channels, quarries, ravines, railroad cuttings, mines, gravel beds, stone fences, &c., furnish most valuable information and healthful recreation. A steel hammer of the form shown in Fig. 1 will be found most generally useful; the edges should be square, the socket large, the handle strong, and the entire weight about two pounds. Rock specimens should not be over three inches square and an inch thick, and should be neatly trimmed. The locality of each specimen should be carefully noted and preserved.

FIG. 1.

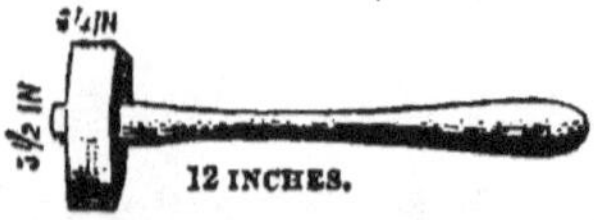

A GEOLOGICAL HAMMER.

The diagram at the commencement of each general subject forms an analysis of the topic. The author is accustomed to have this placed upon the blackboard, and to conduct the recitation from it, without asking questions, excepting as occasion may suggest the necessity of additional information, or a closer investigation of the pupil's knowledge. Questions for review are given in the Appendix. It is suggested that teachers instruct their pupils to assign such fossils as they may find, or have the privilege of examining, *first*, to the sub-kingdom; *second*, to the class; and *third*, to the order, but not to the family, genus, or species, except in case of well-known fossils. Better satisfaction will be given, and results secured, by doing so much well, than by a vain attempt to teach everything in a brief school-term.

Never let a pupil recite a lesson, nor answer a question, except it be a mere definition, *in the language of the book.* The text is designed to interest and instruct the pupil; the recitation should afford him an opportunity of expressing what he has learned, in his own style and words.

CONTENTS.

I.

PAGE

INTRODUCTION, ... 17

II.

LITHOLOGICAL GEOLOGY, ... 35

III.

HISTORICAL GEOLOGY, ... 91

IV.

THE AGE OF MAN, ... 241

APPENDIX.

QUESTIONS, ... 257

GLOSSARY, ... 275

INDEX, ... 277

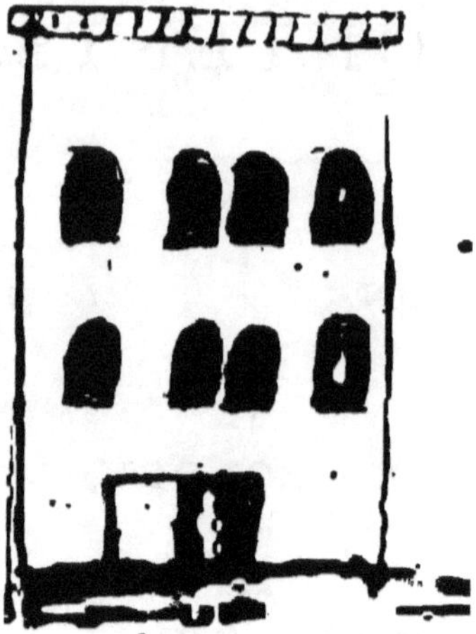

"In the beginning God created the heaven and the earth."

GENESIS i. 1.

ANALYSIS OF INTRODUCTION.

INTRODUCTION.

- I. ORIGIN OF THE EARTH ACCORDING TO THE NEBULAR HYPOTHESIS.
- II. SCENIC DESCRIPTION.
- III. DEFINITION OF GEOLOGY.
- IV. THE EARTH'S CRUST.
  - 1. THE SOLID SHELL.
  - 2. PROOF OF THE INTERNAL HEAT OF THE EARTH.
    - 1. *Temperature.*
    - 2. *Artesian Wells.*
    - 3. *Hot Springs.*
    - 4. *Elevations and Depressions.*
    - 5. *Volcanoes.*
    - 6. *Earthquakes.*
- V. METHODS OF GEOLOGIC STUDY.
  - 1. NATURE'S LAWS UNIVERSAL.
  - 2. SEDIMENTARY ROCKS.
  - 3. TEACHINGS OF SED. ROCKS.
  - 4. IGNEOUS ROCKS.
  - 5. TEACHINGS OF IG. ROCKS.
  - 6. FOSSILS.
  - 7. TEACHINGS OF FOSSILS.
  - 8. GLACIERS.
  - 9. TEACHINGS OF GLACIERS.
  - 10. CHRONOLOGY.
    - a. *Caves.*
    - b. *Lake-bottoms.*
    - c. *Scottish Illustrations.*

Popular Geology.

INTRODUCTION.

*The Origin of the Earth's Crust according to the Nebular Hypothesis.**—Our earth was once, doubtless, a glowing star. In that far off beginning it shone as brilliantly as do now the sun and the fixed stars. In process of time it cooled from a gaseous to a liquid form. It then assumed a spherical figure in obedience to the same familiar laws of force which round a drop of dew. Its atmosphere comprised not only the gases that compose our present atmosphere, but all the oxygen and carbon now locked in the rock and coal masses of the earth—vast quantities of mineral matter vaporized by the fierce heat, and, in the form of superheated steam, all the water which now fills the ocean. The air, thus dense with moisture and poisonous metallic vapors, rested on a seething ocean of fire. Ages passed, and the earth, radiating its heat into space, and thus cooling, began to show on its surface patches of solid substance, like the floating films that first appear

* See Fourteen Weeks in Astronomy, p. 282. THE NEBULAR HYPOTHESIS.

on water as it passes into ice. These, gradually combining, formed at last a thin crust over the entire exterior. This was, however, constantly rent asunder by eruptions from the molten mass beneath. Huge crevices were opened, and torrents of liquid lava, ejected from the cracks and seams, were poured in fiery floods over the scarcely solid crust. The surface, arid and burning, bristled with ragged eminences, or was furrowed with enormous clefts and cracks. But the earth had ceased to shine as a star, and henceforth was itself to be lighted and at last heated from other bodies. As the globe continued to cool, a time arrived when the heat was not sufficient to support the water in the form of vapor. Under the tremendous pressure of the dense atmosphere, the steam was precipitated, boiling hot, upon the heated earth below. Revaporized, it ascended again only to be condensed and returned as rain. This process, long continued, cooled the earth yet more rapidly. The crust, shrinking and cracking as it hardened, became still more uneven with wrinkles and folds, yawning gulfs and fissures. The hot rain falling on the volcanic peaks, the torrents which poured down the mountain sides and through the valleys, all combined to dissolve the rock and sweep the sediment into the deeper hollows. The crust had not yet attained the consistency necessary to resist the pressure of the heated gases and liquids. Hence, in this manner also, enormous dislocations were made, whose folds and uplifts with deep gulfs and belching lavas denoted terrific convulsions. Thus a fierce conflict was raging between fire and water. At last the water triumphed, and the ocean became universal. A hot, muddy, shallow sea surged round the earth from pole to pole. There being no dry land to divert its course, a constant trade-wind must have swept over this primitive ocean spanning the globe.

Astronomy teaches us the probable origin of our globe. As soon as the crust began to be formed by the mingled action of fire and water, Geology steps in to explain the phenomena. In this vague and nebulous border-land the two sciences meet. From that time we find that the earth entered on a regular series of progressive revolutions which gradually fitted it for the introduction of life.

. . . .

The Mosaic Account of the Creation informs us that "the earth was at first without form and void; and darkness was upon the face of the deep." With the first motion of nebulous matter light was developed, or, in the nervous language of Scripture—"God said, Let there be light." Thus ended the work of the first day.*

* The word "day" is of course considered not as a literal day, but as symbolical of a long period of time—ages, during which God was fitting this earth as a home for man. The idea of exact days of twenty-four hours each is neither required by the original nor by the scope of the narration. The word "day" itself is used in four senses in the description. The Christian fathers did not interpret it as a common day. Augustine, in the fourth century, called the days of creation "ineffable days," and described them as "alternate births and pauses in the work of the Almighty—the boundaries of periods in the vast evolution of the worlds." How glorious the idea which we here obtain of God, as, through measureless ages in which he is rich, resting not, hasting not, but slowly and by the steady operation of His own laws, He works out to the finest detail His mighty thought of a world. Moses gives but the grand outline of this creative act, an outline which Geology is filling up rapidly and surely. The Mosaic account is a hymn, full of poetry and grandeur, not a close, exact, scientific record of events. Yet its truths were inspired by the same God who made the world. As such we receive the records of both revelation and nature, and gladly notice their harmony in all their grand teachings. As yet Geology is in its infancy, and we often are able only to suggest and intimate what may hereafter be, firmly believing that God's truth must stand, whether it be revealed in the rock or in the book.

On the second, the firmament or atmosphere was formed, separating the clouds above from the sea below, which, as the revelations of both the rock and the book teach us, as yet covered the entire earth. This was the work of the second day, that long era of cooling and consolidation that separated the formless period of chaos from th birth of the continents.

SCENIC DESCRIPTION.—Let us imagine the scenery of that primitive period. A dark atmosphere of steam, vapor, and sulphurous clouds which conceals the face of the sun, and through which the light of moon or star never penetrates; an ocean of boiling water, heated at a thousand points from the central fire; low, half-molten islands, dim through the fog, and scarcely more fixed than the waves themselves that heave and tremble, lashed into fury by perpetual tempests; roaring geysers, that ever and anon throw up intermittent jets of boiling water and steam from these tremulous lands. In the dim horizon the red gleam of fire shoots forth from yawning chasms, and fragments of molten rock with clouds of ashes are borne aloft; incessant flashes of lightning evoked by the vast chemical changes which are taking place, dart to and fro, shedding a lurid glare upon the seething ocean-cauldron beneath; while bursts of echoing thunder, peal on peal, complete the grand but awful picture.

Geology (*ge* the earth, and *logos* a discourse) may be defined as ***the history of the earth's crust as taught by its rocks and fossils.***

The Earth's Crust.—This is evidently thickening from age to age as the cooling process goes on. Our examination of it is very superficial, extending downward not more than ten miles. On a terrestrial globe, eighteen inches in diameter, the deepest wells, mines, and valleys would be exaggerated by a delicate scratch upon the varnish with a pin. It is generally believed, however, that the solid shell is not over fifty miles in thickness, and that the interior is still a molten mass. The facts upon which this opinion rests are as follows:

(1.) THE TEMPERATURE INCREASES AS WE DESCEND. —The rate varies in different localities, but is always over 1° F. for every hundred feet. At fifty miles this would give a temperature of at least 3000° F., sufficient to melt the most refractory rocks.* Instances illustrating this increase of heat abound in all parts of the world —in frigid Siberia, in temperate Germany, and in tropical Africa. At a depth of fifty or sixty feet in our latitude, there is a uniform temperature unaffected by the vicissitudes of the seasons, and a half mile below us there is summer heat the year round. In a tin mine at Redruth, Cornwall, 1800 feet deep, there is a constant temperature of 100°, equal to that of a hot July day. The miners, it is said, cannot endure their clothing, and are often compelled to ascend part way, and plunge into pools of the cooler water, in order to continue their labor. Similar difficulties also are already experienced in some of the silver mines of the west.

(2.) ARTESIAN WELLS FURNISH WARM WATER.—The hospital at Grenelle is heated by water from an Artesian

* Granite liquefies sooner than soft iron, or at a temperature of about 2,400°.

well 1800 feet deep. At Wurtemburg, large manufactories are warmed in the same manner, the water being conducted through the buildings in metallic pipes. In the Garden of Plants, in Paris, the pipes are laid in the soil; and at Erfurt, Saxony, a salad garden is thus made to yield its proprietor an income of $60,000 per annum. The well at Louisville, Ky., furnishes water of a steady temperature of 76½°, and the one at Charleston, 1250 feet deep, water of 87°.

(3.) Hot Springs and Geysers.—One of the former in Arkansas has a temperature of 180°. The geysers of Iceland and California are fountains of boiling water. The great geyser throws a column of mingled steam and water, eight yards in diameter, to a height of 150 feet. Near the Sahwatch River, Col., is an immense spring so hot that the hunters sometimes cook their provisions in it.

(4.) Elevations and Depressions of the Earth's Crust.—The land in various places has been uplifted or depressed, either by convulsive throes or by a slow movement continued through centuries. This indicates that the ground on which we tread has not an unyielding support.

(5.) Volcanoes.—These throw up great masses of lava, which is merely molten rock. There are estimated to be over 300 volcanoes which are either constantly or occasionally active. The amount of melted matter they eject is enormous. Two streams of lava flowed from Skaptar Jokul, a crater in Iceland, in 1783—one fifty miles long and twelve broad, the other forty miles long and seven broad; each was one hundred feet deep. When we think of such fiery torrents, and that the lava everywhere is essentially the same in its composition, we can but consider the interior of the earth as a melted mass, and the volcanoes as the chimneys of this huge central furnace.

(6.) EARTHQUAKES.—Within the past fifty years, over 2,000 earthquake shocks have been recorded. They are accompanied by volcanic eruptions, jets of boiling water, and heated gases. The only rational explanation is that they are produced by tidal waves or some terrific convulsion in the fiery ocean beneath.

Methods of Geological Study.—UNIFORMITY OF NATURE.—The earth is a microcosm—the universe in miniature. The laws which govern our world govern all worlds. The elements of matter of which it is composed are the same as those which make up the farthest star in space. The earth, therefore, as Prof. Dana beautifully says, though but an atom in immensity, is immensity itself in its revelations of truth; and science, though gathered from our small sphere, is the deciphered science of all spheres. As this world thus reveals to us the laws of other worlds, so the present time makes known to us the laws of past time. The geologist believes in the unchangeableness of God's laws. All results are brought about by established methods. The same effects are always produced by the same causes. The motions of the heavenly bodies, the principles of heat, electricity, chemical affinity, etc., are the same now as they have been from the beginning. The geologist sees God working in nature through the uncounted ages of the past as He works to-day, not fitfully, but uniformly developing the mighty plan of the universe. Thus a knowledge of the present is the magic key whereby the geologist unlocks the history of the past. Let us notice a few of the practical applications of this principle.

Sedimentary Rocks.—The rain which falls on the hills runs down every slope, washing the soil into the brooks and rivers, thence to the lake or sea. It is there deposited as a soft mud or sediment in horizontal layers or strata (singular, *stratum*). The process is necessarily slow, but uninterrupted. Year after year, century after century, adds layer on layer, the more recent deposits concealing the more ancient. If we

FIG. 2.

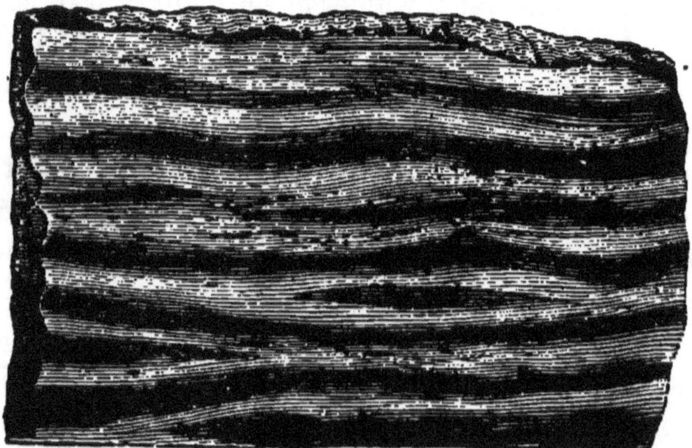

Ripple Marks.

visit the sea-shore, we shall see the fine sand washed up by the waves, and spread, layer upon layer, in a similar manner, each wave rippling its tiny ridges, and covering others beneath its shifting sands. The geologist examines the solid rocks, and finds strata composed of fine sediment arranged in layers, with oftentimes ripple marks curving the surface, appearing as distinct as if the tide had just ebbed. He finds rocks presenting the look of half-dried mud from which the water had been evaporated but yesterday, leaving cracks and even prints of rain-drops so clearly defined that one can tell from what direction the storm came which fell on those mud flats of the olden time. (See Fig. 3.) He notices other strata

FIG. 3.

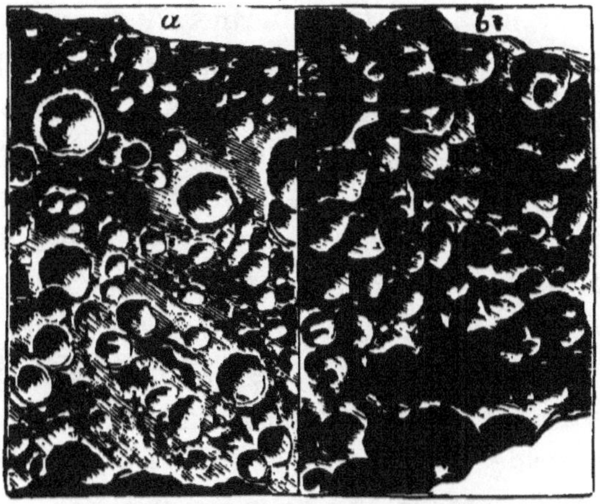

a. Modern impressions of rain-drops.
b. Carboniferous impressions of rain-drops.

composed of sand, gravel, or round water-worn pebbles, such as are now seen along the shore of river or lake among swiftly moving waters. Again he discovers banks of sand or clay where the process of rock-making is still progressing, and the material is in all stages of hardening. He therefore decides that all similar stratified rocks have been formed by the action of water, and hence calls them *sedimentary*.

TEACHINGS OF THE SEDIMENTARY ROCKS.—The water records the history of the land. Not only is the inanimate dust of earth carried into the vast storehouse of the sea, but there lie millions of shells of every shape and hue; there, into the soft, oozy bottom settle the remains of countless fishes which have thronged the waters; thither float leaves and reeds, and trees torn up by the tempest, swept seaward from every shore; there sink skeletons of sea-fowls, exhausted land-birds, and animals borne to the sea by rapid rivers; ships with their unclaimed cargoes, gone on their final voyage, and in harbor at last; drowned mariners lying in their quiet graves unconscious of the fiercest storm that sweeps above them—all these varied relics are slowly buried by the ever-settling sediment. The bottom of the ocean is a cemetery in which lie the dead from the three kingdoms of Nature. Layer by layer are gathered the remains of each passing year, the history of every age being thus deposited and built into the very foundations of the earth. Could we gain access to this sea-bottom, we should find revealed, with each layer turned up by our spade, a fresh page of the history of the world. The ocean is now making up a continuation of this history. The geologist is reading the earlier volumes in the stratified rocks, the sea-bottom of the olden time.

Igneous Rocks.—The geologist watches the action of volcanoes and earthquakes at the present day. He notices that rocks of various consistency and character are formed from the cooling lava, and that stratified or sedimentary rocks are displaced and rent, the fissures being filled with injected matter. In the earth's crust, at various places, the exact counterparts of these rocks and these displacements occur. The rocks are not arranged in layers, but piled up in mountain masses, breaking through the stratified rocks, tilting and throwing them out of their original positions. The observer has no more difficulty in accepting the evidence that the unstratified rocks give of former igneous action and convulsion than in admitting the eruptions and earthquakes of Etna and Vesuvius.

TEACHINGS OF THE IGNEOUS ROCKS.—The geologist calls all rocks which indicate the action of fire *igneous*, and ascribes dislocations of strata and filling up of cracks with igneous products to the operation of ancient volcanoes and earthquakes. If he is not correct in his conclusions, then Nature is not uniform, and is making the same kind of rock on one day by fire and on another by water, and thus all the history of the past is a delusion.

Fossils (*fossilis*, dug up) is a name applied to all animal or vegetable remains which are found embedded in the rocks of the earth's crust. What we have already said concerning the sedimentary rocks shows us how fossils are now forming and have been formed in all time.* As the autumnal leaf drops into the stream, and

* These remains were known to the ancients, and considered "freaks of Nature." Tradition, which attributed to Achilles and other heroes of the Trojan war a height of twenty feet, is traceable, no doubt, to the discovery of elephants' bones near their tombs. Thus, for example, we are assured that, in the time of Pericles, in the tomb of Ajax was found a knee-bone of that hero which was as large as a dinner plate. It was, probably, the fossil knee-bone of an elephant. The Spartans prostrated themselves before the remains of one of these animals, in which they thought they recognized the skeleton of Orestes. Some bones of a mammoth found in Sicily were considered as having belonged to Polyphemus. Even the learned of a later day were not exempt from these blunders. Felix Plater, Professor of Anatomy at Basle, in 1517, referred the bones of an elephant discovered at the roots of a tree torn up by the wind near Lucerne, to a giant at least nineteen feet high. He even restored it in a sketch which was long preserved in the college at Lucerne. In England, similar bones were regarded as those of the fallen angels! When geology first began to be studied, people generally considered the deposition of fossils as having a connection with Noah's flood. Cuvier found the skeleton

becomes imbedded in its mud—as the trees of the forest are borne down by the flooded river and are ultimately entangled in the sediment of its estuary—as the coral reef and shell-bed are gradually increasing and growing as it were into limestone before our eyes—as the skeletons of animals are drifted by the tide and fall to the sea-bottom or sink into rivers and marshes, and are thus preserved from rapid decay—so in all time past have similar agencies been at work; here preserving the broken twig and the fallen forest, there the coral reef and the shell-bed, and anon the remains of animals that were borne by rivers from the land, or drifted by the waves on the muddy sea-shore.

TEACHINGS OF THE FOSSILS.—Digging in the soil, we find a bone. We examine it. It is one of the vertebræ of a horse. We believe it to be real. It is not a "freak of Nature," but was once part of a living horse. We discover some strange fossil bone, and are led irresistibly to a similar conclusion. The skilful geologist, understanding perfectly the relation that exists between the different parts of the animal frame, whereby each portion subserves its part toward the development of life and its functions, can restore the entire form, and even indicate the habits of the creatures that formerly peopled our globe. For example, a sharp claw belongs to a flesh-eating animal with sharp cutting molars; a hoof, to a grazing species

---

of a gigantic salamander preserved as a specimen of the accursed race swallowed up by the deluge.

When we speak of fossils being converted to stone, we do not mean that the particles of the original substance have been *changed to* stone, but that, as they decayed, they have been *replaced by* stone. This is true, however, only of the fossils of the older formations. The new ones retain their original substance. Shells of the Tertiary Period can often scarcely be distinguished from modern ones, while sharks' teeth exhibit their enamel intact.

with broad molars. Knowing, too, the conditions necessary to the life of such animals, he can also decide upon the climate, food, etc., which then existed. Agassiz, from a single scale, reconstructed an entire fish. Subsequent discoveries proved his idea to be singularly accurate. The restoration of the megalosaur by Hawkins is a remarkable instance of a similar character. (See Fig. 83.)

We visit the sea-shore, and gather shells along the beach. On digging, we discover others buried from sight. These are filled with damp sand, which perfectly retains their impress. In the quarry among the layers of sedimentary rocks, we find similar fossil shells. They are certainly the remains of ancient life, and must have existed when the rock was in process of formation. They prove the rock to have been once under water. If the shells are marine, it was the sea; if fresh water, a lake or river; if intermediate, an estuary. The testimony is as conclusive as if we had lived by that ancient shore, and had witnessed their growth, decay, and entombment in the sand.

In certain clay beds of England, shells are found of species now existing only in polar seas. We thence infer that when that clay was deposited, and those shells were inhabited, a climate similar to that of Greenland must have prevailed in British latitudes. Remains of the reindeer and musk ox occur in France. These indicate a former Arctic temperature, unless we are to suppose that the habits of those animals have entirely changed since the time of their existence in southern Europe.

Action of Glaciers (Glā'-seers). — Philosophers have carefully studied the effects of moving masses of ice. They have seen how the glacier pushes its way down the Alpine valley, grinding, rounding, smoothing, and marking the rocks over which it passes, and depositing at the bottom its burden of débris. They have watched the glaciers of polar regions collecting on the sea-shore until at last great mountains of ice break loose and float southward. They have seen these icebergs grounding and melting in a more genial clime, where they finally drop their load of rocky fragments on the sea-bottom.

TEACHINGS OF THE GLACIERS.—The geologist, in regions now far removed from glacial action, finds the lower extremities of mountain glens and valleys heaped with mounds of sand and gravel, and the rocky surface marked with parallel grooves, such as no known agency except the glacier ever produces. Resting on the lower hills and scattered over valley and plain beyond, he sees great bowlders of a weight far exceeding the transporting power of water, miles removed from their parent rocks, and with their sides smoothed and marked. He ascribes these results to glaciers and icebergs. He assumes that these mountains were once covered with snow, these glens once filled with glaciers, and that these lower lands were the bottoms of seas on which floating icebergs grounded, and, melting, left their loads of rocky débris.

Chronology.—Many geological facts aid in determining the relation of different events in respect to time. The following instances illustrate the method:

CAVES.—In certain caves the bones of various animals are found embedded in a calcareous deposit, which has accumulated on the floor by water slowly dripping from the roof. Many of the bones have been gnawed, and the hollow ones split lengthwise. The geologist ascribes the former to den-frequenting, carnivorous animals like the hyena, and the latter to a marrow-sucking race of men. This conclusion is still further substantiated by finding traces of the hyena, and also stone-hatchets, ashes, and charred sticks of wood. Man, alone, lights a fire. Hence we are as sure of the existence of a rude cave-dwelling tribe of men as if we had witnessed their grim countenances lighted up by the fires of which those fragments were the latest embers. The hyena and the cave-dwellers lived at the same epoch. The deeper the layer the older the remains. If we can only determine the rate at which the soil accumulates, we can estimate with some degree of accuracy their antiquity.

LAKE-BOTTOMS.—We drain a level, basin-shaped meadow. The general form and location suggest the idea that it may have been anciently the site of a lake. The moment, however, we dig below the surface, the geologic evidence converts the inference into a matter of certainty. We pass through first the soil, next a layer of peat, then one of marl, and lastly, one of clayey sediment. In the peat we find antlers of deer and bones of oxen; in the marl, fresh-water shells; and in the sediment, a log hollowed out into a rude canoe. Here we have the whole history of the lake, and in reading it we can trace the successive stages as clearly as if we had lived by its shores from the time it was a sheet of shallow water to the hour of its final obliteration. First, the open lake, over which the simple native paddled his rude canoe; second, the shallower sheet, where fresh-water shell-fish luxuriated in myriads, and succeeded each other, generation after generation; third, the peat marsh, over which deer and oxen occasionally ventured, and were mired; and fourth, the level meadow, when the site became too dry for the peat-forming plants to flourish. We have no exact chronology for these events, and can only decide their order. The canoe may have sunk one thousand or five thousand years ago, for aught we know. If, however, we can form some idea of the rate at which the sediment was deposited, or the marl and the peat formed, we can then judge somewhat of its antiquity.

Scottish Illustrations.—Such ancient lake-bottoms are seen in the Lowlands of Scotland. The geologist finds below the peat-bog the bones of horse, pig, deer, dog, and man; deeper still, the Roman eagle or sword; next, the bones of the wild ox, bear, wolf, beaver; then the wooden canoe; below the marl, bones and antlers of the gigantic Irish elk, and tusks of the great mammoth; and at the bottom the solid rock, strewn with ice-borne blocks—the original bed of the lake when its waters were first gathered together. Occasionally, also, raised mounds of piles, plank, branches, stones, and other material are laid bare. These were the foundations of the lake-dwellings of former days, raised by primitive men for their defence. They reveal stone hammers, flint spear-heads, split bones, and fragments of rude pottery-ware. What a marvelous history we read from these records of Nature! In the beginning there is the clear sheet of water rippling in the European landscape—for Great Britain has not yet been separated from the continent—surrounded by forests of pine, birch, and willow. The climate is severe, and the woolly-haired mammoth tramps through the overhanging bushes down to the water's edge. Centuries pass. Reindeer and Irish elk betake themselves to the water in summer, and sink into its miry depths, or seek to cross its frozen crust during the winter's snow, and are buried beneath the treacherous surface. Ages roll on. The climate becomes milder, and Britain is detached from the continent. The lake is gradually becoming shallow; reeds and bulrushes encroach upon its margin; oak clumps adorn its banks, along which prowl the wolf and bear; the beaver builds his dam across the entering stream, and the wild ox and red deer stand lolling in its cool waters. A race of short, broad, round-headed men settle by the shore, pile the mounds and wattle their simple lake-dwellings; with fire and stone adzes scoop out the oak-trunks into canoes, spear the ox and deer in the woods, and enjoy the comforts of a dawning civilization. Time passes. Still the lake grows shallower, and its reedy margin broader. A new race of men—taller, higher-headed, and more nimble —take possession of the scene. They settle the slopes, erect their rude altars in the oak clumps, domesticate the ox, horse, and dog, and attempt a scanty cultivation of the soil. The Roman legions at last—we know the date of that event, about two thousand years ago—invade the country, scatter the natives, and encamp by the lake. They erect their votive altars, make plank roads through the marshy borders, and drop their implements and utensils by the side of those of the ancient Briton. The prehistoric ages have now passed, and we can more easily, but still somewhat confusedly, continue the onward history of the fast lessening waters. The Romans disappear. Celt and Saxon contend for the soil, and we trace in the uppermost bog-earths the remains of existing breeds of oxen, sheep, horses, pigs, dogs, and other domestic animals, and even implements of iron belonging to successive stages of civilization down to the present time.

Lithological Geology.

(A Stone-Discourse.)

> *"And this our life, exempt from public haunt,*
> *Finds tongues in trees, books in the running brooks,*
> *Sermons in stones, and good in everything."*
>
> SHAKESPEARE.

Lithological Geology.

Lithological Geology (*lithos*, a stone, and *logos*, a discourse,) means, literally, a discourse about stones.* It treats of (1) the ***Composition***, (2) the ***Classification***, and (3) the ***Structure*** of the rocks which make up the earth's crust. Underneath the soil and the sea there is everywhere a rocky foundation which protects us from the fiery interior. Along the sea-shore, river-side, road-cuttings, etc., this solid basement is exposed to view. It is generally arranged in layers, sometimes loosely, as sand, clay, or gravel, and sometimes partly hardened into stone. Since it passes thus insensibly

* There is no natural object out of which more can be learned than out of stones. They seem to have been created especially to reward a patient observer. Nearly all other objects in Nature can be seen, to some extent, without patience, and are pleasant even in being half seen. Trees, clouds, and rivers are enjoyable even by the careless. But the stone under the foot has nothing for carelessness but stumbling; no pleasure is to be had out of it, nor food, nor good of any kind; nothing but symbolism of the hard heart and the unfatherly gift. Yet do but give it some reverence and watchfulness, and there is bread of thought in it more than in any other lowly feature of all the landscape. For a stone, when it is examined, will be found a mountain in miniature. The fineness of Nature's work is so great that into a single block, a foot or two in diamèter, she can compress as many changes of form and structure, on a small scale, as she needs for her mountains on a large one; and taking moss for forests, and grains of crystal for crags, the surface of a stone, in most cases, is more interesting than the surface of a hill; more fantastic in form and inconceivably richer in color.—*Ruskin.*

LITHOLOGICAL GEOLOGY.

I. Composition of the Rocks.

- (1.) SILICA
  1. Quartz.
  2. Rock Crystal.
  3. Rose, Smoky, Milky, and Granular Quartz.
  4. Amethyst.
  5. Chalcedony, Sard, Carnelian, Chrysoprase.
  6. Agate, Onyx, Sardonyx, Cameo.
  7. Jasper, Bloodstone, Touchstone.
  8. Opal, Hydrophane.
  9. Sand, Pebbles, etc.
  10. Flint, Hornstone.
  - — Origin of Quartz as Tripoli, Farina, Infusorial Earth, etc.
- (2.) ALUMINA
  - Alumina, Sapphire, Corundum, Emery.
- (3.) LIME
  1. Carbonate of Lime
     - a. Common Limestone.
     - b. Calc Spar.
     - c. Chalk.
     - d. Tufa, Stalactites, etc.
     - e. Oölite.
     - f. Marl.
     - g. Dolomite.
     - h. Marble, Verde Antique, Marble Sawing, etc.
     - — Origin.
  2. Sulphate of Lime
     - a. Uncrystalline—Plaster.
     - b. Crystalline—Satin Spar, Selenite, etc.
- (4.) SILICATES.
  1. Feldspar
     - a. Orthoclase.
     - b. Albite.
     - c. Labradorite.
  2. Mica.
  3. Hornblende, Asbestos, Pyroxene.
  4. Talc, Soapstone, Serpentine, Chlorite.
  5. Garnet.
  6. Tourmaline.

- II. CLASSIFICATION OF THE ROCKS.
  - (1.) SEDIMENTARY ROCKS.
    - 1. SANDSTONE
      - a. Siliceous.
      - b. Argillaceous.
    - 2. CONGLOMERATE
      - a. Pudding Stone. } *Siliceous, Calcareous, or Ferruginous.*
      - b. Breccia. } *Siliceous, Calcareous, or Ferruginous.*
    - 3. SHALE.
    - 4. LIMESTONE (UNCRYSTALLIZED).
    - — SCENIC DESCRIPTION.
  - (2.) IGNEOUS ROCKS.
    - 1. TRAP ROCKS
      - — Description.
      - a. Basalt.
      - b. Greenstone.
      - c. Porphyry.
      - d. Amygdaloid.
      - — Scenic Description.
    - 2. VOLCANIC ROCKS
      - a. Trachyte.
      - b. Lava.
  - (3.) METAMORPHIC ROCKS.
    - 1. GRANITE.
    - — SCENIC DESCRIPTION.
    - 2. GNEISS.
    - — SCENIC DESCRIPTION.
    - 3. MICA SCHIST.
    - — SCENIC DESCRIPTION.
    - 4. SYENITE.
    - 5. QUARTZITE.
    - 6. MARBLE (CRYSTALLIZED LIMESTONE).
- III. STRUCTURE OF THE ROCKS.
  - (1.) STRATIFIED ROCKS.
    - — DESCRIPTION.
    - 1. DISLOCATION OF STRATA.
    - 2. DEFINITIONS.
    - 3. DIVERSE STRATIFICATION.
    - 4. LAMINATION.
    - 5. FAULTS.
    - 6. JOINTED STRUCTURE.
    - 7. FOLDS.
    - 8. CONCRETIONS.
    - 9. SLATE STRUCTURE.
  - (2.) UNSTRATIFIED ROCKS.
    - 1. DEFINITIONS.
    - 2. VEINS.
    - 3. DIKES.
    - 4. ORIGIN OF VEINS AND DIKES.

from one stage of consolidation into another, the geologist applies the term rock alike to all. The desert of Sahara is a sand-rock. Ice is a rock as certainly as is limestone.

1 COMPOSITION OF THE ROCKS.

Rocks are composed, in general, of only three common minerals—*Quartz, Clay,* and *Lime.* Wherever you stand on the solid ground, in any country of the globe, you may be sure that the rock under you is mainly some form or compound of one or more of these earth-builders.*

(I.) SILICA.

1. Quartz (silica, silex) is the oxide of silicon, a rare non-metallic substance known only to the chemist. Silica is the most abundant of all the minerals, comprising one-half of the earth's crust. It is so hard that it strikes fire with steel, scratches glass like a diamond, and

* Since there were so few substances, Nature seems to have set herself about making these three as interesting and beautiful as she can. The clay, being a soft and changeable substance, she doesn't take much pains about—she only brings the color into it when it takes on a permanent form on being baked into brick. (Ruskin's statement does not hold good in America. For examples, the clays of Southern Virginia and North Carolina are beautifully mottled, the cliffs at Gay Head present brilliant tints, and the porcelain clays of Western Kentucky exhibit fine coloring.) But the limestone and flint she paints in her own way, in their native state; and her object in painting them seems to be much the same as in her painting of flowers—to draw us, careless and idle human creatures, to watch her a little, and see what she is about, that being, on the whole, good for us, her children. To lead us to do this she makes picture-books for us of limestone and flint; and tempts us, like foolish children, as we are, to read her books by the pretty colors in them. The pretty colors in her limestone books form those variegated marbles which all mankind have taken pains to polish and build with from the beginning of time; and the pretty

cannot be cut with a knife. It has no cleavage,* and breaks into irregular fragments having a glassy lustre. It is insoluble in any acid (except hydrofluoric), and melts only in the heat of the compound blow-pipe. On

FIG. 4.

A Cluster of Quartz Crystals from Lake Superior.

---

colors in her flint books form agates, jaspers, carnelians, etc., which men have, in like manner, taken delight to cut and polish and make ornaments of from the beginning of time; and yet so much of babies are they, and so fond of looking at the pictures instead of reading the books, that I question whether, after six thousand years of cutting and polishing, there are more than two or three out of any hundred who know, or care to know, how a bit of agate or marble was made or painted.—*Ruskin.*

* Cleavage is the property of splitting with smooth surfaces in certain fixed directions. Many crystals separate very easily in those joinings which Nature has made.

account of its hardness, which resists the action of the elements, it comprises a large part of ordinary pebbles, sand, and much even of the soil. It is found in crystals of the form shown in the figure. When pure, like those of other minerals, they are generally small, and sometimes occur in beautiful clusters. Crystals of great size, though of inferior clearness, are occasionally seen. Dartmouth College cabinet possesses a group weighing 147 pounds. At Milan is a single crystal 3¼ feet long and 5½ feet in circumference, estimated to weigh 870 pounds.

2. *Rock Crystal* is the clear crystalline quartz. The name is derived from the Greek word *krustallos,* meaning ice. The purest specimens are often cut for jewelry, and sold as "white stone" and "California diamonds." They are also used for spectacle glasses. Anciently they were cut into vases and cups, some of which are still preserved as curiosities. It is said that Nero, on learning of the insurrection which led to his fall, dashed into pieces two crystal vases, one valued at $3000. Pure quartz sand is used in large quantities for making glass.

Quartz, when colored by the various metallic oxides, presents a bewildering variety. The young geologist, after having gathered a very respectable collection of minerals, has often been surprised to learn that he has hardly passed outside of this legion family.

3. *Rose or Pink Quartz* is rarely found as crystals, but generally as a massive rock. On exposure to the light, the color fades, but it can be restored by leaving the stone for a time in a damp place.

SMOKY QUARTZ has a dark-brown, smoky tint. It is often black and opaque, except in thin portions, which are semi-transparent.

MILKY QUARTZ is a milk-white, opaque, massive variety, looking not unlike porcelain.

GRANULAR QUARTZ consists of small grains of quartz cemented into a massive rock. It has a texture similar to that of loaf-sugar, and oftentimes crumbles easily into sand. It is used for hearthstones, furnaces, etc., and, when powdered, for making sand-paper, glass, or pottery.

4. *Amethyst* has a beautiful purplish tint from the oxide of manganese, which it contains. The name means "a preservative from intoxication," and was given it from a belief of the ancient Persians, that wine drank from an amethyst cup lost its inebriating properties.

5. *Chalcedony* is distinguished by its waxy, horn-like lustre. It has generally a white or brownish shade. When bright red, it is a *carnelian*. When brownish red, a *sard.* When colored apple-green with nickel, a *chrysoprase.*

6. *Agate* is a kind of chalcedony, in which the different shades of color are arranged in parallel lines—the edges of the layers which compose the stone. These layers are very like the coats of an onion, and represent the successive deposits by which the agate was formed. They are often so thin as to number fifty within an inch. When the lines are zigzag, it is termed a *fortification agate*, from the resemblance to the irregular outlines of a fortress. When the stripes alternate, an opaque with a

transparent band, the stone is termed an *onyx* (*onyx*, a nail), from a fancied resemblance to the alternating lines on the finger-nail. When a deep brownish-red stripe (a *sard*) alternates with a white one, the agate is called a *sardonyx*. When a yellowish-brown oxide of iron is disseminated through the stone in moss-like forms, it is termed a *moss agate*.

Real cameos are cut from the onyx. The most celebrated of the ancient cameos is the Mantuan vase at Brunswick. It was cut from a single stone. It is in the form of a cream-pot, about 7 inches high and 2½ broad. On its outside, which is of a brown color, there are white and yellow groups of raised figures, representing Ceres and Triptolemus in search of Proserpine. The lines of agates sometimes present a striking resemblance to various objects. Some are so remarkable as to be, without doubt, exceedingly ingenious works of art. Thus, Pliny tells of an agate, belonging to Pyrrhus, in which were pictured the nine muses, and Apollo in the midst playing on his lyre. Agates are very abundant on the shores of Lake Superior, and many lakes and rivers of the west. Externally the agate is rough, and exhibits no sign of the beautifully varied appearance it will present when polished.*

* AGATE MANUFACTURE.—The most celebrated agate quarries are at Oberstein, Germany. The nodules are of an ashen-gray color. After being washed, they are placed in a vessel containing honey and water, which, being closely covered, is kept in hot ashes for two or three weeks. The stones are then taken out, cleansed, immersed in sulphuric acid, and then roasted a second time in the hot ashes. The honey, penetrating the pores, is carbonized either by the long-continued heat or the action of the acid. The depth of the color depends on the porosity of the agate. Some become perfectly black, others take a rich brown or chocolate tint, some are striped alternately like the onyx, while others resist all attempts to change the natural hue. By soaking the porous agates in a solution of sulphate of iron, and then heating in an oven, a fine

7. Jasper is a dull, massive variety of quartz, with a little clay. It has shades of red, yellow, brown, and green, owing to the presence of iron in different stages of oxidation. The yellow becomes red by heat, which changes the yellow oxide of iron to red. When the colors are arranged in stripes, it is termed *ribbon* jasper. It is susceptible of high polish, and is therefore much prized for ornamental purposes. When of a deep green, with dark red spots, it is named *blood-stone.* At Paris there is a bust of Christ carved from this stone in such a manner that the red spots represent the drops of blood. A hard, velvet black jasper is called the *touchstone.* It is used for testing the purity of gold alloys. This is done by rubbing the alloy on the stone, and comparing the color with that of some known alloy. The stone is adapted for this purpose because of its hardness and smoothness, and also because it presents a good background on which to compare colors.

8. Opal is a most beautiful variety of quartz. It contains ten per cent of water, which is combined with the silica. It is softer than quartz, and, unlike it, is easily soluble in a hot solution of potash. Its external color is a pure white, but when broken it exhibits a play of rich and delicate internal reflection. A kind called

---

carnelian red is produced. A blue color, which has all the effect of a turquoise, is also developed by a process not yet divulged. By roasting, the natural colors are heightened and rendered more permanent. In these various ways a coarse and valueless stone may be so changed as to pass for a gem of the first quality. The agates are ground on rough stones, turned by water-power from the numerous little brooks which abound in that neighborhood, and polished on soft wooden wheels with powder of tripoli (see page 48) found near by. Vases, cups, seals, knife-blades, agate mortars for the chemist's use, etc., are made in such abundance as to become articles of commerce.

hydrophane is remarkable for becoming transparent when dipped into water.*

9. Sand, Pebbles, Gravel, Cobblestones, etc., consist largely of quartz, since it resists the action of the water longer than other rock materials. The color is due to the various oxides of iron; † although it is sometimes a mere stain produced by vegetable matter.

10. Flint is a compact form of quartz of various colors—white, brown, and even black. It breaks into fragments having a sharp edge and a conchoidal ‡ surface. Its use formerly for gun-flints and by the Indians for arrow-heads is well known.

HORNSTONE is an impure variety of flint, so named from its color and appearance. *Buhrstone* is a kind of flint possessing a cellular texture, which makes its surface very rough. In many of the best stones the cavities equal the solid portions. It is found in various States

* The same phenomenon is shown in an ox's eyeball. When plunged into water, it vanishes instantly from the sight. They refract light at the same angle as water, and hence the eye has no power of distinguishing them.

† Iron is Nature's universal dye. Without it the soil would be a dirty white—the color of snow in a time of thaw. Instead of the pretty lively color of sand and pebbles, we should see the dull and somber hue of ashes; and instead of the glittering sand of the sea and lake shore, a plain drab or gray, which no wealth of sunshine or of spray could turn to beauty. The slates used for roofing have a warm rich tint; oxide of iron puts vermillion into them as it does into our bricks, which else would be only a plain pepper and salt. The ruddy hues of brown now seen in ploughing sandy fields, contrasting so richly with the green of woods and meadow, would be, without the iron, only the cold repulsive gray of clayey soils. Many marbles, too, are colored with this same familiar dye. "The violet veinings and variegations of the marbles of Sicily and Spain, the glowing orange and amber of Sienna, the blood-red color of precious jasper that enriches the temples of Italy," are all painted with iron-rust. Thus by an infinity of design does God, from the simplest, commonest material, interweaving the beautiful in Nature everywhere, cultivate our taste and adorn the world for our happiness.

‡ A conchoidal surface is one that is curved like the outside of a watch-crystal.

—Ohio, Massachusetts, Arkansas, Georgia, etc. The buhrstone of Ohio contains some lime, and it has been thought that the cellular character may be due to the *partial dissolving of the lime out of the stone.*

ORIGIN OF QUARTZ.—Though quartz is a mineral, probably most of the flint and hornstone which we find is of animal or vegetable origin. Sponges secrete little spicules or points of silica. *Diatoms* are minute one-celled vegetable organisms, too small to be seen singly by the naked eye. Yet when gathered in countless myriads, they appear as a brown or reddish slime.* They have the power of separating the silex from the water in some unknown way. These plants grow in such numbers that after their death their indestructible siliceous coverings so accumulate as to form strata of great thickness and extent. The hardness, sharpness, minute size and fragility of the particles, whereby

FIG. 5.

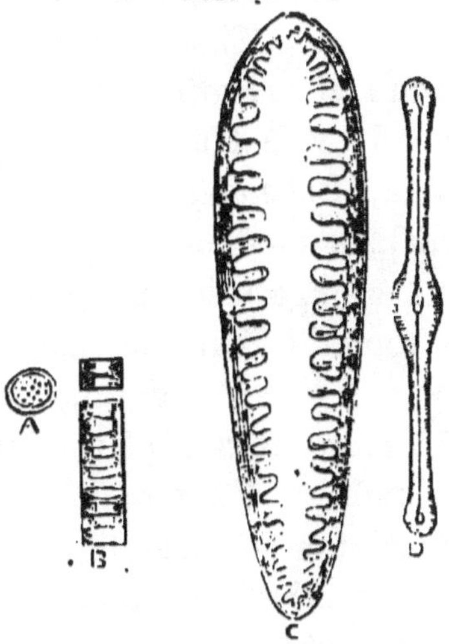

Diatoms from Albany and Waterford, Maine.

B is magnified 25 Diameters.
C is magnified 250 Diameters.
D is magnified 200 Diameters.

* Dr. Hooker, in his account of the Antarctic regions, says: "Everywhere the waters and the ice abounded in these microscopic vegetables. They stained the iceberg and pack-ice wherever the latter was washed into the sea, and imparted to it a pale ocherous color. In the 80th deg. of S. latitude, all the surface ice carried along by currents, and the sides of every berg, and the base of the great Victoria barrier itself—a perpendicular wall of ice from one to two hundred feet above the sea level—were tinged brown from this cause, as if the waters were charged with oxyd of iron." It is a curious fact that these minute, flint-secreting diatoms are the food of the soft, almost impalpable, jelly fish, and, as has been lately stated, that this in turn constitutes the food of the huge whale.

they fall to pieces at the least touch, make the mass useful as a polishing material. *Tripoli*, or polishing slate, is composed of these siliceous remains, a single cubic inch containing 41,000,000, so that at every stroke made with the powder millions of perfect fossils are crushed to atoms. The *mountain meal*, or *fossil farina* of Tuscany, is a mass of these organisms. In Lapland a similar earth is found, which in times of scarcity the inhabitants mix with the ground bark of trees, and use for food. This *infusorial earth*, as it is termed, is found at various localities in this country, as at Richmond, Va., Maidstone, Vt., Waterford, Me., etc. At Bilin, Bohemia, besides a stratum of tripoli 14 feet thick, a kind of semi-opal occurs, composed of diatoms and sponge spicules, cemented with siliceous matter. It is thought that the more delicate shells were dissolved by the water, and thus formed opal cement, in which the more durable of the fossils are preserved, like insects in amber. Flint and hornstone, under the microscope, reveal the outlines of spicules of sponges, of diatoms, and of other animalcules. We are thence led to believe that perhaps the larger part of the quartz we find, in all its Protean forms, has impressed upon it an organic structure which it received at an inconceivably remote time, when it was animated by microscopic life.

(2.) ALUMINA.

Alumina is the oxide of the metal aluminum, which, on account of its abundance in clay, is called the "clay metal." In hardness, alumina is only inferior to the diamond, and will easily scratch quartz. Pure crystallized alumina, when [redacted] (red), constitutes the [redacted] (ruby). This ranks in value next to the diamond, and some perfect specimens have sold at even a higher rate. The dull-colored variety is called *corundum*, and the coarse granular kind *emery*. (See feldspar and common clay, page 53.)

(3.) LIME.

1. Carbonate of Lime is more commonly called "limestone."

(a.) LIMESTONE is a compound of lime and carbonic acid. It embraces all shades from white and cream color to a dense black. It may be known by its softness—being easily scratched with a knife—and by its effervescing with an acid. Limestone is useful for building purposes, and when the carbonic acid is expelled by heat, quick-lime is produced.

(b.) CALC-SPAR (Calcite).—Pure crystals of limestone are called calc-spar. Those having the fundamental form —the rhombohedron—are familiarly termed Iceland spar, as they were first brought from that country. They illustrate double refraction very beautifully.

FIG. 6.

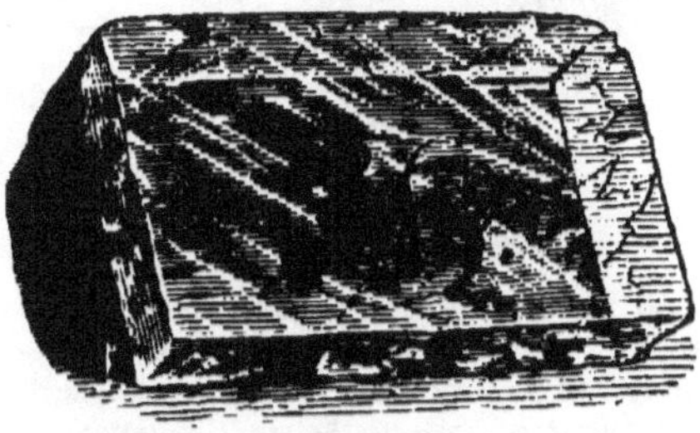

Object seen through Iceland Spar. Crystal from Rossie, N. Y.

(c.) CHALK is a porous, uncompacted variety of limestone.

(d.) CALCAREOUS TUFA * is formed by deposition from

* Calcareous tufa, or travertine, often forms beds of limestone, which can be

water charged with carbonate of lime in solution. (Rev. Chem., page 138.) *Stalactites* depend from the roof of caverns in limestone regions. They are produced, like tufa, from calcareous waters. The water, dripping down from crevices in the rock, evaporates, deposits its limestone, and thus forms pendants of curious and grotesque figures. Some hang like icicles, while others look like falling sheets of water caught in mid-air, and turned to stone. The drippings upon the floor produce calcareous mounds, called *stalagmites*. The two, meeting, often form pillars strangely grouped and interwoven like trees in a forest, and sometimes even combined into broad curtains of semi-transparent rock.

FIG. 7.

Oölitic Marble, Chester, England.

(e.) OÖLITE (*oön*, an egg, and *lithos*, a stone) is a limestone consisting of numerous small, rounded grains, resembling the roe of a fish.

(f.) MARL is a mixture of clay and carbonate of lime. It is loose, friable, and generally full of small shells. It is valuable as a fertilizer.

(g.) MAGNESIAN LIME-

---

used for architectural purposes. The Coliseum at Rome is built of this rock. In the vicinity of Rome a solid layer of this stone, a foot in thickness, has been formed in four months. Springs near the Tiber are famous for their production of travertine.. Indeed, the term travertine means simply Tiber stone. The water of the river near them is so charged with mineral matter that it is said that even fish have been entangled and petrified. In certain regions, springs deposit the tufa so readily that incrustations may be obtained upon sticks, leaves, baskets, etc. At the baths of San Filipo, Tuscany, the preparation of casts in this way forms a regular business. Moss petrified in this manner is so plentiful in Caledonia, N. Y., that it is used for building fences. It is also found in abundance at Chittenango and Sharon Springs.

STONE, or dolomite, contains magnesia. It is harder than limestone, and does not readily effervesce with an acid unless heat is applied.

(h.) MARBLE is crystallized limestone. When pure, it is clear and fine-grained, like loaf-sugar. It is of great value in the arts.* The finest statuary marble comes from Carrara and the island of Păros, whence the term, Parian marble, so famous among the Greek sculptors. The pure whiteness of Parian marble was thought to be especially pleasing to the gods, hence it was selected for the work of Praxiteles and other celebrated artists. The Venus de Medici, the Oxford marbles, and many noted statues are wrought from this stone. An excellent building marble is quarried at Rutland, Vt., in Massachusetts, and in Connecticut. Marble often contains mica and other impurities, which give it a clouded and mottled appearance. This detracts from its value, and ruins it for statuary purposes. *Verde Antique* is a variety of marble streaked with serpentine.

Marble is sawed into slabs by means of a thin iron plate, a saw without teeth, driven by machinery. The friction is produced by sharp sand and water, which are

---

* What are marbles made for? Over the greater part of the surface of the earth we find that a rock has been providentially distributed in a manner particularly pointing it out as intended for the service of man. It is exactly of the consistence which is best adapted for sculpture and architecture. It is neither hard nor brittle, nor flaky, nor splintery, but uniform and delicately, yet not ignobly soft—exactly soft enough to allow the sculptor to work it without force, and trace on it the finest lines of finished form; yet it is so hard as never to betray the touch or moulder away beneath the steel; and so admirably crystallized and of such permanent elements, that no rains dissolve it, no time changes it, no atmosphere decomposes it; once shaped, it is shaped forever, unless subjected to actual violence or attrition. This rock, then, is prepared by Nature for the sculptor and architect, as paper is by the manufacturer for the artist; nay, with greater care and more perfect adaptation.—*Ruskin.*

constantly applied. The saws penetrate very slowly, not more than an inch per hour.

ORIGIN OF LIMESTONE.—Limestone forms a prominent constituent of shells, bones, corals, etc. Animals have the power of secreting the lime from the water in which they live, or from the food they eat. When they die their mineral remains accumulate in great quantities, and gradually harden into rock. Chalk was formed by the consolidation of minute shells, smaller than a grain of sand. As each particle is thus cellular, and not solid, the chalk has a soft porous structure. The microscope reveals these tiny shells in the glazing on a visiting-card. Even when the rock contains no trace of fossils, it may have been made by the sea breaking and grinding shells and corals into a fine powder, just as it grinds rock and pebbles into fine sand. We see this process now going on in the formation of coral-reefs, as, for example, off the coast of Florida. From the vast extent of the limestone rock on the earth, we can form some estimate of the amount of animal life which has existed in past ages.

2. Sulphate of Lime, or, as it is generally called, "gypsum," is a compound of lime and sulphuric acid.

GYPSUM is readily distinguished from limestone by its superior softness. It may be scratched with the finger-nail, and carved with a knife into any desired shape. It does not effervesce with the acids.

(a.) UNCRYSTALLINE GYPSUM is commonly known as "plaster stone." When the stone is crushed and ground it forms a white powder sold as *plaster*, and used as a fertilizer.

(b.) CRYSTALLINE GYPSUM occurs in fibrous masses with a pearly lustre, known as *satin spar;* in scales, layers, and crystals, pellucid as glass, *selenite;* and as a snowy-white solid, *alabaster.*

At Grand Rapids, Mich., a mottled variety is found, which is turned in a lathe into beautiful vases, goblets, and other ornamental objects. In the mammoth cave, Kentucky, are found exquisite forms resembling leaves, flowers, and vines. When burned, gypsum is known as "plaster of Paris."

(4.) THE SILICATES.

The Silicates are compounds of silica with other substances, such as alumina, lime, magnesia, potash, oxide of iron, etc. The following are the most common ones:

1. Feldspar. This is somewhat softer than quartz, and, unlike it, has a regular cleavage on two sides, each crystal showing a flat surface and pearly lustre. It has usually a white or flesh-red color. There are three varieties which are silicates of alumina with an additional substance, viz: *orthoclase* or potash-feldspar, *albite* or soda-feldspar, and *labradorite* or lime-feldspar. Albite (*albus,* white) may always be distinguished by its marked whiteness. Labradorite (originally from Labrador) exhibits often a beautiful play of colors from internal reflection, and is susceptible of polish. *Clinkstone,* so named because of the metallic ring it emits when struck with a hammer, is a compact variety of feldspar.

COMMON CLAY is formed by the decomposition of feldspar rocks mixed with a large proportion of quartz sand. Pure feldspar, when decomposed, produces *kaolin* (high ridge, the name of a hill near Jauchu Fu, where it is obtained), a kind of clay used for making porcelain or China-ware. The red color of bricks is due to the iron contained in the clay. Pipe-clay is free from iron. The beautiful pipe-stone used by the Indians was a compacted red clay from Coteau des Prairies. A bed of similar clay is now accumulating in Lake Superior.

2. ***Mica*** (*micare*, to glisten) is commonly called "isinglass." It is easily known by its lustre and by its separating readily into thin elastic plates, which may again be subdivided until many thousand would be required to make an inch in thickness. It is often seen in sand as bright, glittering particles. On account of its transparency it is used in Siberia for windows. It is employed on board of ships where the concussion would be liable to break glass, and for windows in stoves. At several places in New Hampshire, perfectly transparent plates, two or three feet in diameter, have been obtained.

3. ***Hornblende*** is so named from its toughness. It has generally a black or greenish-black color and a pearly lustre. Some varieties present long, slender, needle-shaped crystals of a delicate green tint and a glassy lustre. *Asbestos* (unconsumed) is so fibrous that it can be spun and woven like cotton. The ancients made it into napkins, which, when soiled, were cleansed by being thrown into the fire, where they were burned clean and white in a few minutes. The Greenlanders use it for lampwicks, and it formerly served a similar

purpose in keeping the perpetual fire in the temples, its incombustibility being thought to render it sacred. It is said that in Siberia and Spain, gloves, purses, etc., are made from *amianthus* (undefiled), a variety of asbestos having a beautiful satin lustre. The finest locality for asbestos in this country is at the Quarantine, New York.

FIG. 8.

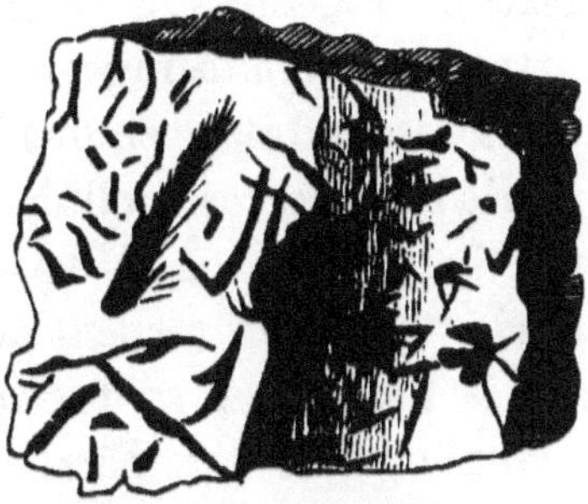

Hornblende Crystals in Quartz. Berkshire, Mass.

PYROXENE, often called augite (from *auge*, lustre), is a dark-green mineral, very like hornblende, and some of its massive specimens can hardly be distinguished from it. Its crystals, however, are stouter and thicker, and are never needle-shaped, though it has a fibrous asbestos which can hardly be distinguished from hornblende except by analysis. Augite is a characteristic constituent of igneous rocks.

4. Talc is so soft that it can be cut with a knife, and even scratched by the finger-nail. It separates readily into thin pearly layers, which are not elastic and tough like those of mica. It has usually a light-green color, and an unctuous feel from the magnesia it contains. A compact variety of talc is familiarly known as "French chalk."

SOAPSTONE or steatite (*stear*, fat) is a massive crystalline variety which is susceptible of being worked into any desired form, and of receiving a high polish. It can be sawed into slabs or turned in a lathe. It is made into inkstands, water-pipes, and fire-stones for furnaces and culinary vessels.

SERPENTINE is a sort of compact talc. It differs from steatite in being less granular and more compact in its texture, and in being sometimes separable into layers; it has also a dull, resinous lustre. It was named from its mottled colors, resembling the skin of a serpent. Stoves have been made of it, as it bears heat well. When polished, "precious serpentine" has a rich, oil-green tint, and is highly valued for inlaid work.

CHLORITE is a mineral somewhat resembling talc and serpentine. It has, however, a dark, olive-green color, a granular texture, and is much less unctuous to the touch. It forms a slaty rock very common in some localities.

5. *Garnet* is a common mineral in connection with mica, hornblende, and granite. It is found usually in dark-red crystals of 12 or 24 sides. This dodecahedral form, and its fracture presenting an entire want of cleavage, with its glassy lustre, sufficiently distinguish it. The garnet is the ancient carbuncle. When clear-colored it is a beautiful gem.

FIG. 9.

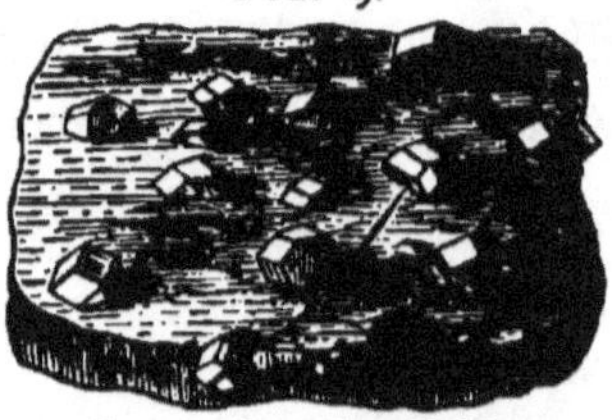

Garnets in Mica Schist.

FIG. 10.

Tourmaline Crystals in Quartz
Alexandria Bay, N. Y.

6. *Tourmaline* is found in long prisms of 3, 6, 9, or 12 sides, each of

which is generally deeply furrowed lengthwise. It is of various colors—black, red, green, and even white. The black crystals are highly polished, have no cleavage, and break like resin. They are often found as small as a knitting-needle, and several inches long, radiating in every direction through the rock which contains them.

II. CLASSIFICATION OF THE ROCKS.

In the earth's crust we find two kinds of rocks, produced respectively by the action of fire and of water. The former was poured out from the furnace within the earth, and the latter spread out by the waters above. These two agents, fire and water, seem to have worked jointly in laying the solid foundations. Rocks are divided into three different classes according to their mode of formation: *Sedimentary, igneous,* and *metamorphic.*

(1.) SEDIMENTARY ROCKS.

Sedimentary Rocks are those which have been deposited by water. They are arranged in strata or layers, and are hence sometimes called the *stratified rocks.* They comprise the following kinds:

1. ***Sandstone,*** which is only consolidated sand, and may be either *siliceous* or *argillaceous* (clayey).

2. ***Conglomerate,*** which is only consolidated gravel —the conglomerate taking the name siliceous, calcare-

ous, or ferruginous (*ferrum*, iron), from the character of the sandy paste which cements together its pebbles. If the conglomerate is composed of rounded pebbles, it is often stylèd a "pudding stone;" if of angular fragments, a "breccia" (brek-cea). The Potomac marble, seen in the capitol at Washington, is a very beautiful calcareous breccia.

3. *Shale*, or argillaceous rock, which is composed mainly of clay, and separates easily into thin, fragile, irregular plates.

4. *Limestone*, which has been pulverized from shells, corals, etc., by the action of the water, and been deposited in sediment at the bottom of the sea.

SCENIC DESCRIPTION.—Sandy regions, from the shifting character of the material, must be sometimes abruptly uneven and irregular, and may, therefore, occasionally afford a pleasing diversity; the tendency, however, is to a flat and monotonous surface. Shaly, and especially slaty formations, consisting usually of harder and softer layers, which weather unevenly, present oftentimes wild ravines and picturesque waterfalls, as in the Watkins Glen, near Seneca Lake, N. Y. The streams cut deep channels and make abrupt plunges with unaccountable leaps, while the tops of the hills form escarpments with sharp edges. When the clay shale is more uniform, it presents a scenery less picturesque, but not less beautiful. Gracefully contoured hills and grass-carpeted meadows in wide-spreading valleys mark the softer aspects of the rural landscape.

(2.) IGNEOUS ROCKS.

Igneous Rocks are those which have been thrown out in a melted state. They are usually not arranged in layers, and are hence termed the *unstratified rocks.* They are divided into two classes—*trap* and *volcanic rocks.*

1. Trap Rocks are so called from the Swedish word *trappa,* a stair, because they frequently occur in terrace-like bluffs, in the form of massive steps. They are generally black or of a dark color, often with shades of green or brown. Their hardness renders them very serviceable in paving and "macadamizing" roads, for which purpose they are largely used. Their dull and unattractive hues, and the difficulty of dressing them into shape, unfit them for general purposes. They are, however, very appropriate for Gothic edifices on account of the appearance of age which they give. There are four common varieties of the trap-rock.

(a.) BASALT is also called *dolerite* (*doleiros,* deceptive), because of the difficulty in distinguishing its constituent minerals. These are principally augite and feldspar. It sometimes contains, scattered through it, crystals of a bottle-glass green color, called *chrysolite* (olivine). When the rock weathers, these little grains fall out. They are found of considerable size at Isle Royale, Lake Superior. They are used as gems, though they are quite soft and have little lustre.

(b.) GREENSTONE—known sometimes as "ironstone"—

is also called *diorite* (*dioros*, distinct), because its composition is so readily determined. It consists of hornblende and feldspar. Most of the trap-rocks of the Eastern States are diorite.

(c.) PORPHYRY (*porphura*, purple) is so named from a purple variety which was highly prized in Egypt. It consisted of a red feldspar with rose-colored crystals scattered through it. It was susceptible of a high polish, and was very enduring, hence it was much sought after by the ancients, who wrought it into sepulchres, baths, obelisks, etc. Any trap-rock in which the feldspar is disseminated in distinct crystals is said to be porphyritic.

FIG. 11.

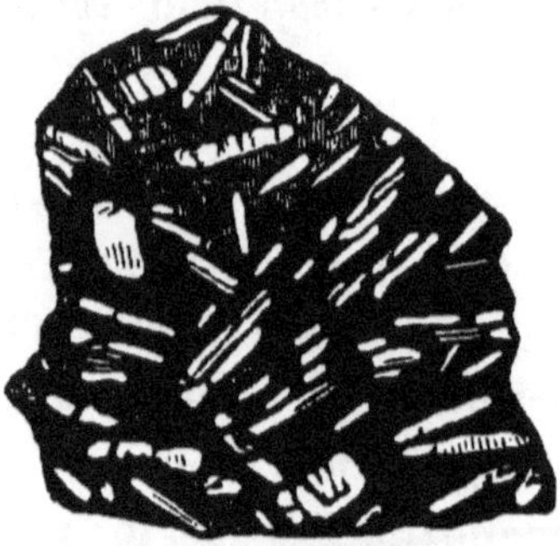

Porphyry.

FIG. 12.

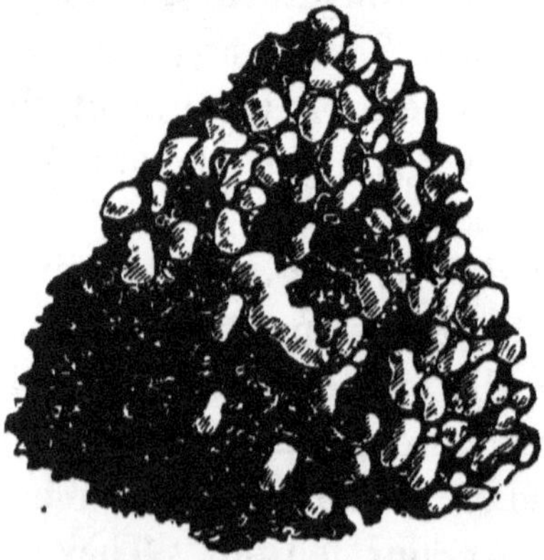

Lava (Scoria), in part turned into an Amygdaloid.

(d.) AMYGDALOID (*amygdala*, an almond) is a name applied to certain trap-rocks which contain rounded cavities often filled with quartz, calcite, etc., so that the rock appears like a cake stuck full of almonds.

SCENIC DESCRIPTION.—The most striking characteristic of the trap-rocks is their columnar structure.* They are crystallized into prisms more or less regular, with from three to eight sides, a diameter of from one inch to many feet, and a height often of several hundred feet. These pillars are frequently jointed, and the sections are concave at the top and convex at the bottom. The columns often stand perpendicularly, and when broken and disintegrated by the action of the weather or of the sea, present most picturesque appearances as of old castles and of ruined fortifications. Some of the most remarkable scenery in the world is of this character. Fingal's Cave, Isle of Staffa, and the Giant's

FIG. 13.

Fingal's Cave. (From a Photograph.)

* We suppose that the columnar structure of trap-rocks has resulted from a sort of crystallization while cooling under pressure from a melted state, for two reasons: 1, similar columns are found in recent lavas; and, 2, from experiment. Mr. Watt melted 700 lbs. of basalt, and caused it to cool slowly, when globular masses were formed, which enlarged and pressed against one another until regular columns were the result.

This can be illustrated by putting balls of putty into a vessel, and gently pressing

Causeway* in the north of Ireland, are familiar examples. On the north shore of Lake Superior, among the Palisades on the Hudson, upon Mts. Tom and Holyoke, Mass., along the banks of the Columbia River, and the Penobscot in Maine, are presented many similar scenes. Trap-rocks, when weathered, acquire a dull, dark brown appearance, and are often colored with patches of white lichens. There are cases of the existence of basalt in well-defined flows, which still adhere to craters visible at the present day, and in regard to the igneous origin of which there can be no doubt. One of the most striking examples of a basaltic crater is that of La Coupé in the south of France. Upon the flank of this mountain, the traces left by the current of liquefied basalt are still seen occupying the bottom of a narrow valley, except at those places where the river Volant has cut away portions of the lava. Trappean regions abound in perpendicular walls, sharp ascents, and abrupt precipices. The eruptive masses often rise from amid level plains, while hard dikes alternate with rich strata which decompose into

---

upon them, when they will be seen to arrange themselves in five and six-sided columns, precisely similar to the five and six-sided columns of Staffa or the Giant's Causeway.—*Page.*

* Hogg, the "Ettrick Shepherd," thus graphically refers to these grandeurs of Nature:

"Awed to deep silence, they tread the strand
Where furnaced pillars in order stand;
All framed of the liquid burning levin,
And bent like the bow that spans the heaven;
Or upright ranged, in wondrous array
With purple of green o'er the darksome gray.
The solemn rows in that ocean den
Were dimly seen like the forms of men;
Like giant monks in ages agone,
Whom the god of the ocean had seared to stone;
And their path was on wondrous pavement old
In blocks all cast in some giant mould."

FIG. 14.

Basaltic Pillars, near La Coupé, France.

fertile soils. The soft plain ascends often at one stride into a hill fantastically rugged; and bare, fractured precipices overtop level fields and terraced slopes rich in verdure.*

2. *Volcanic Rocks* are of two common varieties.

(a.) TRACHYTE (*trachus*, rough) is so named because of its rough, gritty feel. It is porous, has a white, gray, or black color, and is usually porphyritic. It is abundant in South America—the colossal Chimborazo being a lofty trachytic cone—in the extinct volcanic regions of the west, on the banks of the Rhine, and in France.

(b.) LAVA is a term applied to all melted matter observed to flow in streams from volcanoes. It consists almost entirely of augite (pyroxene) and feldspar.† The former constitutes dark colored, and the latter light colored lava. When cooled, the upper part of the stream is light and porous as a sponge, from the expansion of

---

* Hugh Miller has mentioned the curious fact that all, or nearly all, the noted Scottish fortresses are built upon trappean rocks. Thus the early geologic history of a country seems typical of its subsequent civil history. A stormy morning, during which its strata have been tilted into abrupt angles and yawning chasms, is generally succeeded by a stormy day of fierce wars, protracted sieges, and all the turmoil of human passion. Amid the centers of disturbance, the natural strongholds of the earth, the true battles of the race have been fought. Greece, the Holy Land, the Swiss Cantons, Scotland, New England, all have been grand theatres alike of geologic and of patriotic strife.

† Other simple minerals occur in lava. At least 100 species have been detected in that of Vesuvius, but they bear so small a proportion to the whole mass as to render it incompatible with the design of this work to devote space to them here. There are also thrown out from volcanoes "fragments of granite and other rocks scarcely altered; cinders and ashes of various degrees of fineness, which are sometimes converted into mud by the water that accompanies them; also sulphur in a pure state; various salts and acids; and several gases, among which are the hydrochloric, sulphurous, and sulphuric acids: alum, gypsum, sulphates of iron and magnesia, chlorides of sodium and potassium, of iron, copper, and cobalt; chlorine, nitrogen, sulphuretted hydrogen," etc.—*Hitchcock.*

the steam bubbles, and will swim in water, while the lower portions are hard and compact like the ancient basalt. The porous lava is called *scoria*. *Pumice* is a feldspathic scoria with long, slender air-cavities, drawn out by the forward movement of the lava stream; large quantities of it are often found floating in the ocean. It is much used in polishing marble. *Obsidian* is a glassy-like lava.

SCENIC DESCRIPTION.—Regions of frequent volcanic action contain cones and craters surrounded by beds of lava and scoria. These features are well exhibited in the accompanying view of a scene near Mono Lake, Sierra Nevada region.

FIG. 15.

Volcanic Cones, near Mono Lake.

(3.) METAMORPHIC ROCKS.

Metamorphic Rocks are those which have been altered by heat. A mass of melted lava penetrating sedimentary rocks would materially modify their character; the clay would be changed to slate, the limestone converted into marble, earthy sandstone and clay rocks into granite-like rocks, and the impurities crystallized into various minerals.* The stratification would be destroyed, and the fossils in part, if not entirely, obliterated. Sometimes, however, the original fossils may be still distinguished. There is a kind of marble found at Kilkenny which contains shells of the ammonite. They look exactly like the prints of a careless heel, and many a housekeeper has wearied herself in vainly trying to scour out these fossil remains. The famous Carrara marble is a metamorphic limestone. On examination with a lens it reveals spangles of graphite, and frequently nodules of ironstone lined with perfectly limpid crystals of quartz. These accidental defects, resulting from impurities in the limestone, are very annoying to the sculptor, since nothing in the exterior of a block betrays their existence.

1. Granite (from the Italian *grano*, because of its granular structure) consists of feldspar, mica, and quartz. The feldspar shows a smooth surface of cleavage in two directions, and is usually of a white or flesh color; the mica may be readily recognized by its glistening look,

* In Whitney's Geological Survey of California, constant illustrations are given of the effects of metamorphism. Places were found where the line of separation between the sedimentary and metamorphic rocks is sharply drawn. Near the junction of the two kinds, the latter seem to have retained their original stratification. Patches of sedimentary rocks which entirely escaped the igneous action are inclosed in the metamorphic rocks. Here is a layer of quartz, which beyond is converted into jasper; a clayey sandstone into serpentine, or into mica slate with disseminated garnets. The metamorphic and sedimentary rocks give each a distinctive character to the landscape. The former furnish hills of sharper outline, richer soil, and more abundant vegetation, so as to be readily recognized even at a distance.

and by being easily separated into thin layers; the quartz has a glassy lustre and no cleavage. *Graphic granite* is a variety in which the quartz is imperfectly crystallized into long, slender crystals. When the rock is broken crosswise, the ends of these crystals present forms somewhat resembling Hebrew characters. Sometimes granite has a very coarse structure, the crystals being a foot or more in diameter; at other times it is so fine that one can with difficulty distinguish the constituent minerals. When sound, it is an excellent building stone, but does not merit the character of extreme hardness which is proverbially ascribed to it. Its granular texture unfits it for road-making, since it is crushed into dust so readily by tramping feet. In the Crimean war it was shown that granite ramparts were as easily demolished as those of limestone. Granite seems to be the lowest rock in the earth's formation, and yet, strangely enough, it is found on Mt. Blanc—the highest in Europe, and crowns many of the Rocky Mountains.

FIG. 16.

Graphic Granite, Berkshire, Mass.

Granite is quarried in great quantities in the Eastern States for building purposes. New Hampshire and Massachusetts are noted for their extensive beds. They may be called the Granite States of the Union. The granite is detached in blocks by drilling a series of holes, one every few inches, to a depth of three inches, and then driving in wedges of iron between steel cheeks.

In this manner, masses of any size are split out. There is a choice of direction, as the granite has certain directions of easiest fracture. Masses 120 feet in length have been obtained at some of the quarries. Granite was highly prized by the ancients. There are granite obelisks in Egypt which have stood for 3,000 years. Pompey's Pillar and several of the principal Pyramids are composed of this material.

FORMATION OF GRANITE.—Granite is often styled the primitive rock, since it seems to be the one which constitutes the basement of the earth's crust. Though it may now lie at the foundation, it may still be a metamorphic rock, and not the first product of the slowly cooling globe. It is more likely that most of the granite rocks have resulted from the wearing down of the primeval crust of true igneous rocks. These were carried into the sea and deposited as stratified rock. Buried afterward beneath vast accumulations of other rocks, by the internal heat and the influx of hot water charged with various chemical agents,* they were crystallized, and their fossils and stratification obliterated. Again, they may have been worn by the sea, deposited, and afterward

* In the account given of the Pluton Geysers, California, we seem to have an insight into the laboratory of the world, and can learn something of the chemical changes which have been going on in past ages. These geysers are hot springs, which throw out intermittingly and spasmodically powerful jets of steam and scalding water, their temperature varying from 93° to 169° F. The water contains sulphuric acid, sulphuretted hydrogen, and probably other active solvents. The rocks are rapidly dissolving under this powerful metamorphic action. Porphyry and jasper are transformed into a kind of potter's clay. Trap and magnesian rocks are consumed, much like wood in a slow fire, forming sulphate of magnesia and other products. Granite is rendered so soft that one can crush it between his fingers as easily as unbaked bread. The feldspar is converted partly into alum. The boulders and angular fragments brought down the ravine by floods are being converted into a firm conglomerate, so that it is difficult to dislodge even a small pebble, the pebble itself sometimes breaking before the cement will yield.—*Shepherd, Am. Journ. of Science.*

metamorphosed. How many times this cycle of change has taken place, we have no way of judging. The entire crust of the earth has doubtless undergone metamorphic action, to some extent at least, and is unlike what it was when created. What made up that primeval crust we do not know, and hence cannot tell whether any of the ancient formation survives. It is generally believed that granite could not be produced directly by the cooling of the melted lava that then composed the globe. There are, however, places where it has been found at a great depth, and, by some powerful convulsion, has been ejected to the surface in a melted state, like a true igneous rock. It may even now be in the process of formation in the lower portions of the earth's crust. It is certain that as the crust wears away above, new rocks must be cooling underneath, since the point of fusion is constantly passing downward. Granite has, however, been formed in all ages of the world, and cannot be thought a primitive rock merely, although specially characteristic of the earlier periods. We shall, therefore, consider it, *in general, as a metamorphic rock crystallized by the combined action of heat, water, and other chemical agents, from sedimentary or more ancient rocks.*

SCENIC DESCRIPTION.—The ancient granite, having been exposed for so long a time to the wear of the elements, rarely imparts boldness or grandeur to the landscape, unless more recent convulsions have broken it up and rendered it picturesque. When containing little feldspar, and being therefore more durable, it forms lofty pyramidal peaks of sharp outline that rise in enormous spires, as in the vicinity of Mt. Blanc. There seems to be often a tendency to rounded concentric outlines,* which render the view sombre and uninteresting. The

FIG. 17.

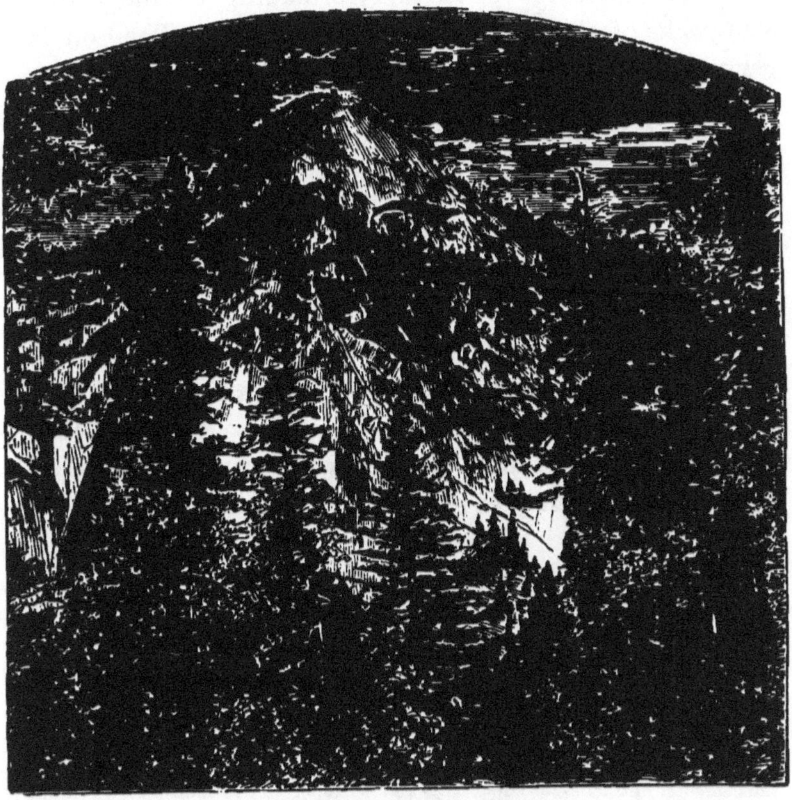

North Dome—Yosemite Valley.

peculiar dome-like appearance of granite mountains is beautifully illustrated in the magnificent scenery of the

* Humboldt says: "All formations are common to every quarter of the globe, and assume the like forms. Everywhere basalt rises in twin mountains and truncated cones; everywhere trap porphyry presents itself to the eye under the form of grotesquely shaped masses of rock; while granite terminates in gently rounded summits." As the pupil will observe, however, this latter is but one of the aspects which granite presents.

Yosemite. Its colossal peaks are of solid granite, the North Dome being 3568 feet in height. Granite forms, in general, lofty hills and elevated table-lands, which are rendered still more bleak and forbidding by the snow-clad peaks of the more elevated mountains. The soil is generally scanty and barren. The clay from the decomposed granite is the finest and best that can be found; the sand, often of the purest white, always lustrous and bright. As a result, the landscape wears a peculiar aspect of purity.* It cannot become muddy, foul, or unwholesome. The streams may indeed be opaque and white as cream with the churned substance of the weathered granite; but the water is good and pure, and the shores not slimy nor treacherous, but pebbly or of firm and sparkling sand. The quiet springs and lakes are of exquisite clearness, and the sea, which washes a granite coast, is as unsullied as a flawless emerald.

2. *Gneiss* (nīce) differs from granite only in being stratified. Indeed, the two kinds of rock pass into each other so insensibly that they are often difficult to dis-

* It is remarkable how this intense purity in the country seems to influence the character of the inhabitants. It is almost impossible to make a cottage built in a granite country look absolutely miserable. Rough it may be, neglected, cold, full of aspect of hardship, but it never can look foul; no matter how carelessly, how indolently its inhabitants may live, the water at their doors will not stagnate, the soil at their feet will not allow itself to be trodden into slime; they cannot so much as dirty their faces or hands if they try. Do the worst they can, there will still be a feeling of firm ground under them and pure air about them, and an inherent wholesomeness which it will need the misery of years to conquer. The inhabitants of granite countries have, too, a force and healthiness of character about them, abated or modified according to their other circumstances of life, that clearly distinguish them from the inhabitants of less pure districts.—*Ruskin.*

tinguish.* Its origin, therefore, is doubtless the same as that of granite, both being made from stratified rocks; when the stratification entirely disappeared, granite being the result; and when only partially or not at all, gneiss. Because of the ease with which it divides into thin layers, this rock is much used for flagging.

SCENIC DESCRIPTION.—In our own country we find much of the grand scenery of the White Mountains, Blue Ridge, and Rocky Mountains, among rocks of this formation. Hugh Miller, humorously speaking of the gneiss hills of Scotland, says: A gneiss hill is usually massive, rounded, broad of base, and withal somewhat squat, as if it were a mountain well begun, but interdicted somehow in the building, rather than a finished mountain. It seems almost always to lack the upper stories and the pinnacles. It is, if I may so express myself, a hill of one heave; whereas all our more imposing Scottish hills—such as Ben Nevis and Ben Lomond—are hills of at least two heaves; and hence in journeying through a gneiss district, there is a frequent feeling on the part of the traveler that the scenery is incomplete, but that a few hills, judiciously set down upon the tops of the other hills, would give it the

* Doubtless some gneiss has been formed by the action of water, and is perhaps a sedimentary rock. Thus granite being worn away by the waves, the granite débris would be deposited in regular strata at the bottom of the sea, constituting gneiss. Most of it is, however, the product of an incomplete metamorphic action, which, if made complete, would have produced true granite by destruction of all fossils and stratification. Thus Dawson, in his Acadian Geology, says that in Nova Scotia, near the Nictaux river, there are beds of slate in which the granite has been intruded, and the slates near the junction have been altered into gneiss containing garnets. Here is a case of clear metamorphism of shale into gneiss.

proper finish. No hill, however, accomplishes more with a single heave than a gneiss one.

3. *Mica Schist* is a gneiss rock, consisting mostly of mica. The dust in the roads of places abounding in this rock is full of the fine glistening particles of mica.

SCENIC DESCRIPTION.—The scenery of regions where mica schist predominates is bold, rugged, and unfertile. Thrown into lofty mountains by the protruding granite, and often tilted in nearly vertical positions, they present that rugged and abrupt aspect so characteristic of the Scottish highlands and some of the mountain ranges of our own country. Loch Katrine and many other places, classic for their picturesque beauty, owe their origin to the peculiarities of this formation. Hugh Miller says: "Their gray locks of silky lustre are curved, wrinkled, contorted, so as to remind us of pieces of ill-laid-by satin, that bear on their crushed surfaces the creases and crumplings of a thousand careless foldings."

4. *Syenite* is a granite in which the mica is replaced by hornblende. It is so called from the city of Syene, Upper Egypt, where the ancient Egyptians quarried it for monumental purposes.* The celebrated Quincy granite is mostly of this class. It is largely used in architecture, many public edifices being composed of it; for example, the Bunker Hill monument, the custom-

* It has since been found, however, that the ancient syenite is only a granite with black mica, and not hornblende as was supposed. As the upper part of Mt. Sinai is a mass of true syenite, it has been proposed to rename this rock as *sinaite*.

houses at Boston and New Orleans, and the Astor House in New York.

5. Quartzite is a rock composed of quartz sand cemented by heat. In a quartz district, because of the slow weathering, the hills present a scenery of savage wildness, but wonderful grandeur.

6. Marble is metamorphosed limestone. The different varieties have already been described on page 51. Limestone is one of the rocks in which the metamorphic action can be most easily traced. When not thus modified we find it as common limestone, chalk, etc. By heat its character is entirely changed; it takes on a crystalline structure, its color is varied, the fossils are generally destroyed, and the various impurities form new minerals which often fill the veins of the marble with beautiful colored figures, as seen in the variegated marbles of California.

There are also other varieties of metamorphic rocks, viz., *talcose schist*, a slate which contains much talc, *chlorite* schist, one which contains chlorite (an olive-green mineral very like talc), and *slate rock*, which passes almost insensibly into an argillaceous or clayey shale.

III. STRUCTURE OF THE ROCKS.

The rocks of the earth's crust are divided according to their structure into two classes, the *stratified* and the *unstratified* rocks. The former are arranged in layers, the latter are not. The former were generally produced by aqueous, the latter by igneous agencies. The former mark the periods of rest in the world's history, the latter chronicle its convulsions. Upon the exterior of the crust the stratified rocks are largely in excess, occupying probably $\frac{19}{20}$ of the surface; upon the interior, however, the unstratified comprise the whole mass, and extend to a depth of perhaps 50 miles. Historical geology deals almost entirely with the stratified rocks, and nearly all of its principles are based upon facts which they disclose.

(I.) STRATIFIED ROCKS.

As soon as dry land was formed, it began to be worn away by the ceaseless action of the rain and the restless sea, depositing the débris at the bottom of the ocean.* Thus, while the earth's crust has been growing from below by the formation of unstratified, it has been growing above by the formation of stratified rocks. These materials are arranged in comparatively flat layers as in Fig. 18. In this way the earth would be covered over by successive deposits like the coats of an onion.

FIG. 18.

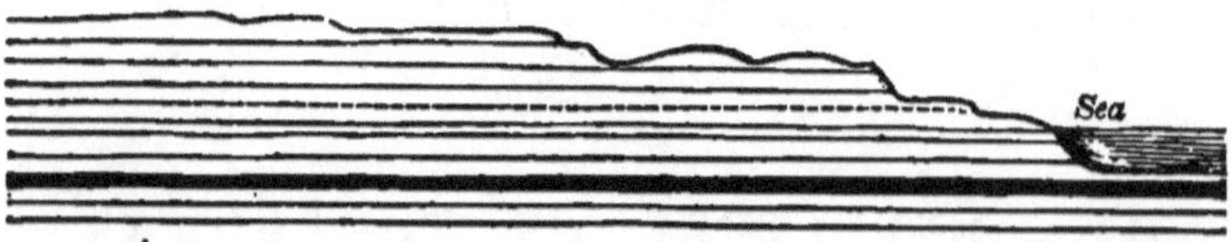

1. Dislocations of Strata.—Had these wrap-

---

* It is probable also that submarine volcanoes poured their liquid streams into the primeval ocean. These materials were worked over and deposited as stratified rocks. The earliest strata, says Agassiz, are pierced with numerous funnels, which were outlets for the fierce floods beneath.

pings remained undisturbed, we could have made little progress in deciphering their history, since we have not pierced the crust much more than half a mile in perpendicular line. But by igneous action, the rocks which would have lain as in Fig. 18 have been upheaved, and present a form similar to that shown in Fig. 19, where

FIG 19.

we can examine, on the top, the edges of various sedimentary strata, and also the igneous rocks which were hidden below. Oftentimes the geologist, in tracing the course of a river, will find successive strata tilted up on edge, presenting the appearance represented in Fig. 20.

FIG. 20.

Here, had the rocks remained in their original position, the river in its descent might not have disclosed more than two or three layers; now, by the *outcropping*, as it is termed, many successive strata can be examined oftentimes within a few miles.

2. *Definitions.*—A *stratum* includes one or more layers, or laminæ, of any particular kind of rock. A *formation* is composed of several strata which were deposited in the same period. A *group* is a part of a formation, including such strata as are in any way related to each other. The laminæ, or layers, of a group bear the same relation to each other that the groups of a formation do.

In Fig. 21 the strata at A are said to be *horizontal*,

FIG. 21.

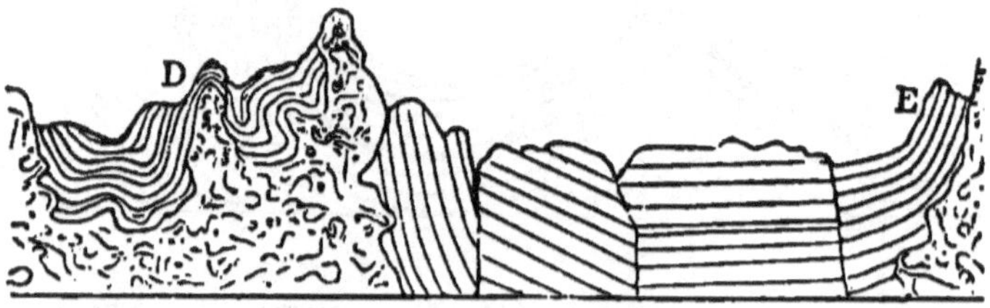

those at B *inclined* (and the angle which they form with the horizon is called the *dip*), those at E to be *tilted up*, at C to be *vertical*, and at D to be *contorted*. In Fig. 22, strata dipping in opposite directions, *a*, are

FIG. 22.

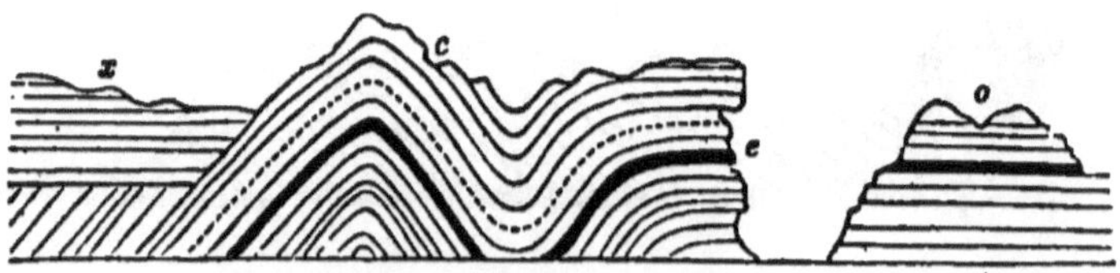

called *anticlinal;* when dipping toward each other, *s*, *synclinal;* *e* is an *escarpment* or bluff; strata, as *c*, coming to the surface, are called an *outcrop;* strata arranged regularly above each other, as at *o*, are said to be *conformable;* those not, as at *x*, are styled *unconformable.*

3. Diverse Stratification.—Sedimentary rocks were not always originally deposited in horizontal layers.

FIG. 23.

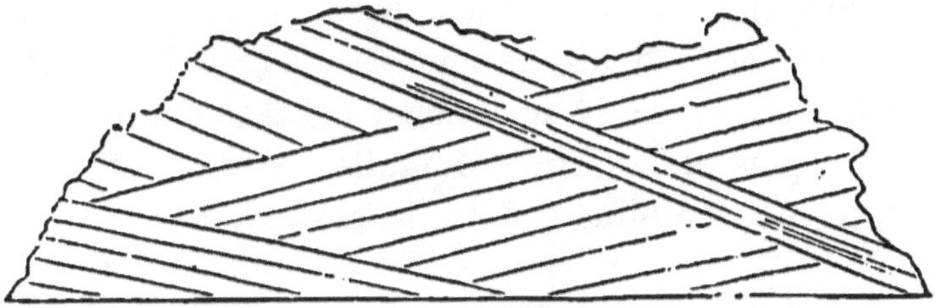

Diverse Stratification.

Along the sea-shore we can see the deposits being made on its sloping bottom. The ebb and flow of the tide, the sand blown by the wind, and the action of the waves, which often undermine one part and elevate another, may cause a rock to present the diverse stratification seen in Fig. 23.

4. Lamination.—It is necessary to distinguish between stratification and lamination. Separate laminæ, as well as strata, indicate a pause in the process of deposition, whereby the sediment had time to partially harden. The former denote a shorter time, so that the laminæ, in general, do not easily separate from each other. In some stones it requires as much force to split them along the planes of lamination as "across the grain." The different kinds of lamination are instructive, since they indicate the circumstances under which the rock was formed. Quiet deposition always produced *parallel,* slowly rippling waves, *curved,* and pressure, *contorted* lamination.

5. *Faults.*—Vertical cracks or seams frequently traverse the rocks, and the strata on one side slipping away from those on the other, the layers on the two sides do not correspond. During the unequal movements which have produced the dislocation, the edges have often ground together so as to become polished and grooved. Fig. 24 represents a series of faults, *offsets,* as they are called, in the iron mine at Mt. Pleasant, N. J.

FIG. 24.

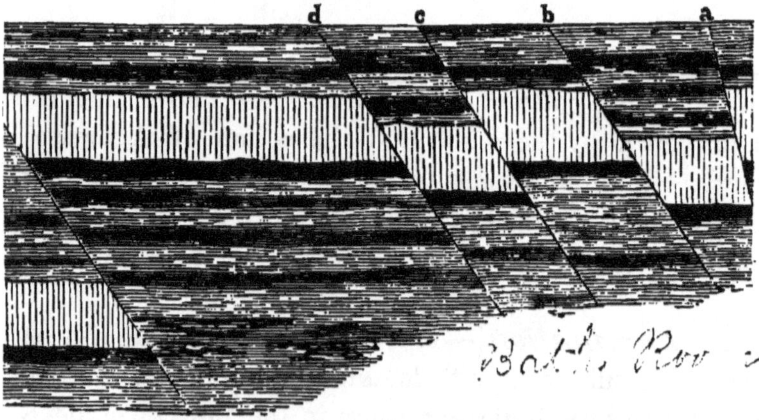

Faults (offsets) in Mt. Pleasant Iron Mine, Rockaway, N. J.

6. *Jointed Structure.*—When these vertical cracks are parallel to each other, and, in addition, a second system crosses the first at right angles, the rocks are divided into regular blocks, forming a *jointed structure.* On Cayuga Lake the rocky bluffs resemble fortifications

with towers and bastions. Joints in the rocks are almost invaluable to the quarrymen. It would be a most difficult task indeed to quarry a rock destitute of stratifica-

FIG. 25.

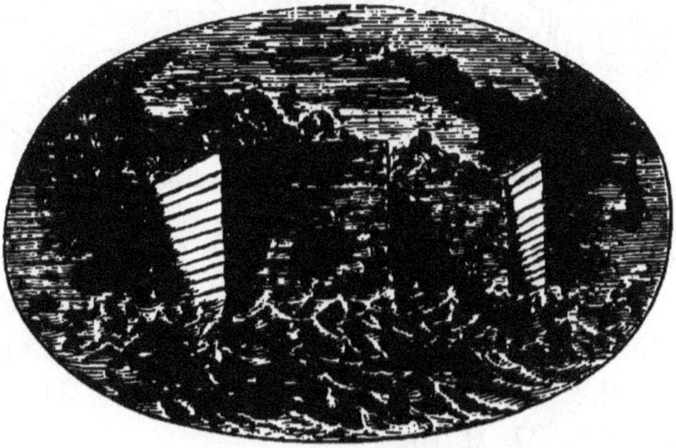

Jointed Structure, Cayuga Lake.

tion and joints. These seams have doubtless been produced partly by shrinkage as the earth has cooled, and partly also by long-continued lateral pressure consequent upon movements of the earth's crust. The fact that the joints of any region are parallel to each other indicates a common origin.

7. *Folds.*—Strata are often so folded upon each other that it is difficult to decide upon their relative age. Huge mountains consist of rocks twisted and contorted as if they had been "crumpled up" by some mighty hand. Fig. 26 represents a section of slate 1000 feet long and 300 feet high, taken in the coast ranges of California. After these were deposited as sediment, they were crushed together and bent over by steady lateral

pressure.* "How prodigious the force which could fold the rocky strata of a mountain as one would the leaves

FIG. 26.

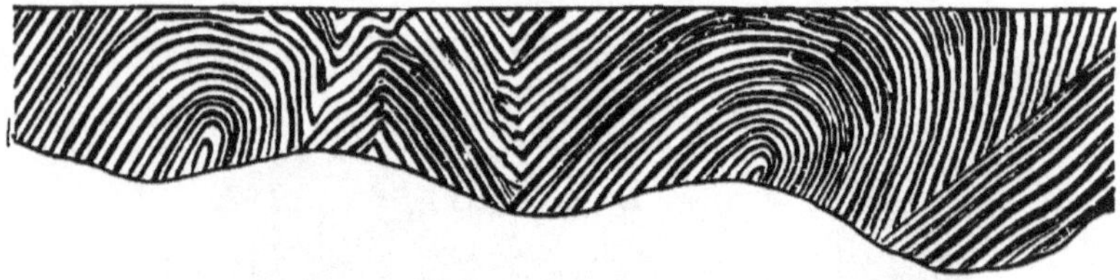

Flexures in Slate, Coast Range, California.

of a book." After rocks have been folded in this manner, the top has often been removed by *denudation,*† *i. e.*, the action of water, leaving parallel strata standing on edge, the older or lower being above the newer. Thus, in Fig. 27, if the fold were swept off down to the line D E, there would be no appearance of anything more than a mere tilting up of the strata; yet the layer A would lie above C, when it was really deposited below it.

FIG. 27.

A Decapitated Fold.

---

* Lyell illustrates the effects which pressure would produce on flexible strata by laying several pieces of cloth upon each other in a pile, and then placing a book on top; apply other books at each end and force them toward each other. The folding of the cloth will exactly imitate the folding seen in the rock strata.

† Near Chambersburg, Pa., there is a fault 20 miles in length, and the depth of the dislocation is 20,000 feet, and yet a man can stand with one foot on one side of this fracture and the other foot on the other side. What has become, then, of this immense mass of material 20,000 feet in height. It must have been swept into the Atlantic by the denuding flood. If this had not been done, a bold precipice would have stood there nearly four miles in height and twenty miles in length. Long ages must have been required for water to effect such a denudation.—*Lesley.*

8. *Concretions* are rounded nodules formed by the tendency of matter to collect about a center. They are usually flattened, though they are sometimes quite spherical. At the center there is most commonly some foreign object, a fossil, shell, twig, or the like, which was the nucleus of the crystallization. In some iron mines are found balls of ore, which, from their peculiar form, are termed "kidney shaped." Calcareous concretions, washed up by the waves, abound along the shores of Lake Erie. They have been found as large as six feet in diameter. They sometimes have the shape of large sea-turtles, and the cracks formed by shrinkage often resembling the plates of the shell, they are considered by the neighboring people as petrified relics of that animal. On the coast of Durham, England, the magnesian limestone forms bold cliffs, which look as if made up of irregularly piled cannon balls. When the internal cracks formed in drying have become filled with spar, the concretions are termed *septaria* (*septum*, a division), and,

FIG. 28.

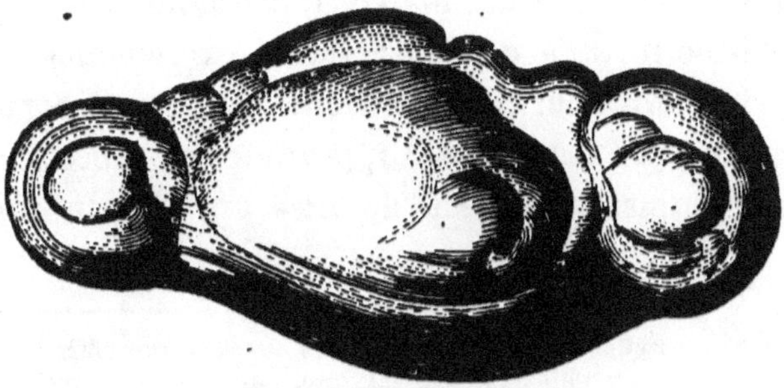

Claystone, Springfield, Mass.

when cut and polished, present an ornamental appearance. They are so abundant as to be used in making the famous Roman cement. In beds of clay containing considerable carbonate of lime are found peculiar concretions called *claystones.* They are popularly supposed to be worn by the water. They often assume most fantastic shapes, resembling familiar objects, such as a hat, bird, ring, etc. A variety of limestone composed of minute concretions, often as small as a grain of sand, is termed oölitic (see Fig. 7). Along the limestone bluffs of the Mississippi beautiful "geodes" are found. Externally they are merely rough stones, but a blow of the hammer reveals the interior lined with delicate quartz crystals.* Fig. 29 represents iron nodules, found in coal mines,

FIGS. 29-3

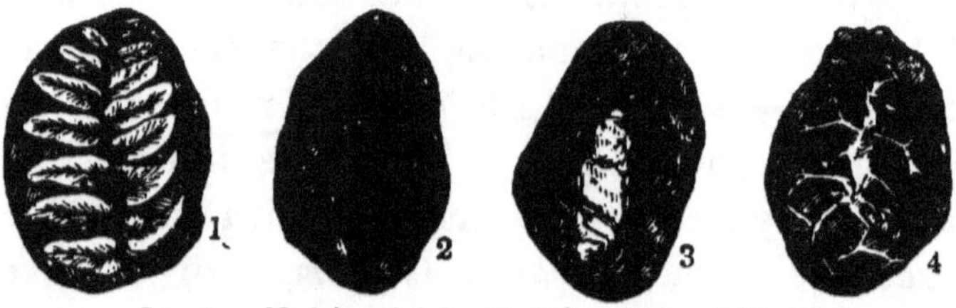

Ironstone Nodules, showing Varieties of Central Nuclei.

with their central nuclei—No. 1, a fragment of a plant; 2, a fish-tooth; 3, a coprolite (fossil excrement); and 4, a septarium, with curious partitions of white carbonate of lime, giving the section the appearance of a beetle; from which circumstance such nodules are known in some places as *beetle stones.*

---

* "Water is sometimes found in the geodes, holding the silex in solution, and making with it a milky looking mixture. As the water evaporates, the silex has been known to suddenly form into delicate crystals. Such geodes were at one time abundantly found on Briar Creek, in Scriven or Burke County, Ga., in a rock composed of hornstone and jasper; the milky fluid contained in them was used by the inhabitants as a paint or whitewash."—*Am. Journal of Science.*

9. *Slate Structure.*—This term is commonly applied to any rock which splits into thin layers. The true

FIG. 33.

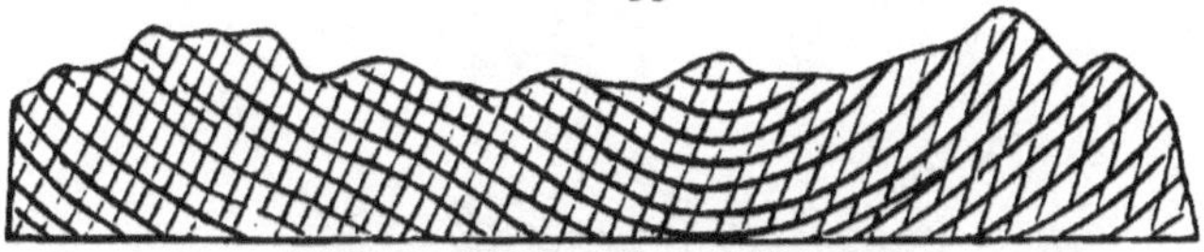

Section exhibiting Lines of Cleavage.

slate, however, splits in layers transverse, often at right angles to the strata. Such rocks have been changed from clay shales by metamorphic action, in which process they have been hardened and partially crystallized, while at the same time they have been submitted to long-continued lateral pressure. Prof. Tyndall has shown that even soft clay will in this manner divide into thin laminæ.

(2.) UNSTRATIFIED ROCKS.

The unstratified rocks are found as shapeless masses *underlying, overlying,* and sometimes penetrating the stratified rocks.

1. *Definitions.*—In Fig. 34, C is an underlying mass of granite, *e* is a stratum forced between two

FIG. 34.

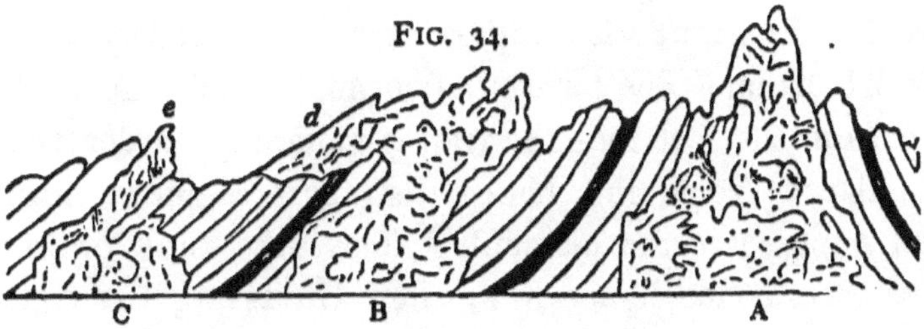

strata of sedimentary rocks, *d* is an overlying mass, and

A simply a mass thrown up from below, and disrupting the regular stratified rocks above it. In Fig. 35,

FIG. 35.

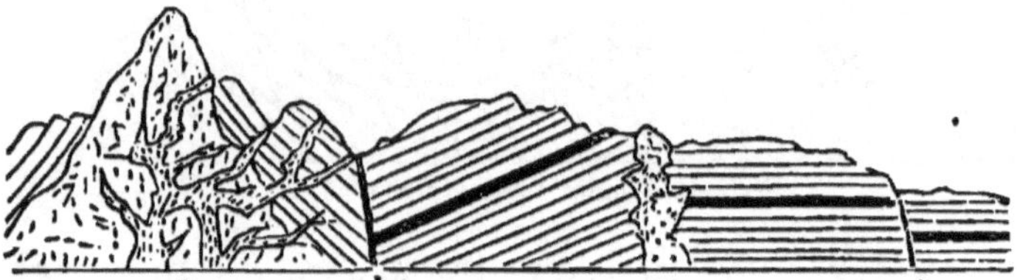

at c is a fault in the rocks, and the joint at that point filled with igneous rock is called a *dike*. At *a* is a series of *veins* traversing a stratified and an unstratified rock.

2. ***Veins*** are fissures in the rock strata, filled with crystallized mineral matter, such as fluor spar, quartz, etc. They are of all sizes, from an inch to many feet in thickness. We often find rocks and even pebbles crowded with veins sometimes not thicker than a sheet of paper (see Fig. 39).

3. ***Dikes*** are wide fissures filled with igneous rocks or recent lava. They are generally larger than veins, have their sides more nearly parallel, ramify less commonly in branching veins, and contain but a single kind of rock. In Fig. 36 is a representation of modern dikes near Mt. Etna. The term dike means a wall. It is derived from the fact that the trap is generally harder than the adjacent rock, and hence disintegrates more slowly when exposed to the elements. The dike thus projects above the surface like a wall, often traversing the country for many miles. Hugh Miller, in speaking of the

FIG. 36.

Modern Dikes near Mt. Etna.

scenery about Edinburgh, compares the denuding influences to the work of the sculptor; as he brings out his

FIG. 37.

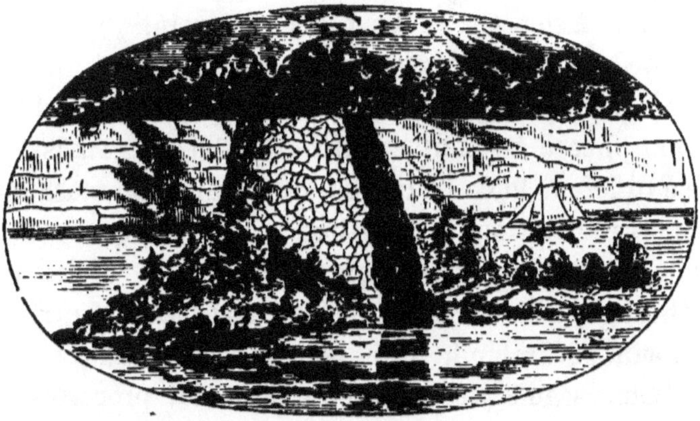

Trap Dike, Lake Superior.

figures in relief by cutting away about them, so Time scoops away the sand rock and shale, and leaves the bold, rugged features of the trap ridges.

When veins cross each other, it is easy to decide upon their relative age, the one which is separated being necessarily the older. Thus in Fig. 38 there is a trap-dike protruding through a bed of gneiss, and crossing that is a vein of quartz, *a b*. Prof. Hitchcock describes a block of greenstone which exhibits eleven series of veins.

FIG. 38

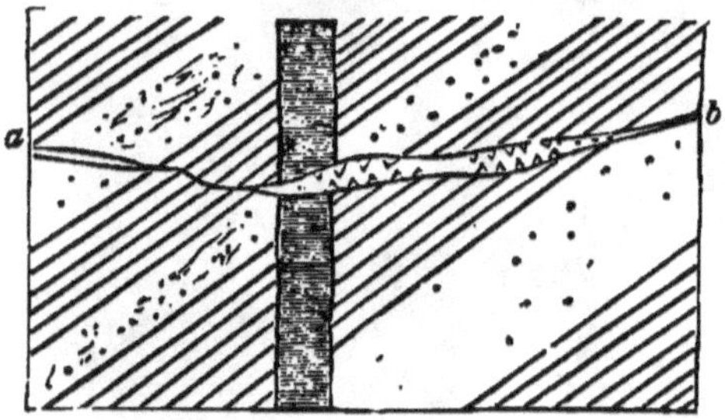

Dike.

a b. A Quartz Vein passing through a Greenstone Dike and Layers of Gneiss.

4. Origin of Veins and Dikes.—When the rocks cooled from a melted, or dried from a moist state, they naturally shrank so as to form cracks or seams of varying size. In different ways Nature collected material to fasten the rocks together again. Some clefts were filled by melted rocks injected from below, and then cooled. This is known, because the adjacent rocks are metamorphosed by contact with the burning mass, and wear a different look from the rest, while the mass itself, by its crystallization, shows that it cooled sooner on the outside against the walls than at the center. Dikes passing through beds of chalk in the county of Antrim, in the north of Ireland, have changed the chalk to marble. Some seams were filled by chemical processes with matter which crystallized out from the adjacent rocks, as, for example, a plaster rock dark and muddy is often found crossed with layers and filaments of white, transparent selenite crystals, which have doubtless been formed from the parent stone. The larger number, however, of these rents were mended with rock material from highly-heated water charged with mineral matter.* This water filtering through the finest seams of the rock would fill them with a crystalline paste. We often see this process

FIG. 39.

Vein-form Pebble from Drift, Elmira.

* Large rocks are sometimes as full of veins as your hand is, and of veins nearly as fine (only a rock-vein does not mean a tube but a crack). These clefts are mended usually with the strongest material the rock can find, and often literally with threads; for the gradually opening rent seems to draw the substance it is filled with into fibers which cross from one side to the other, so that when the crystals become distinct, the fissure has often the look of a rent brought together with strong cross stitches. When all has been fastened, a new change of temperature may occur, and the rock contract again. The old vein must open or a new one be formed. If the old one be well filled the cross stitches will be too strong to break, so that it can only give away at the sides; and thus this space being filled afterward, a supplementary vein is added. In this manner three or four parallel veins have been made.—*Ruskin.*

FIG. 40.

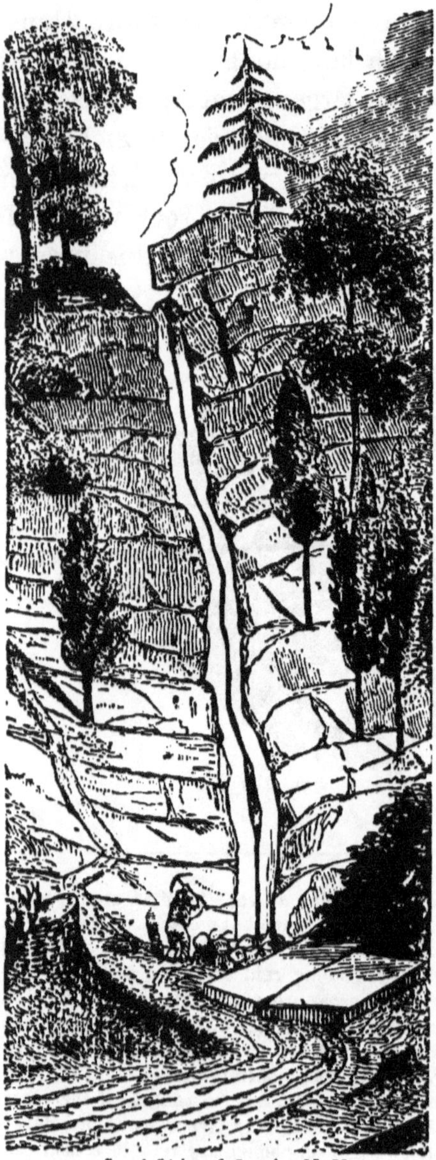

Lead Vein of Rossie, N. Y.

beautifully illustrated in an opaque uncrystalline rock, and in pebbles threaded with fine crystalline veins of a different variety. (Fig. 39.) Veins are often rich in metallic ores. Probably the metal in such cases has been sublimed by heat below, and carried up either with steam or melted matter, and deposited in the rock fissures above. In the figure is shown a valuable vein of lead-ore formerly worked at Rossie, N. Y. This is the simplest form of a metallic vein (lode), as it is a mere vertical sheet.

Historical Geology.

"The crust of our earth is a great cemetery, where the rocks are tombstones on which the buried dead have written their own epitaphs."—Agassiz.

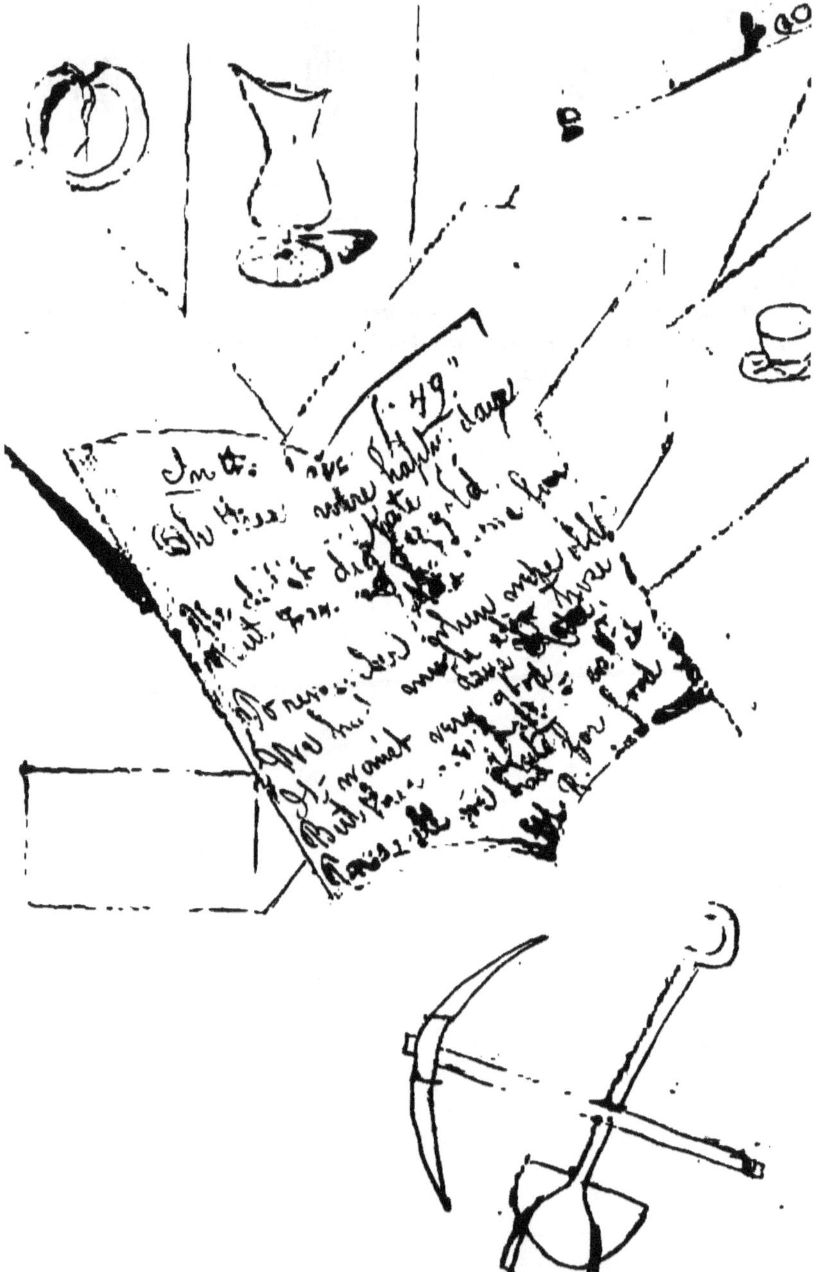

Historical Geology.

THE history of the formation of the earth's crust is not yet fully written. In its investigation many difficulties are met. Strata were not made over the whole earth at the same time, so that the coatings of rock are not uniform. Again, some are found in one section which are wanting in others, and the same strata even are composed frequently of diverse material in different parts of the earth. Thus, the chalk formation of England is represented by a limestone in this country, though both belong to the same era. It is therefore a difficult task to reconstruct these scattered fragments, and put them together. "The world is to the geologist a great puzzle box." He is to trace the resemblances and learn how to combine all the widely strewn parts of the world's history, and to arrange them in order and symmetry. He is, however, constantly learning to read more accurately the rocky leaves of the book of nature. In his work the fossils are his chief reliance. They have been well termed "the Medals of Creation," since by their means the geologist identifies different strata, and judges of the successive creations of animals and plants through the ages of the past. As the seals, medals, coins, etc., found in a ruined city concerning which history is silent, declare its nationality, so the organic remains of a stratum determine its geologic period and characteristics. Each epoch recorded in its rocks and fossils the history of the life which it supported, and the changes through which it passed.* Each formation possesses its peculiar fossils. This similarity obtains in a great degree over the entire world. Thus, the identification of fossils is the identification of formations. We can therefore understand with what eagerness these are gathered and preserved. Fragments which the ignorant would spurn from his feet are invested with as high an interest as the obelisks of Egypt or the sculptures of Nineveh. The antiquarian pores over those with intensest enthusiasm, seeking to read the history of a few thousand years. The geologist bends with equal delight over the forms and impressions of the rocks, seeking to gather information with regard to a past, compared to the duration of which the chronology of man is but as the moments of yesterday. The print of a leaf, a petrified shell, a tooth, the fragment of a bone, a fish-scale even, may serve to unriddle the most puzzling problem. Rough and mutilated

---

* "Nature has all her facts stereotyped. She writes her events often upon the most fragile plants and flowers, on the very winds and waters—all the most evanescent and changing forms, as well as the most permanent. Her record is as enduring as the phases of the object upon which she writes, and sometimes, as if fearing both would be lost, she petrifies the whole, and leaves it thus to endure for the ages. She has often preserved in stone the history of her frailest leaves, her most ephemeral and minutest insects and infusoria, the record of her ebbing and flowing tides, of the piles of dust blown together by her winds, the footprints of her smallest birds, and of her rain-drops falling upon the sand."—*Blackwell.*

though the fragments may be, to the educated eye they embody a tale as legible as any sculpture or hieroglyphics, and far more comprehensive. That tiny stem, a mere discoloration on the rock, once floated as sea-weed in the waters; that reed once luxuriated in a primeval marsh; that delicate rock impression was a fern that once waved in the sunshine; and that simple leaf, now only a film of coal-like matter, sparkled with the dew of heaven as certainly as the tender herb is cherished by the dew to-day, or existing verdure grows to beauty in the sunlight. Every trace, then, becomes a letter, every fragment a word, every perfect fossil a chapter in the world's history. Each tells of races that lived, multiplied and died, of lands that were tenanted, and waters thronged with life,—so oft repeated, again and again, that the mind, at first excited by the marvels, at last grows weary and loses itself in the contemplation of the works of the Infinite Creator.

There are no sharply-drawn lines between the different ages. They fade into each other as insensibly as the mountain blends with the plain. Yet each has a prominent idea, and chronicles a grand transition in the world's history.* Lesser changes are denoted by Periods, Epochs, and Groups. Some, at least, of the revolutions marking the separate ages were nearly if not quite universal. Those denoting the other divisions were more local in their character. The periods and epochs are therefore

* The land now lay low in the water, and anon was lifted into arid, mountainous regions. Consequent upon each change was a new set of climatic influences, winds, ocean currents, rains, etc., each necessarily producing its impress on the vegetable and animal life of the period. Thus there were pauses, as it were, in the deposition of sediment, each pause making a break in the strata.

not the same in Europe and America. They vary much in the formations which are represented even on the Atlantic slope and in the Mississippi valley.

Geological Divisions.—The first land, swept by a boiling ocean, was lifeless. The age during which it was formed has received a corresponding name, The Azoic Time (without life). Following this, we have the successive stages in the development of life on the globe.

As the history of man upon the earth's crust is divided into three portions, *Ancient*, *Medieval*, and *Modern* history, so the history of the crust itself is separated into three grand eras, the *Palæozoic* time (ancient life), the *Mesozoic* time (middle life), and the *Cenozoic* time (recent life). Under these are classified those ages which resemble each other in their dominant types of life.

I. PALÆOZOIC TIME.

1. Silurian Age (*Age of Mollusks*).
2. Devonian Age (*Age of Fishes*).
3. Carboniferous Age (*Age of Coal-Plants.*)

II. MESOZOIC TIME.

The Age of Reptiles.

III. CENOZOIC TIME.

The Age of Mammals.

The following table contains the geological subdivisions now generally received:

Age	Division	Period	Epoch	
I. SILURIAN AGE. (*Age of Mollusks.*)	LOWER SILURIAN.	1. POTSDAM PERIOD.	a. Potsdam Epoch.	
			b. Calciferous Epoch.	
		2. TRENTON PERIOD	a. Chazy Epoch.	
			b. Birdseye Epoch.	
			c. Black River Epoch.	
			d. Trenton Epoch.	
		3. HUDSON PERIOD.		
	UPPER SILURIAN.	1. NIAGARA PERIOD	a. Oneida Epoch.	
			b. Medina Epoch.	
			c. Clinton Epoch.	
			d. Niagara Epoch.	
		2. SALINA PERIOD.		
		3. LOWER HELDERBERG PERIOD.		
II. DEVONIAN AGE (*Age of Fishes.*)		1. ORISKANY PERIOD.		
		2. UPPER HELDERBERG PERIOD	a. Cauda-Galli and Schoharie Grit.	
			b. Upper Helderberg	*Onondaga Group.*
				Corniferous Group.
		3. HAMILTON PERIOD	a. Marcellus Epoch.	
			b. Hamilton Epoch.	
			c. Genesee Epoch.	
		4. CHEMUNG PERIOD	a. Portage Epoch.	
			b. Chemung Epoch.	
			c. Catskill Epoch.	
III. CARBONIFEROUS AGE (*Age of Coal-Plants.*)		1. SUB-CARBONIFEROUS PERIOD.		
		2. CARBONIFEROUS PERIOD.		
		3. PERMIAN PERIOD.		
IV. AGE OF REPTILES		1. TRIASSIC PERIOD.		
		2. JURASSIC PERIOD.		
		3. CRETACEOUS PERIOD.		
V. AGE OF MAMMALS		1. TERTIARY PERIOD	a. Eocene Epoch.	*Claiborne Epoch.*
			b. Miocene Epoch.	*Jackson Epoch.*
			c. Pliocene Epoch.	*Vicksburg Epoch.*
				Yorktown Epoch.
		2. POST-TERTIARY (QUATERNARY) PERIOD.	a. Glacial or Drift Epoch.	
			b. Champlain Epoch.	
			c. Terrace Epoch.	

The Duration of Time represented by these geological periods and epochs we have no means of judging. Estimating the past, however, by the present rate of change, it must be immense, so that even if we could express it in centuries and years, we could form no idea of the aggregate any more than we can comprehend the distances that separate our earth from the fixed stars. This idea of immense duration of time is suggested at the first examination of the stratified rocks. All that Geology attempts, at present, is to arrange in regular order the various stages of progress in the history of the earth's crust, leaving it for the future to decide upon the length of the different epochs. As yet we only know that "*time is long,*" and hence estimate it by ages, eras, and periods, rarely venturing more than an occasional hint at their relative duration. There is an eternity of time as well as of space in which God works out His almighty plan of creation. Whatever may have been our preconceived notions, we should come to the study of Nature with a reverent, teachable spirit, seeking to learn its mysteries, to comprehend its plan, and to understand the ways of Him who created all things.

THE AZOIC TIME.

Location.—The Azoic rocks probably constitute the foundation rock over the entire globe, but are generally covered deeply with later deposits. On our continent they form the surface rock of a V-shaped region resting on the great lakes, one arm reaching N.W. to the Arctic

Ocean, and the other N.E. to Labrador; in addition there are isolated sections, as shown in the map (Fig. 41). These constitute the oldest dry land of our globe—the Canada area representing the ancient continent, and he other portions widely scattered islands. America is,

FIG. 41.

Azoic Continent (Dana).

geologically speaking, the old rather than the new world, being the first-born among the continents. "We may walk," says Agassiz, "along its summit, and feel that we are treading upon the granite ridge that first divided the waters into a Northern and a Southern ocean; and if our imagination carry us so far, we can look down to its base, and fancy how the sea washed against this earliest shore of a lifeless world."

Kinds of Rock.—The rocks are generally metamorphic, such as granite, gneiss, etc. Statuary marble, schists, porphyry, soapstone, slates, and the like, also occur. All were doubtless deposited as sedimentary strata from the washings of the original crust, and perhaps also the eruptions of submarine volcanoes, and afterward crystallized. The iron mountains of Missouri, and the iron-ore beds of northern New York, date from this time.

Fossils.—Of the life of this era we know nothing definitely, except that if any existed it must have been of the lowest order. The term Azoic indicates that the land and sea were devoid of inhabitants. There was, without doubt, such a time when the boiling water and the heated earth could not support either animal or vegetable life. Some of the slates and sandstones are not more altered than rocks of a later period which abound in fossils, so that organic remains may reasonably be sought. Should any be hereafter definitely discovered in what we have termed the Azoic time, this will simply remove the "dawn of life" back to an earlier period.

Logan found in a bed of marble, near the River St. Lawrence, what seemed to be fossil corals. Prof. Dawson, of Montreal, after a careful microscopic examination, pronounced them to be shells of Rhizopods * (root-

* They were so called because the shell was full of holes, through which passed fleshy filaments or stems. The higher orders of these animals laid hold of objects by means of these stems, and dragged themselves along. The Eozoön, however, simply grew in patches on the sea-bottom.

footed). The name Eozoön Canadense (Canadian early life) has been given to this remarkable fossil. Since then it is said to have been found in the serpentine rocks of Chelmsford, Bolton, Boxboro', and at many other localities in Massachusetts.

FIG. 42.

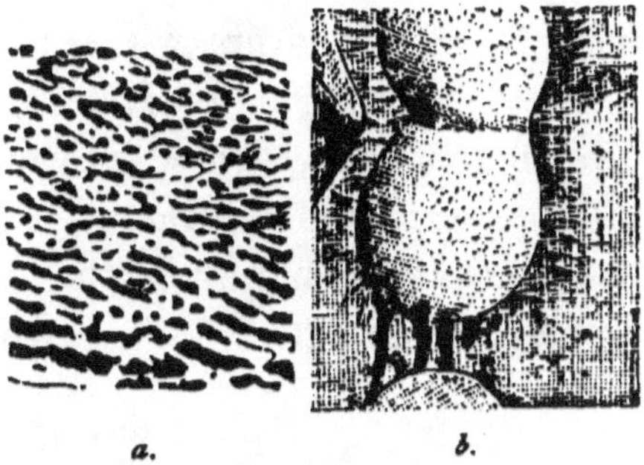

a. Serpentine Marble of Canada.
b. Chamber-Wall of Eozoön magnified (Carpenter).

Still, the hypothesis of the organic structure of these remains is not universally accepted. Should it be established, it will remove the beginning of life back through an era represented by 30,000 feet of rocks.

Remarks.—*1. Mountains.*—Between Canada and New York runs a low range of hills called the Laurentian, named from the River St. Lawrence.* They are probably the oldest mountains upon the earth.

---

* "Their low stature, as compared with that of other more lofty mountain ranges, is in accordance with an invariable rule, by which the relative age of mountains may be estimated. The oldest mountains are the lowest, while the younger and more recent ones tower above their elders, and are usually more torn and dislocated also. This is easily understood when we remember that all mountains and mountain chains are the result of upheavals, and that the violence of the outbreak must have been in proportion to the strength of the resistance. When the crust of the earth was so thin that the heated masses within easily broke through it, they were not thrown to so great a height, and formed comparatively low elevations, such as the Canadian hills or the mountains of Bretagne and Wales. But in later times, when young, vigorous giants, such as the Alps, the Himalayas, or, later still, the Rocky Mountains, forced their way out from their fiery prison-house, the crust of the earth was much thicker, and fearful indeed must have been the convulsions which attended their exit."—*Geological Sketches, Agassiz.*

2. *Convulsions.*—The metamorphism of the Azoic rocks was closely attended by extensive upheavals, which twisted and folded them, throughout vast areas, into every conceivable form. They, however, commonly remain in regular layers, which can be traced. This would indicate a uniform force acting at right angles to the dip of the beds. These movements must have taken place prior to the Silurian age, since the Silurian rocks rest unconformably upon the Azôic, as is shown in the accompanying figure. We see here that the sedimentary

FIG. 43.

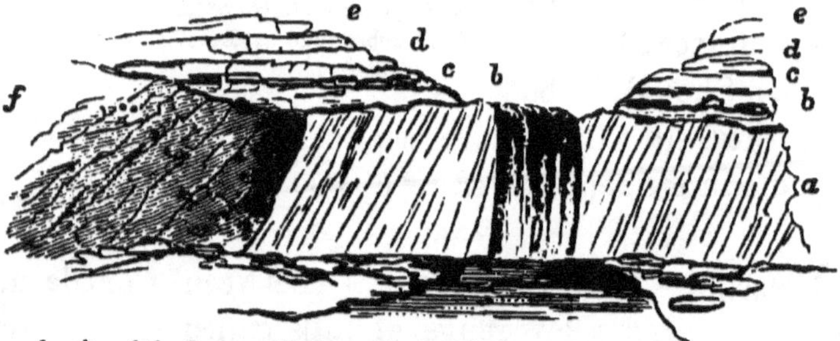

Unconformity of the Lower Silurian with the Gneiss at Montmorency, Canada East. *e, d, c, b.* Lower Silurian. *a.* Gneiss. *f.* Black Slate.

rocks *e, d, c, b,* lie horizontally upon tilted gneiss, *a,* and black slate, *f.* The Azoic rocks at Montmorency are about 12,000 feet in thickness. Through what ages those vast deposits must have slowly gathered in the primeval ocean!*

---

* In the Azoic rocks are conglomerates bearing no resemblance to the beds in which they are found. They are fragments of other rocks, other continents perhaps, broken up and destroyed. There is, then, little hope of our discovering the origin of life on the globe, since this page of the genesis of the facts has been torn. For some years geologists loved to rest their eyes in this long night of ages upon an ideal limit, beyond which plants and animals would cease to appear. Now, this line of demarcation between the rocks which are without

3. Canadian Divisions.—The Azoic rocks of Canada have been divided by Logan into two distinct systems, the Laurentian and the Huronian. They have a total thickness of about 30,000 feet. The former includes nearly all the Azoic area; the latter, a section near Lake Huron.

4. Probability of Life.—The presence of limestone, graphite and anthracite coal would indicate the existence of life. It would seem reasonable to suppose that vegetable life had the precedence, since the animal kingdom is wholly dependent on the vegetable for its subsistence; and that the vegetation consisted of land-plants, since the earth would be cooled sufficiently to admit of life sooner than the water. Geology is, however, as yet silent on this subject, and no plants of that period are known.

5. The Outlines of the Continent.—This V-shaped Azoic land was the nucleus around which the continent grew. Through the subsequent ages additions were made to this germ upon the southeast and southwest sides. Its very shape was thus a prophecy of the shape of North America. The direction of the two

---

vestiges of organized beings and those which contain fossils is nearly effaced among the surrounding ruins. On the horizon of the primitive world we see vaguely indicated a series of other worlds which have altogether disappeared; perhaps it is necessary to resign ourselves to the fact that the dawn of life is lost in this silent epoch where age succeeds age till they are clothed in the garb of eternity. The river of creation is like the river Nile, which, as Bossuet says, hides its head—a figure of speech which time has falsified; but the endless speculations opened up by these and similar considerations led Lyell to say: "Here I am almost prepared to believe in the ancient existence of the Atlantis of Plato."—*M. Esquiros.*

arms was parallel to that of the Atlantic and Pacific oceans (see Fig. 41). The land and sea have from the beginning maintained these relative positions. We are thus led to believe that the thought of God, as ultimately revealed in the form of this continent, was fairly outlined in the first land that appeared. In the early part of the next age the Appalachian and Rocky mountains began to rise, thus forming the framework of the continent, and still further developing the plan.

How accurately did the ancient "backbones" define the present contour of the finished continent! The St. Lawrence flows to the sea through a valley parallel to the Laurentian ridge; the Mississippi river in a second valley inclosed between the Appalachian and Rocky mountains; the Mackenzie finds its way to the Arctic sea in a third valley between the Rocky and Laurentian mountains; while Hudson's Bay is snugly locked in the arms of the Laurentian mountains.

6. *The Mosaic Account* informs us that on the third day the waters were gathered into one place and the dry land appeared, and, as a later creation of the same day, that vegetation was brought forth. The geologic record of the Azoic age agrees with the first portion, and upon the second gives as yet only hints of possible discoveries. The direct rays of the sun could not penetrate the thick mists which then enshrouded the warm, damp earth, and hence, although the sun and moon had shone since the first, these luminaries were not yet set in the firmament to rule the day and the night.

[The following leaf of Natural History is inserted for the benefit of those pupils who may not be familiar with that delightful branch of knowledge. This brief analysis will enable us to speak more understandingly of the ancient life of our globe. It may be studied separately or used merely for reference.]

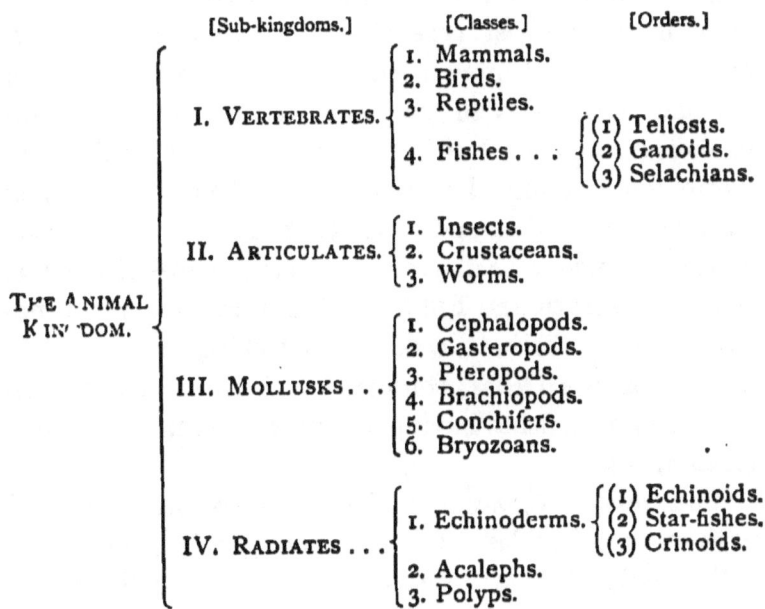

	[Sub-kingdoms.]	[Classes.]	[Orders.]
THE ANIMAL KINGDOM.	I. VERTEBRATES.	1. Mammals.	
		2. Birds.	
		3. Reptiles.	
		4. Fishes . . .	(1) Teliosts.
			(2) Ganoids.
			(3) Selachians.
	II. ARTICULATES.	1. Insects.	
		2. Crustaceans.	
		3. Worms.	
	III. MOLLUSKS . . .	1. Cephalopods.	
		2. Gasteropods.	
		3. Pteropods.	
		4. Brachiopods.	
		5. Conchifers.	
		6. Bryozoans.	
	IV. RADIATES . . .	1. Echinoderms.	(1) Echinoids.
			(2) Star-fishes.
			(3) Crinoids.
		2. Acalephs.	
		3. Polyps.	

All animals are constructed upon one of four* different types which constitute the sub-kingdoms of the animal creation. Each type is a thought of God worked out in a multitude of ways. The design of nature seems to be to have an infinity of detail and variety, with the utmost simplicity of elements, or, as Agassiz beautifully says, a fundamental harmony upon which an endless set of vari-

* Some authorities give a fifth class, which includes what are termed Protozoans, or systemless animals. It embraces sponges, infusoria, and other similar animals which seem to have no distinct plan of structure.

ations may be played. It is our privilege to trace out these four ideas in their curious ramifications, and thus classify the animals of the present as well as the fossils of the past.

I. Sub-kingdom of Vertebrates.—The verte brate is the highest type of structure. Fishes, reptiles, birds and man all agree in having an axis running from one end of the body to the other, which in the lowest animals is a soft cord, but in most is a series of small bones (vertebræ), making what we call a backbone. The spinal cord lies above this, and expands at one end into a brain. This sub-kingdom is divided into four classes—MAMMALS, BIRDS, REPTILES, and FISHES. Fishes are subdivided into three orders—*Teliosts, Ganoids,* and *Selachians.*

The *Teliosts* (*telios,* complete, and *osteon,* a bone) include common fishes having a bony skeleton. Ex., perch, salmon, etc.

The *Ganoids* (*ganos,* splendor) comprise fishes covered with enameled scales. Ex., sturgeon, garpike, etc.

The *Selachians* (*selachos,* cartilage) embrace those having a cartilaginous skeleton and a rough skin, often called shagreen. Ex., shark.

II. Sub-kingdom of Articulates.—The articulate type is a jointed structure, *i. e.,* one composed of rings. Ex., spider, centipede, shrimp, etc. It is expressed in three different ways, and thus there are three classes—INSECTS, CRUSTACEANS, and WORMS. Crustaceans have a shelly covering. Ex., crab, lobster, etc.

III. Sub-kingdom of Mollusks.—The mollusk type is a soft sack, usually inclosed in a hard shell. Ex., oyster, clam, etc. There are six classes—CEPHALOPODS, GASTEROPODS, PTEROPODS, BRACHIOPODS, CONCHIFERS, and BRYOZOANS.

The CEPHALOPODS (head-footed) have arms attached to their head. Ex., nautilus, cuttle-fish, etc.

The GASTEROPODS (body-footed) move on the under part of their body, which forms a fleshy foot. Ex., snail, slug, etc.

The PTEROPODS (wing-footed) live only in the sea, and swim with a pair of fins extending out like wings from the side of the head. They are the food of the right whale.

The BRACHIOPODS (arm-footed) are bivalves having arms by which they stir the water, and thus bring their food within their reach. The two parts of the shell are unequal; the larger is called the ventral and the smaller the dorsal valve. Each valve is, however, equal sided, so that if a line be dropped from the beak to the opposite side, it will divide the valve into equal parts.

The CONCHIFERS have their gills in thin, membranous plates on each side of the body, which may be easily seen in the oyster, clam, etc. (For this reason they are sometimes called Lamellibranchs, *lamella*, a plate.) A line let fall as in the case of the brachiopods, will divide the shell into two unequal parts.

The BRYOZOANS (moss-like animals) grow in clusters, and form moss-like incrustations on rocks. They resemble corals.

IV. Sub-kingdom of Radiates.—The radiate type is a structure arranged around a central axis. Ex., star-fish. There are three classes—ECHINODERMS, ACALEPHS, and POLYPS.

The ECHINODERMS (hedge-hog skin) are covered with spines. They are divided into three orders: (1) The *Echinoids*, which have a hard shell, as sea-urchins and the like; (2) *Star-fishes;* and (3) *Crinoids*, or "stone-lilies," as they are called, since they grow on a stem like a flower.

The ACALEPHS (headless) are soft, jelly-like animals. Ex., jelly-fish, medusa. Some of them, however, formed corals, and have hence left remains among fossils.

The POLYPS (many-footed) are the true coral-producing animals. They have a mouth around which is arranged a row of tiny arms, like the petals of a China aster. The coral is the bone of the polyp, which it secretes from the water. As the animal dies below, it leaves its skeleton of bone behind, and grows above.

THE PALÆOZOIC TIME.

PALÆOZOIC TIME.
1. Silurian Age.
2. Devonian Age.
3. Carboniferous Age.

The Palæozoic time is divided into three ages to mark the great life-changes which occurred. These are called the Silurian or Age of mollusks, the Devonian or Age of fishes, and the Carboniferous or Age of coal-plants. These ages, though unlike in marked particulars, are yet distinguished by certain common features in the life they supported, while they are all very dissimilar to any later formations. Neither birds nor mammals were known, and many extensive classes of animals which peculiarly characterized these ages disappeared with them.

I. THE SILURIAN AGE.

I. SILURIAN AGE (AGE OF MOLLUSKS.)	LOWER.	1. Potsdam Period. 2. Trenton Period. 3. Hudson Period.
	UPPER.	1. Niagara Period. 2. Salina Period. 3. Lower Helderberg Period.

This first great stage in the progress of life on the globe was so called by Murchison, the celebrated English geologist, who first fully investigated it in Wales, and so named it from the ancient Silures, a tribe of Britons formerly inhabiting that region. The subdivisions of the age vary greatly in different portions even of the United States. The Silurian and Devonian rocks are very distinctly developed in New York, and the epochs established in the geologic survey of that State are therefore taken as the basis for study and comparison. In

FIG. 44.

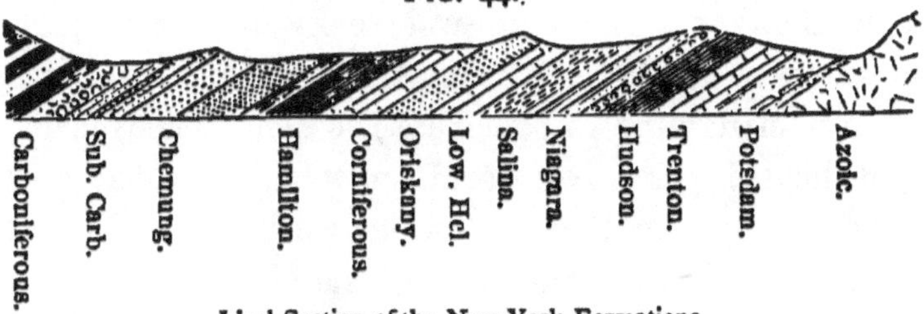

Ideal Section of the New York Formations.

Fig. 44 is shown an ideal section extending from the Azoic rocks in the northeastern part of the State to the carboniferous in the southern. It will be seen that the different epochs succeed each other regularly. The dip of the strata is by no means as uniform as is represented, nor is there any attempt to indicate their relative thickness. This illustrates on a grand scale the fact stated on page 77 concerning the method of geologic study.

We shall see that, with each period, a narrow, irregular belt was added to the Azoic area, from which, as a germ, the continent grew by successive additions.

General Characteristics.—It is probable that at this early day the Appalachians on the east and the Rocky Mountains on the west were already being lifted above the floor of the sea, thus rendering the interior of the continent an immense lagoon, protected in great measure from the ocean. At the bottom of this shallow basin, sandstone, shale and limestone were formed. The kind of rock varied with different sections of the country and periods of the age, according to the peculiar circumstances which influenced the deposit of sediment at any specified place or time. There were broad areas of low mud-flats and wave-washed sand beaches. There may have been rivers and lakes on the Azoic continent, but if so, they have entirely disappeared in the wreck of subsequent changes. The land was rocky and barren, while the waters swarmed with crustaceans and mollusks. The pale sun, struggling to penetrate the dense atmosphere of a yet heated primitive world, now first yielded a dim imperfect light to these, as far as we know, earliest created beings* that left the hand of the Creator.

* We have already spoken of the Eozoön of the Laurentian rocks, which, if accepted as a true fossil, is the oldest known inhabitant of our globe. Among the Longmynd rocks of Ireland, Dr. Oldham discovered a zoöphite (*zō-o-fite*, plant-animal, a class of polyps, so named because they resemble both plants and

POTSDAM PERIOD.

Location.—This period is named from Potsdam, a town in northern New York, where the rock is well developed. The formation is very thick in Pennsylvania, and can be traced westward through Michigan, along the southern shore of Lake Superior, through Wisconsin and Minnesota to the Black Hills of Dacotah, and southward along the Appalachian range from Vermont to Alabama. It outcrops at many other places, and generally underlies all the newer sedimentary rocks, forming over the entire continent the floor, as it were, on which the more recent deposits rest.

Kind of Rock.—The rock varies much throughout this wide extent. At Potsdam it is a coarse, hard sandstone; at Malone, N. Y., a friable one; at Keeseville, a quartzite; and at other localities, a fine white sand, fit for glass-making. At some points east it is a good building-stone, while at the west it is often so friable as to crumble in the fingers. The colors are brown, gray, yellowish, and even red. In many localities it is worm-burrowed,* ripple-marked, mud-cracked, and rain-pitted,

---

animals), which in his honor has been named the Oldhamia antiqua. These rocks are called by Sedgwick and Murchison the Cambrian. The latter authority places them on the same geologic horizon with the Huronian. American geologists, however, believe them to be the equivalent, in part, of Barrande's Primordial Zone of Bohemia, and in part of the Potsdam sandstone. The pupil will see from this that the question of the "dawn of life" on our globe is yet an unsettled one, although we have traced it back to where organisms of the lowest type seem to just emerge out of the igneous rocks of the primitive earth.

* The holes burrowed out by marine worms were filled with sand, which hardened like the rock itself, and, when the rock is broken, form regular casts of the worm-burrow. The holes are like those now made along the sea-shore in the same way.

showing the mode of its formation on a low sand-beach or mud-flat. The upper portion of this period, known as the Calciferous Epoch, is in part calcareous, so that some layers are even burned for lime. In the Mississippi valley its character changes, and it is called the *Lower Magnesian Limestone.**

FIG. 45.

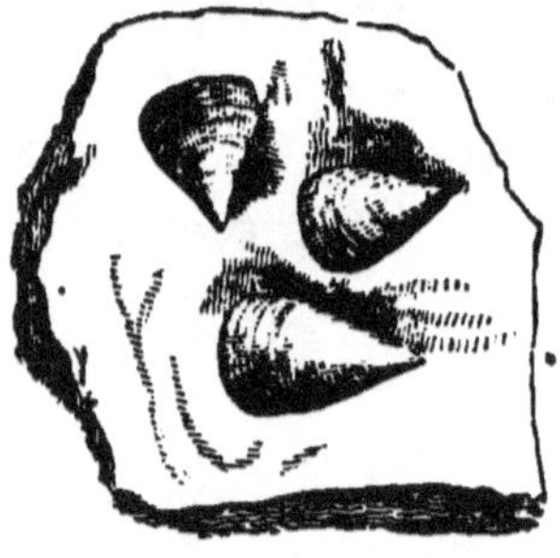

Lingula antiqua.

FIG. 46.

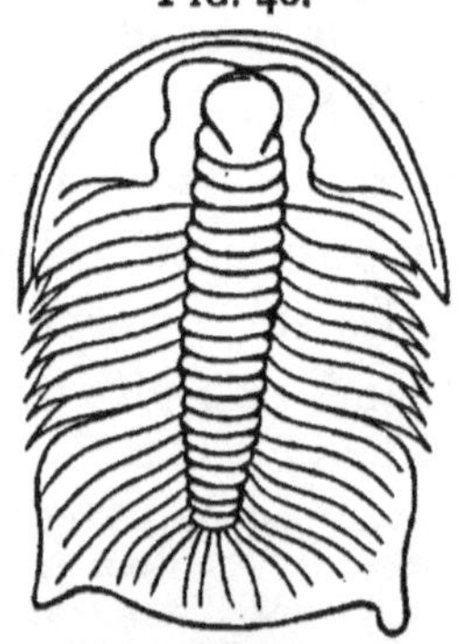

A Trilobite (Dikelocephalus Minnesotensis).

Fossils.—A brachiopod, the *lingula* (little tongue), so named from its peculiar shape, is a characteristic fossil. The form and size of the shell are similar to that of the finger-nail. The peculiarity of this mollusk was that, when alive, it grew on a fleshy stem which anchored it to the rock. Several species of the lingula still exist in the Moluccas. A crustacean, the *trilobite* (three-lobed), is the most conspicuous fossil. This family was prominent in the early creations, but disappeared in the Carboniferous Age. It is perfectly preserved, and the various stages of growth, from the egg to the adult, have been more accurately traced than even those of the crab, a

* In Wisconsin, Iowa, Minnesota, and Illinois, this is overlaid by the St. Peter's sandstone,—a soft, white, incoherent rock, composed of grains of quartz that crumble easily under the hammer, though in some localities it is hardened by a calcareous cement. It is used in Chicago for glass-making. Like the Lower Magnesian Limestone, it is destitute of fossils.—*Whitney.*

living crustacean. It was of wonderful variety, more than 400 species having been discovered. It had an oval figure, and was from $\frac{1}{6}$ of an inch to 24 inches in length. The body, divided into three lobes, was covered with small plates which folded over each other as in the tail of the lobster. Some species could roll themselves up into a ball, and thus present a hard armor in every direction. The head was protected by a buckler of a crescent shape. Its eyes were very curious. They were of a conical shape, and each one was composed of from 40 to 6000 separate facets or lenses,* by means of which

FIG. 47.

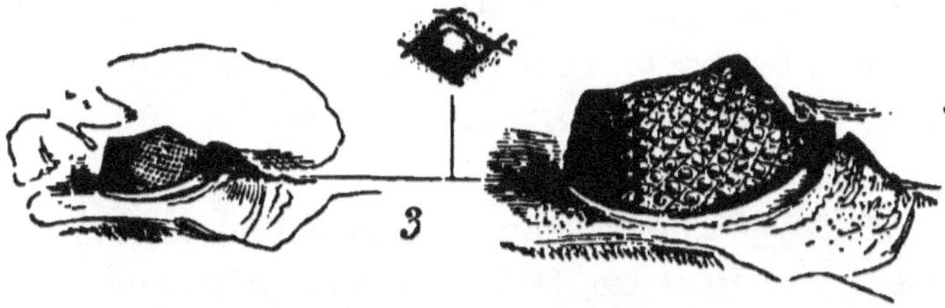

Eyes of Trilobites, showing that the eyes of insects of the present day are constructed on the same plan. 3. Enlarged Lens.

the animal could see in every direction at once. The inner side of each eye being of no practical value, Nature, on her principle of economy, placed no lenses there. The trilobite is supposed to have gathered in shoals in the shallow water, swimming slowly on its back by means of membranous appendages now lost.

---

* The construction of the eye was very like that of certain insects at the present day. The house-fly has 14,000 of these facets, the butterfly 35,000, and the dragon-fly 60,000.

Remarks.—*1. The Atmosphere.*—The eyes of the trilobite would have been useless unless the atmosphere had been clear enough to permit sufficient sunlight to reach the earth to render objects visible in some degree. God makes all things for a purpose; hence we conclude that at this early period the sun had pierced the clouds, and the air was being purified.

2. Early Silurian Beach.—Where the Potsdam rock lies on the surface, we are assured that that locality was raised above the sea at or near the close of this period (unless uncovered by subsequent denudation), else it would have been concealed by the sediment of the succeeding one. The narrow zone of the Potsdam rock along the borders of the Azoic area, was doubtless the beach of the early Silurian sea.

3. Life.—The organic remains found in this period represent the Radiates, Mollusks, and Articulates among animals, and the sea-weeds among plants. The trilobite was the highest type. Three of the four general ideas of expressing animal life were thus simultaneously developed at the beginning; the fourth does not appear until long after. There is, says Dana, no proof that the dry, primordial hills bore a moss or lichen, or that the ocean contained a single fish. No sounds were heard in the air save those of inanimate Nature—the moving waters, the tempest, and the earthquake.

4. Climate.—No difference is seen in the life of different latitudes; hence it is thought that there was a uniformity of temperature existing over the earth, and that the diversity of zone and climate had not yet been established. Various reasons have been assigned for this, among which are—(a) the greater interior heat of the earth on account of the thinness of the crust, (b) the dense atmosphere which retained the sun's heat more fully, (c) the great expanse of the ocean which tended to equalize the temperature, and (d) the greater size and heat of the sun in that era, according to the nebular hypothesis.

5. Changes in the Sea, Life, and Rock.—Shales were produced in the muddy water, and limestones in the shallow, clearer sea; since the coral animal thrives best in pure water less than a hundred feet deep. The crust of the still unsteady earth, as it rose and fell, shallowing or deepening the waters, rendering them muddier or purer, varied the character of the life supported and the rock formed. There were frequent transitions of this kind during the Potsdam Period, and especially in passing into the Calciferous Epoch, when there was almost a complete extermination of the different species.

6. Lake Superior Region.—In connection with the deposit of Potsdam sandstone, there was a depression of the crust, thus forming the bed of Lake Superior, and also igneous ejections, making the trap-rocks and dikes so characteristic of that section. The sandstone has since been worn into grotesque and curious forms as seen in the famous Sculptured and Pillared Rocks.*

* These strata form a wall 50 to 100 feet high, and line the shore for a distance of five miles. Their brilliant hues and fantastic shape excite the imagination

7. *The Mosaic Account* tells us that the sun and moon were created on the fourth day. Geology shows us that the distinctive feature of the early Silurian Age was the partial clearing of the sky after the murky

FIG. 48.

Sculptured Rocks, Lake Superior. "The Inverted Volcano."

clouds of the Azoic. The first glimpse of the sun would have seemed to an observer as a new creation, and, in popular language, it is thus described in Genesis. We also read that on the fifth day the waters brought forth

of every beholder. Here is "Miner's Castle," with its turrets and bastions; there "Sail Rock," a ship with sails full spread; and yonder "The Amphitheatre," with its symmetrical curves. A closer inspection only reveals more curious details and resemblances. For a very interesting account of these rocks see Harpers' Magazine, Vol. XXXIV, p. 681.

abundantly the moving creature that hath life. We shall see how perfectly the swarming seas of the Silurian and Devonian Ages justify this description.

TRENTON PERIOD.

Location.—The Trenton formation extends along the great Appalachian chain of mountains on the east, thence outcrops at various points westward to the Mississippi river, and beyond to the Rocky Mountains. It is more widely distributed than any similar deposit.

Kinds of Rock.—This was the first great limestone period of the continent. In New York there are four epochs—(1) the *Chazy limestone*, a dark, irregular rock, named from a locality near Lake Champlain; (2) the *Bird's Eye limestone*, a dove-colored rock containing fine white crystalline points scattered through it; (3) the *Black River limestone*, a black, hard-grained marble capable of a high polish,* named from the river of that name, east of Lake Ontario; (4) the *Trenton* proper,† a hard, compact rock of a grayish or black color, so called from the well-known gorge at Trenton Falls. This epoch of the period has been identified in Canada and throughout the south and west, but the other epochs vary somewhat, and their equivalents are not so well established.

* At Watertown, N. Y., it is lumpy, and breaks into rhomboidal fragments, while the Bird's Eye has a conchoidal fracture. The river takes its name from the dark color of the rocks over which it flows.

† The massive pillars of the court-house at St. Louis are from the Trenton limestone quarries of Sulphur Spring. The crest of the Falls of St. Anthony is of Trenton limestone. In Kentucky and Tennessee this rock is termed the Stone River group.

(5) In Illinois, Wisconsin, and Iowa, the *Galena limestone* overlies the Trenton. It is the great lead and zinc bearing rock of a region embracing about 3,000 square miles. The streams have cut deeply down into this stone, so that they are bordered by precipitous bluffs crowned by perpendicular ledges, having frequently a castellated appearance like the walls of some half-ruined city, while isolated masses sometimes rise abruptly from the valleys like lofty watch-towers. Dubuque and Galena are partly situated on picturesque bluffs of this character.*

Fossils.—The Chazy limestone is not characterized by many very distinctive fossils. The principal ones are gasteropods. Fig. 49 represents the characteristic marine

FIG. 49.

The Bird's Eye Coral (Phytopsis tubulosum).

---

* The QUEBEC GROUP is thought by Hall to underlie the Chazy (Shăz-ĕe) in New York, and to be the equivalent of Emmons' much disputed TACONIC SYSTEM. Others refer both to the Calciferous epoch.

plant which is found in the Bird's Eye limestone. The ends of the stems give the rock the dotted appearance from which it takes its name. Fig. 50 gives an idea of a coral common in the Black River limestone. It has been found in masses of a ton's weight. The Trenton limestone abounds in organic remains. The flagstones in the streets of Ottawa show branching sea-weeds spread out on their surface; at Cincinnati, where the rock is known as the *Blue limestone*, at Nashville, Tenn., and at many other widely-scattered localities, corals, crinoids, and shells are found crowded together in the greatest profusion. Thin, semi-transparent slices, apparently devoid of fossils, under the microscope reveal their animal origin.

FIG. 50.

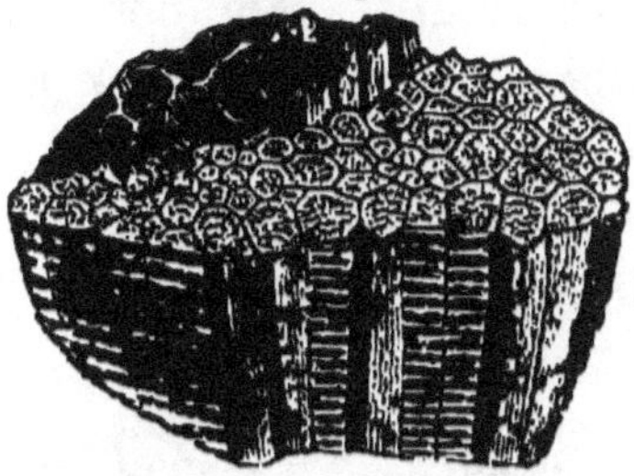

Black River Coral (Columnaria alveolata).

Brachiopods occur in wonderful variety. Trilobites, the highest type of the Potsdam, appear of a dozen species, varying in size from that of a finger-nail to a foot in length. They, however, now yield in abundance, activity and power to the cephalopods. A family of these, the *Orthoceratite* (straight-horn), distinguishes the entire period. It had a long straight shell, divided into sometimes as many as seventy chambers. These were formed to accommodate the growth of the animal. As it increased in size, it moved forward in its room, and extending its shell at the larger end, partitioned off its new quarters from the rest by a shelly wall. Thus, in time, a long series of chambers were made, each larger than its predecessor.* They were connected, however, by a membranous tube ("siphuncle"), which passed from the animal in the newest and largest chamber at one end to the oldest and smallest room at the other. These empty chambers are thought to have acted as a buoy to float the heavy animal. Some of the fossil orthoceratites are not larger than a lead pencil, while others are a foot thick and thirty feet in length. They had many muscular arms, with which they seized and strangled their prey in their powerful grasp. They were doubtless the sea-rovers of the Lower Silurian Ocean.

Remarks.—*1. Life and Death* were coeval from the first—one species giving place to another, most commonly at the close of a period, but frequently within its duration. After the exterminations of the last period,

---

* "Year after year beheld the silent toil
That spread his lustrous coil;
Still as the spiral grew,
He left the past year's dwelling for the new.
Stole with soft step its shining archway through,
Built up its idle door,
Stretched in his last-found home, and knew the old no more.

"Thanks for the heavenly message brought by thee,
Child of the wandering sea,
Cast from her lap forlorn.
Cast from thy dead lips, a clearer note is born
Than ever Triton blew from wreathed horn;
While on my ear it rings,
Through the deep caves of thought, I hear a voice that sings:

"'Build thee more stately mansions, oh, my soul,
As the swift seasons roll!
Leave thy low-vaulted past!
Let each new temple, nobler than the last,
Shut thee from heaven with a dome more vast
Till thou at length art free;
Leaving thine outgrown shell by life's unresting sea.'"

TRILOBITES OF TRENTON PERIOD.

FIG. 51.

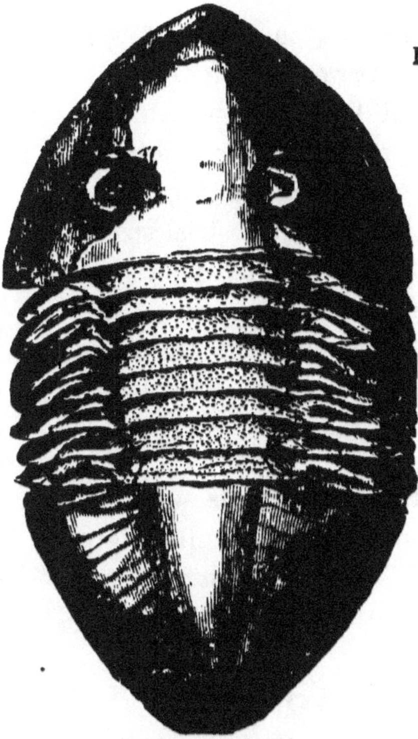

1. Asaphus (Isotelus) gigas.

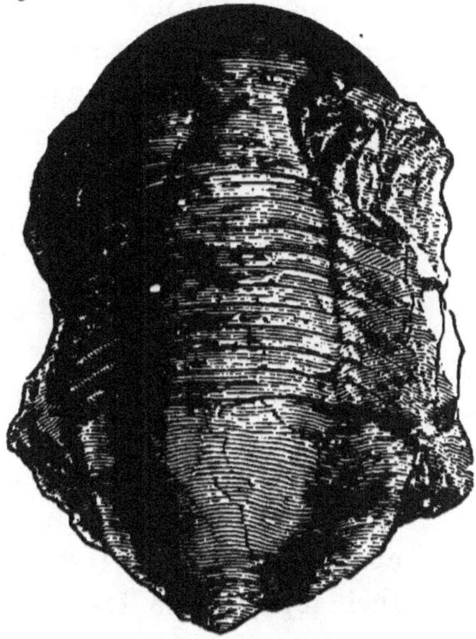

2. Illænus trentonensis.

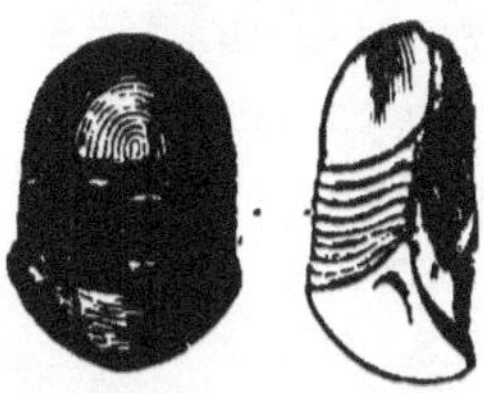

3. Illænus crassicauda.

4. Calymene senaria.

FIG. 52.

Orthoceras multicamerntum (Black River Epoch).

the sea was repopulated by new species, but of the old genera represented in the Potsdam. It was still, however, the reign of mollusks, since that sub-kingdom was exhibited in its various classes, while the articulates had not progressed above the crustaceans and worms, and no vertebrates have been discovered as yet. No terrestrial species of any kind have been found. The only plants yet known were sea-weeds. The land, so far as geology teaches, remained leafless and lifeless as at the beginning. The sea, however, in its shallower places, resembled a flower-garden, with its abundant corals.

2. *Geography.*—The Green Mountains were elevated above the sea, though not to their full height, about the close of this period. We know this because their tops contain Trenton, but no Hudson River rocks.

HUDSON PERIOD.

Location.—This formation is exposed to view along the Mohawk river, N. Y., on the shores of Lake Huron, and in many of the western and southern States; also along the Appalachian range to Alabama. From its abundance near that city, it has also received the name of the "Cincinnati Limestone."

Kinds of Rock.—It consists mainly of soft clay or shales, and even the Cincinnati limestone is interlaminated with shale or marl. Its color is dark, and it is frequently bituminous, so as to afford a black pigment. There are thin seams of coal which have many times tantalized those ignorant of geology with unfounded hopes of the discovery of profitable beds of coal.

Fossils.—In the limestone regions corals, shells, trilobites, etc., are abundant as in the Trenton Period. In the shales, however, they are sparingly distributed, being mostly those which flourish in muddy waters. The graptolites (rock-writing) of the kingdom of Radiates are striking fossils (see Fig. 53). They are found in the Potsdam, but become very plentiful in the Hudson Period. They are merely a delicate, plume-like tracery upon the rock. They have been therefore poetically styled *sea-pens.* They delighted in foul, as the corals in clear water, and must have thickly covered the muddy bottom of the shallow sea with their fragile, mossy branches. They are found commonly in scattered fragments, the arms only of the entire animal as seen in Fig. 53.

FIG. 53.

A Graptolite with Eight Arms (Graptolithus octobrachiatus).

Remarks.—*Geography.*—The River St. Lawrence was fast assuming its present proportions. Lake Champlain and Hudson River probably date from this time. The continent was steadily pushing its way southward, and had reached the central part of New York, western Vermont had emerged from the sea, while the then low, narrow Rocky Mountains represented the western part of the continent.

NIAGARA PERIOD.

Location.—This is a widespread formation like the Trenton. It is found in Canada, south through the Appalachian region, and west through the Mississippi valley. It takes its name from the fact that the great cataract of Niagara pours over a rocky wall of this period. The peculiar form of the fall is owing to the fact that the soft shale below wears away more rapidly than the hard rock above, thus leaving a cavern behind the falling sheet.

Kinds of Rock.—In New York there are four epochs of this period.

1. THE ONEIDA GROUP, called from a county of that name in central New York, is a gritty, hard rock, so rough as to form millstones.

2. THE MEDINA GROUP, named from the locality in western New York where the rock is extensively quarried for building purposes, is a thickly laminated sandstone, of red, gray, and beautifully mottled colors.

3. THE CLINTON GROUP, so called from a village in central New York, is a shaly sandstone.*

4. THE NIAGARA proper is a limestone of a light gray

* In Michigan and some of the western States it assumes more of a limestone character, and in New York, Ohio, and Wisconsin, has beds of oölitic iron ore of great value. In Tennessee it is called "dye-stone," being extensively used for dyeing cloth.

or cream color, and of an enduring hardness, but yet soft enough to be easily wrought to any desired form. At Chicago it is called the "Athens marble," and is almost a pure dolomite. At Lockport, New York, dog-tooth and pearl-spar, also gypsum and other minerals, are found in beautiful crystals lining the cavities in the rock. At the west the Niagara limestone—including also the Helderberg—stands in bold bluffs along the river banks. It contains nodules of hornstone ("chert"), often arranged in layers parallel to the strata. The Niagara rock is frequently found capping small hills or knobs, and has hence received the name "Mound limestone."*

Fossils.—In the Clinton beds a brachiopod (the *pentamerus*, five-parted) is very abundant. This is peculiarly interesting because it is known to be spread in strata of this period from Europe to the west of the Mississippi. *Sea-weeds* (fucoids) cover the Medina sandstone in many places with their interlacing stems, curiously wrought, like the intricate carving of some old Gothic cornice. The Niagara rocks abound in corals, crinoids, shells, etc. They are doubtless the remains of old coral reefs.

The crinoids appeared in preceding periods, but now became very plentiful. They grew on a stem, and had somewhat the form of a lily, hence have received the

* The Blue Mounds, the Platte Mounds, Sinsinnewa Mound, in Wisconsin; Sherald's, in Iowa; Scales's, Charles's, Waddell's, Pilot's Knob, etc., in Illinois, are striking examples of this peculiarity, since they form conspicuous landmarks in the scenery of those States. These outliers of the Niagara limestone assume a great variety of forms, but are always graceful in their outlines, and, as they are generally covered with forest trees, present a striking contrast to the rocky bluffs of the Galena limestone.

name of "stone-lilies." Their cup-shaped body sent out, star-like, five arms; these branched sometimes into as

FIG. 55.

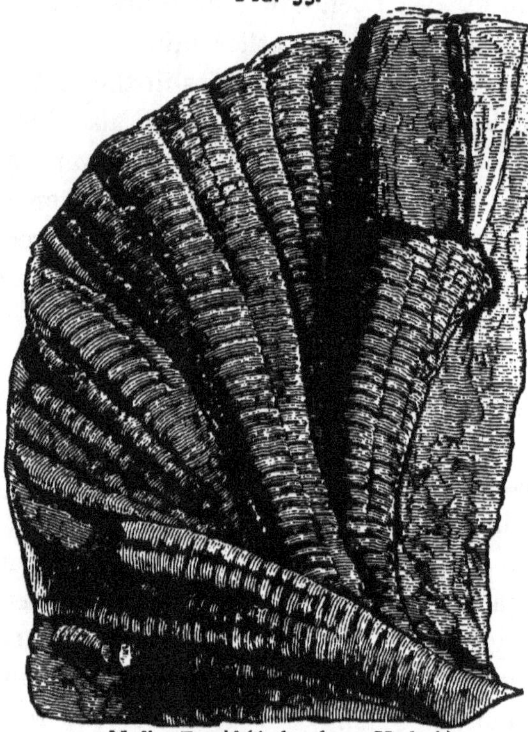

Medina Fucoid (Arthrophycus Harlani.)

many as a thousand, each composed of a hundred little bones, firmly and exquisitely jointed together. The stalk was also jointed, like the vertebræ of the spine, and was curiously grooved and ornamented on the surface. The arms were adapted to be spread out, and to seize and draw into the centre shoals of animals, the food of the crinoid. In many places the rock is a confused mass of crinoidal stems (Figs. 58 and 75).

FIG. 56.

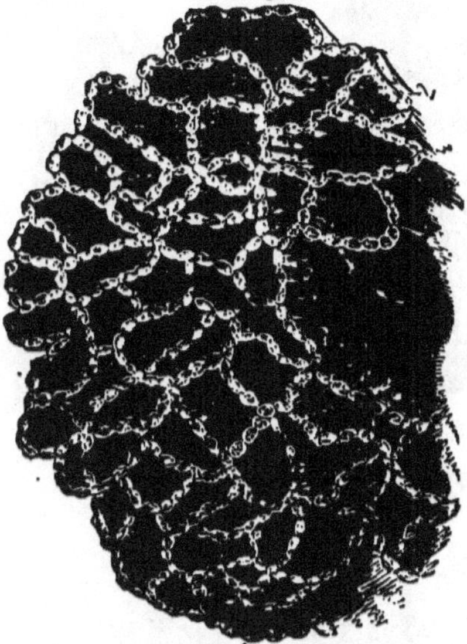

A Niagara Coral.

Remark.—The Appalachian region does not seem to have received any Niagara deposits from the clear sea which covered the central part of the continent and produced limestones. It appears rather to have been a reef bordering the Atlantic Ocean, from which mud and clay were constantly washed in great quantities. Under its lee the interior sea protected the corals, mollusks, and crinoids that during the great limestone periods swarmed in the clear shallow waters.

SALINA PERIOD.

Location.—The Salina period is named from the salt springs near Syracuse, N. Y. The rock occurs in Michigan, and perhaps at the west and south.

NIAGARA CRINOIDS.

Fig. 57

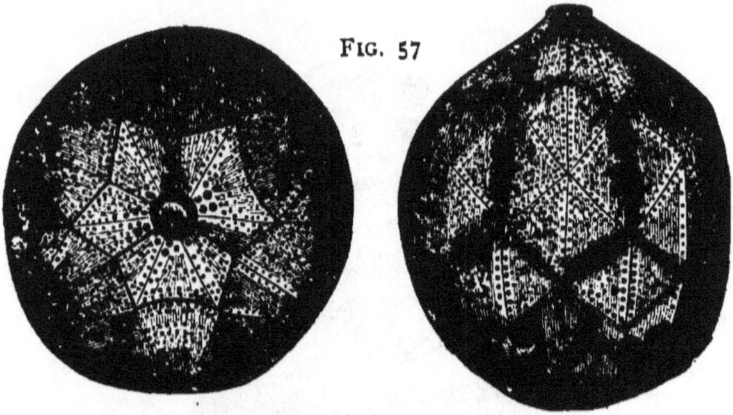

Caryocrinus ornatus.

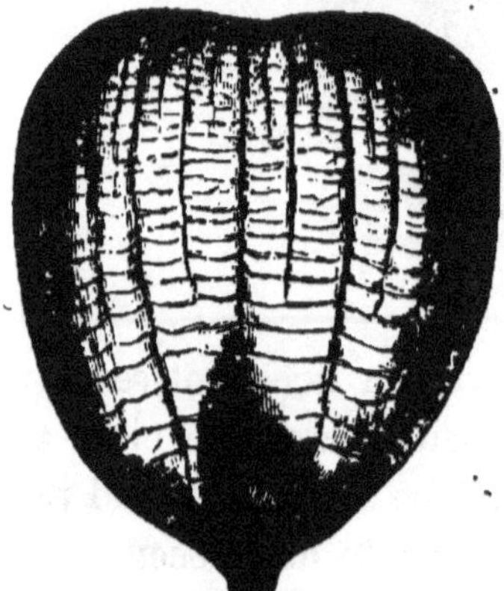

Eucalyptocrinus decorus.

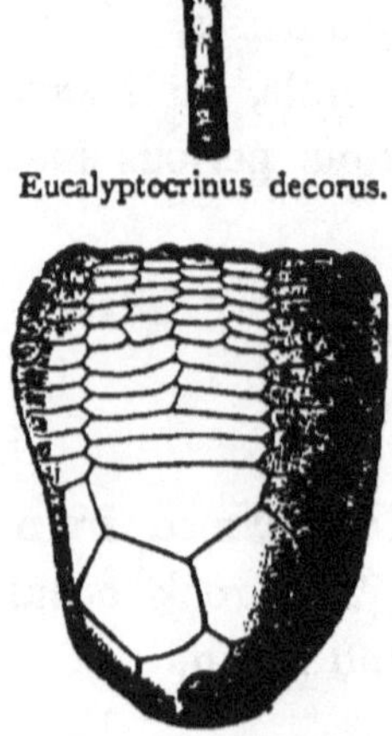

Lecanocrinus macropetalus.

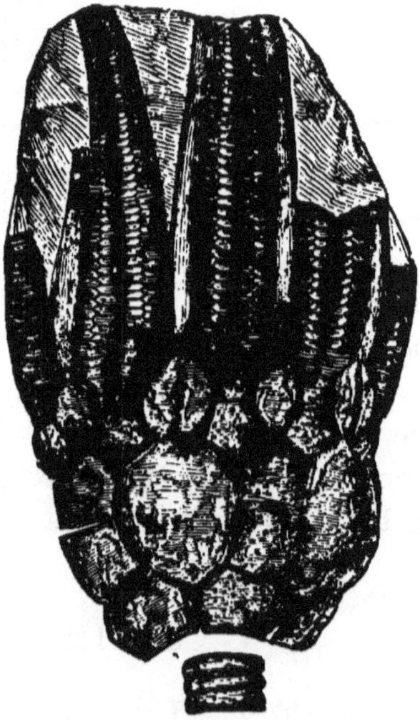

Ichthyocrinus lævis.

FIG. 58.

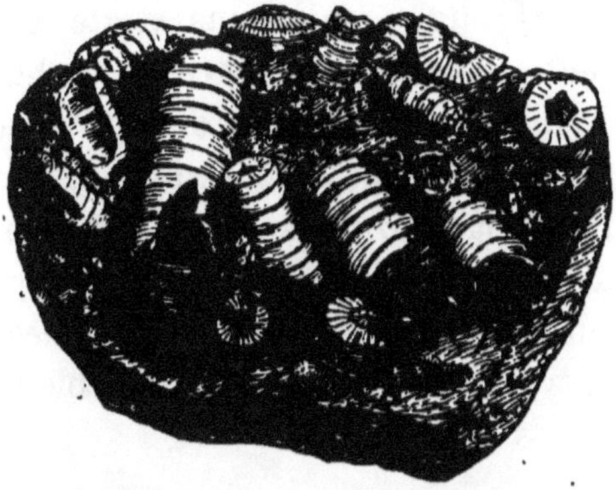

Fragment of Encrinital Limestone, Niagara Period.

Kinds of Rock.—The rocks consist mainly of shales, marls, and some limestone. The saliferous beds are about 1,000 feet in thickness, showing a long continuance of the peculiar conditions under which they were formed.

Fossils.—It seems nearly destitute of fossils. The conditions of the water, sometimes too salt for any life, and sometimes too fresh for marine life, were unfavorable for the existence of animals.

Remarks.—*1. The Salt Springs* of Syracuse have been accounted for in the following manner: Central New York is considered to have been at that time a great salt lake, shut off mainly from the sea. By continued evaporation, by fresh overflows of the brine from the ocean, and by washings of rains and streams from the adjacent land, muddy deposits were formed, thoroughly impregnated with salt.

2. Gypsum abounds in many localities. It seems to have been formed after the limestone was deposited, since in places where the gypsum has been dug out, well-like holes, passing through continuous strata of limestone, have been left. The process appears to have been as follows: Sulphur springs produce sulphuric acid by oxydation from the air. This acid acting on the carbonate of lime, converts it into the sulphate of lime (gypsum). Sulphur springs still abound in this group, and there is a very celebrated sulphuric acid spring near Alabama, Genesee county, N. Y.; hence it is probable that gypsum is still in process of formation.

LOWER HELDERBERG PERIOD.

Location.—This period takes its name from the Helderberg Mountains, near Albany, N. Y. The rocks gradually disappear in the western part of the State, but are conspicuous southward along the Appalachian range, and reappear in Maine, and also in Illinois and Missouri.

Kind of Rock.—This is also a great limestone formation, but differs from the Trenton and Niagara groups in being thickest on the eastern border. The lower beds in New York and Virginia are used for hydraulic cement, whence their name—the "*Water-lime group.*"

Fossils.—The conditions of life seem to have been eminently favorable. About four hundred species of animals have been discovered. A brachiopod (*Pentamerus galeatus*) is so common in some sections as to give its name to the rock. A peculiar crustacean, the *eurypterus* (broad-fin), is allied to the trilobite. Crab-like in its organs of mastication, lobster-like in its prolonged and segmented body, with its broad swimming-limbs and huge claws,

FIG. 59.

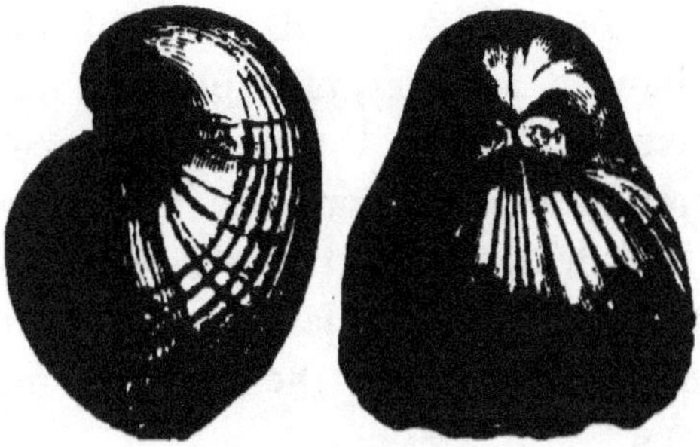

Pentamerus galeatus.

FIG. 60.

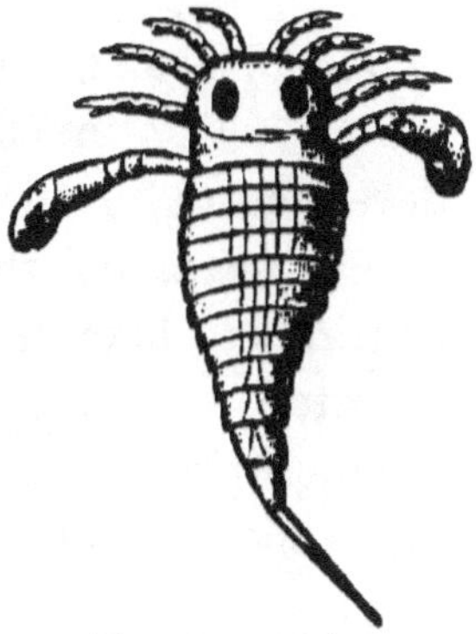

Eurypterus remipes.

it presents a new and striking family. Some seem to have been six or eight feet in length. They were the scavengers of their time, living on the lower forms and garbage by the sea-shore. Small cones, called Tentaculites, are so abundant in some places as to compose the mass of the rock.

FIG. 61.

Tentaculites ornatus.

Remarks.—*1. Geography.*—The formation of limestone in this period in eastern New York and in the Green Mountain region shows that these sections must have been depressed, and the mountains, in part at least, again submerged in the sea. More than half of New York, nearly all of Canada and Wisconsin, had now become dry land. A great bay, however, covered a large part of Michigan. The rivers were probably small, and fresh water lakes, if any existed, have disappeared.

2. *Climate.*—The fossils, constituting a kind of life-thermometer, indicate that the climate of the Silurian was uniform.

3. *Progress of Life.*—The grand types of life remain. Continued changes, however, take place in the development of the creative idea by the disappearance* of old genera and the appearance of new ones. Mollusks continue to take the lead, while the articulates are represented as yet only by the second class—crustaceans. Neither plant nor animal is seen on the land, and no fishes sport in the waters.

4. *Uniformity of Nature.*—The construction of the eyes of the trilobite shows that the laws of light were the same then as now. The animal itself was very like the king-crab of the Atlantic coast. The orthoceratites were the progenitors of the nautilus, the shell being uncoiled in those early species. The sea-shore was clad in weeds, and in favorable localities the waters were thronged with inhabitants. Species and genera took their places in the grand sub-kingdoms of animal life. It requires no great stretch of the fancy to people those early seas, and imagine them busy and joyous on a summer's eve as the tribes that throng our existing oceans.

SCENIC DESCRIPTION.—Let us picture to ourselves the scenery of the Silurian Age. The air, damp

* For example, the chain-coral and graptolites passed away with the Upper Silurian, while the crinoids greatly increased. Dana says that not one species belonging to the latter part of the Lower Silurian existed at the close of the Upper Silurian.

with fogs and foul with noxious gases, hangs heavy over land and sea. The sun sheds a strange lurid glare. The land, faintly visible in the dim light, presents few attractions. The new-born continent is yet crude and unfinished. Vapor is rising in clouds from the heated surface. With no song of bird, nor hum of insect, nor garment of verdure, it is a broad, low, barren, rocky desert. Everywhere are seams, and gulfs, and ridges, rent and upheaved by earthquake shocks, and swept by volcanic floods. The sea is the only centre of life. The low rocky beach is garnished with innumerable sea-weeds, whose long trailing branches rise and fall with the tide, while every wave strews the sand with shells and broken corals, heaped in lengthened rows like the grass from the mower's scythe. Trilobites, in swarming shoals, scull their tiny boats in animated pursuit of food. Huge orthoceratites lie quietly floating their many-chambered shells on the surface, or speed through the water with long arms spread to grasp their prey. The sea-bottom is gay with the lily-shaped crinoids that, blossoming with life, foreshadow the flowers which are yet to deck the barren earth. Coral reefs stretch away in lines of beauty, where myriad workers toil to build their many-colored fragile homes. In shallower places, too, there is somewhat of grace, for the graptolites cover the muddy bottom with their quaint mossy branches, overshadowing mollusks that sluggishly luxuriate in endless profusion below. Yet as the long age goes by, continued changes take place. The land rises and falls. The sea retires, and anon pours swelling in again. The scene of life shifts from one locality to another. The great drama of life and death has begun, and is to be played while the earth endures.

II. THE DEVONIAN AGE.

THE DEVONIAN AGE.
1. Oriskany Period.
2. Corniferous Period.
3. Hamilton Period.
4. Chemung Period.

This second great stage in the progress of life on the earth takes its name from the county of Devon, England, where the formation is very clearly and extensively developed. It is often styled the OLD RED SANDSTONE, from the prevalent color of the rock, and has been immortalized by Hugh Miller under that name. On this continent its color and character are very different, although it is similar in its dominant fossils.

General Characteristics.—The continent is still small, low, and rocky. The Silurian sea is gradually retiring southward, as period after period adds its belt to the growing margin of the land. The earth, however, is no longer lifeless. Flags and rushes abound by the water-courses, while ferns of rare beauty and plants very like our rushes, flourish in the marshes. There are some cone-bearing trees, but no flowering tree or shrub like the maple, elm, or rose. The graptolites have become extinct, the trilobites are reduced to about a dozen species, while that curious crustacean, the eurypterus, appears in profusion in Europe, but rarely in America.

The most marked feature is the fishes which swarm in

the seas.* They were nearly all Ganoids, *i. e.*, they had beautifully enameled scales encasing them as with an armor, and often a bony helmet large enough to cover the skull of an elephant, strong enough to resist a musket-ball, and hard enough to strike fire like a flint. The tail was nearly always of unequal lobes, instead of equal lobes or rounded forms, as at the present. Thus, says Agassiz, the progress of life through the ages has

FIG. 61.

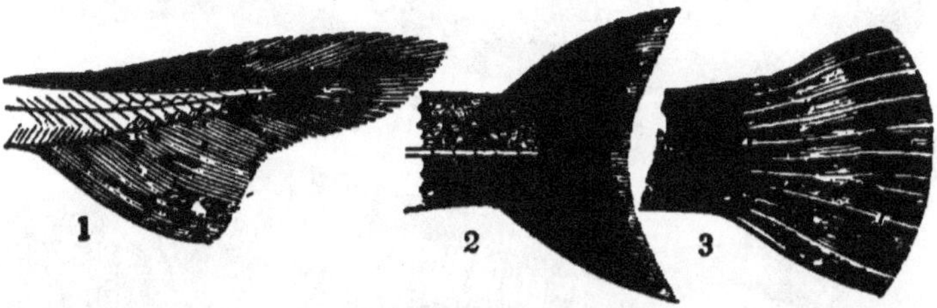

1. Heterocercal, or Unequally bilobate; 2. Equally bilobate; and, 3. Single and rounded form of tail.

been marked in the tails of the fishes. Among the most peculiar of these fishes we notice—

1. THE COCCOSTEUS (berry-bone), which takes its name from the tiny berry-like projections ornamenting its plated armor. Its teeth are chiseled, as it were, out of the solid jaw, just as the teeth of a saw are cut out of the solid metal.

2. THE PTERICHTHYS (wing-fish) had two arms or wings, combining the broad blade of a paddle with the

---

* Anderson says the remains of these Ganoid fishes are so abundant in the yellow sandstone deposit of Dura Den, Scotland, that a space of little more than three square yards yielded above 1,000 fishes, most of them perfect in their outline, with scales and fins quite entire, and the forms of the creatures often starting freely out of their hard, stony matrix into their complete armature of scale, fin and bone.

FIG. 62.

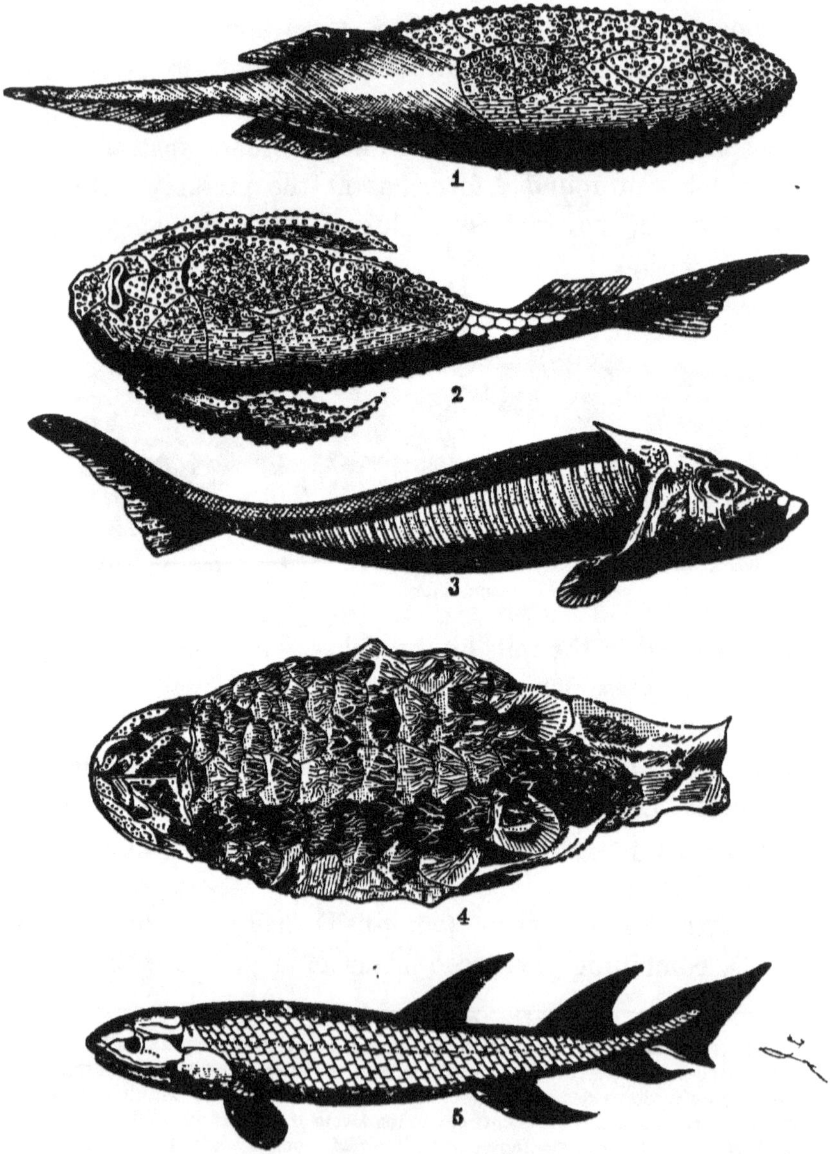

Fishes of Devonian Sea. 1. Coccosteus. 2. Pterichthys. 3. Cephalaspis. 4. Holoptychius. 5. Osteolepis.

sharp point of a spear, which served both for propulsion and for offence. The head was covered with a strong helmet, perforated in front by two circular holes, through which the eyes looked out. Its chest was protected by a curiously constructed cuirass formed of plates, and the tail was sheathed in a flexible mail of bony scales.

3. THE CEPHALASPIS (buckler-head) had a head-plate of a single bone of a crescent shape.

4. THE HOLOPTYCHIUS (all-wrinkled) is so called from the curiously wrinkled sculpturing that adorned its scales.

5. THE OSTEOLEPIS (bony-scale), whose bony scales are placed alongside each other like the bricks in a building, thus affording protection, and at the same time yielding readily to the bending of the body.

In these fishes there is a singular union of reptilian and fishy traits. The structure of their skull resembled that in reptiles, while their air-bladders had a lung-like character. They could move the head upon the neck independently of the body. Like reptiles, also, their vertebræ were connected by ball and socket joints instead of inverted cones, as in common fishes.

✓ *Comprehensive Types.*—The Creative purpose seemed at the beginning to be sketched in broad, general characters, and to include in the first expression of the plan all the structural possibilities. This combination of higher with lower features in the early organic forms is a very striking peculiarity, and becomes still more significant when we notice that many of the later types recall the more ancient ones. The latter may be styled prophetic and the former retrospective types, since the one anticipates the future and the other recalls the past. The crinoids, with closed cups in some, and open, star-like forms in others, united features of the present star-fishes and sea-urchins, and by their stems, which fastened them to the ground, included also a polyp-like character. The armor-plated pterichthys propelled itself with paddle-arms, like the turtle, instead of with the tail, like other fishes. The trilobites, with their uniform rings and head-shield, partook at once of worm and crustacean types. The chambered shells of the orthoceratite and goniatite gave hints of the ammonite of a later age. The early fishes prophesied not only the reptiles which were to come, but also the birds and even mammals. Though the ancient types have become obsolete and have been replaced by modern ones, as Agassiz happily remarks, a few old-fashioned individuals have been left behind to give, as it were, the key to the history of the race. The gar-pike explains the ancient Devonian fishes; the Millepore coral, the old Silurian corals; the nautilus, the ammonite and orthoceratite. The thought of God thus includes all that have gone before as well as all that now exist. The study of nature reveals to us the present linked with the past, which is not lost and dead, but perpetually revivified and reproduced in the life of to-day.

ORISKANY PERIOD.*

Location.—This formation is named from Oriskany Falls. The rock crops out at points in Maine, and extends southward along the Appalachian region.

Kind of Rock.—It is mostly a light, rough sandstone. Its thickness in New York varies from twenty feet at the typical locality to only a few inches at other places; in Pennsylvania it is 200 feet thick. Its color is white, passing to a reddish-brown where iron is present.

Fossils.—The most common fossil is a brachiopod (Fig. 63). The rock is often made up of these charac-

FIG. 63.

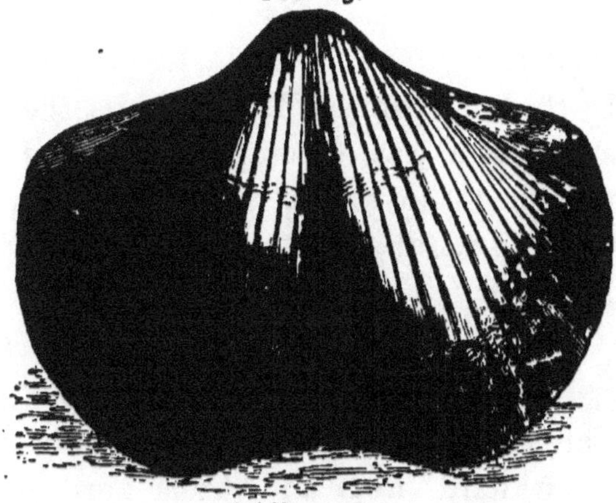

Spirifer arenosus.

* In Southern Illinois there is a formation termed the *Clear Creek limestone*, which seems to mark a transition from the Silurian to the Devonian, since it contains well-marked fossils of both ages. It forms the Mississippi Bluffs south of Thebes.

teristic shells or of thin casts. The latter are represented in Fig. 64. It is a mould of the interior of the shell

FIG. 64.

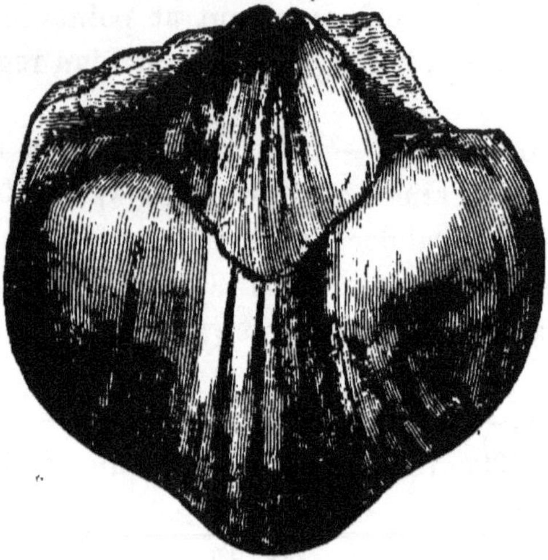

A Cast.

formed by the sand which filled it, while the substance of the shell itself has decomposed. These casts are very abundant, as in Cumberland, Md., and have received many fanciful names, such as "colts' tracks," "butterflies," etc.

Remark.—This formation is another feature of the old Appalachian sea-beach. The thickness of the rock, as it extends southward from the Azoic area, indicates a deepening of the water* which covered both New York and New England, while the Green Mountains were a narrow island separating them.

---

* The material for making the continent came always from the north-east. For this reason formations are generally coarser east, and finer west. Shales and sandstones east often become limestones west.

UPPER HELDERBERG OR CORNIFEROUS PERIOD.

Location.—The lower group is found in New York, and somewhat in New Jersey and Pennsylvania; the upper group is widely distributed through the interior to the States beyond the Mississippi. At the west, owing to the absence of the Oriskany, the Corniferous rocks lie directly upon the Niagara limestone, except where the Salina intervenes.

Kinds of Rock.—This formation in New York comprises two epochs:

1. THE CAUDA GALLI AND SCHOHARIE GRITS, which are named—the former from a peculiar feathery sea-weed common in it, and the latter from the typical locality in eastern New York.

2. THE HELDERBERG LIMESTONE—the last great limestone formation in New York—the lower beds of which are termed the *Onondaga,* and the upper the *Corniferous limestone.*

The Helderberg beds lose their distinctive features westward and blend into one group, which is called by either of these names. The Corniferous limestone (*cornu,* a horn) derives its appellation from disseminated nodules of hornstone ("chert"). The Onondaga is a dark-gray rock which takes an excellent polish. These limestones are quarried as a building-stone at multitudes of points throughout western New York, Ohio, Michigan, Indiana, Illinois, and Iowa.

Fossils.—This was the great Palæozoic coral reef. Corals are found in every conceivable form—standing, lying down, broken into fragments, or preserved as perfectly as if they had grown but yesterday. They flourished luxuriantly and may have exhibited all the wealth of coloring now manifested in the tropical seas. They are especially abundant at the Falls of the Ohio, near Louisville. Some have a diameter of five or six feet. Crinoids and mollusks, in all their orders, present a bewildering variety and profusion.

HAMILTON PERIOD.

Location.—This formation extends across New York, Michigan, thence west of the Mississippi river, and southward through Pennsylvania, Virginia, and Tennessee.

Kinds of Rock.—In New York this period comprises three epochs.*

---

* The entire Hamilton series in New York makes one enormous formation, the strata being in all 5,000 or more feet in thickness. They are nearly destitute of lime, and thus differ widely from the Onondaga, Trenton, and Niagara limestones which overlie them on the north. They give rise to marked peculiarities in the country which they underlie, and also affect its soil and productions. Containing little lime, we find the culture of wheat does not generally succeed well upon them; nor does the central wheat-growing district extend upon them more than a few miles south of the limestone range, except in a few alluvial valleys, or places where calcareous materials from the limestone belts have been strewed over the southern slates by the Drift, of which we shall speak hereafter. Grazing and dairying are almost exclusively the pursuits of the farmer.

The most marked physical features of all this great extent of country consist in its deep valleys and long ridgy hills, usually extending in a north and south direction, as an inspection on any map of the rivers which follow the valleys will show. Some of these long north and south valleys having been excavated

1. THE MARCELLUS SHALE is a soft, clayey rock, often nearly jet-black. It is very fissile, and breaks under the hammer into thin, slaty fragments, not more than six or eight inches across. It abounds in septaria, such as those spoken of on page 83, as resembling turtles. It contains so much carbonaceous matter as to sometimes burn quite freely. This fact has led to much waste of money in exploring it for coal. The attempts are always futile, since the formation lies thousands of feet below the coal measures.

2. THE HAMILTON GROUP* consists of a harder and lighter shaly sandstone, often calcareous. The layers are remarkable for the abundance of ripple-marks. They present also a very perfect jointed structure, some fine examples of which are seen on Cayuga Lake (Fig. 25). It is extensively used as a flagging-stone, since it breaks into slabs of great size and of uniform thickness.

3. THE GENESEE SLATE which overlies the Hamilton

---

so deeply below their outlets as to retain the accumulated waters of the rains and streams, form that remarkable series of lakes beginning with the Otsego, and comprising the Canaseraga, Cazenovia, Otisco, Skaneateles, Owasco, Cayuga, Seneca, Crooked, Canandaigua, Honeoye, Canadice, Hemlock, and Conesus lakes; all so similar in their general form and direction, and in the shape and geological formation of their inclosing hills. Over the whole extent of these rocks, the country is "rolling" or broken into ridges generally running north and south, and rising from one to eight hundred feet above their main dividing valleys; and it is rarely that we find among them a plain half a mile in width, excepting in a few of the "bottom-flats" or alluvial lands along the larger rivers.

The Hamilton Group in New York is overlaid by a dark, impure rock, termed the Tully limestone. It is about twenty feet in thickness, and contains a few distinguishing fossils.

* The absence of the Marcellus Group at the west, drops the Hamilton directly upon the Corniferous, forming the appearance of a single mass. Thus, four limestone formations—the Niagara, Salina, Corniferous, and Hamilton—are there brought into juxtaposition. Before they were closely distinguished, the entire mass was known as the "*Cliff limestone*," because they often formed bold bluffs along the river-banks.

beds derives its name from the gorge in the Genesee river, where it is well developed. It is a dark-blue, green, and often black slate, by which last name it is known through the Mississippi valley.

Fossils.—The Marcellus shale contains few fossils, mostly small except the orthoceratite and goniatite. The

FIG. 65.

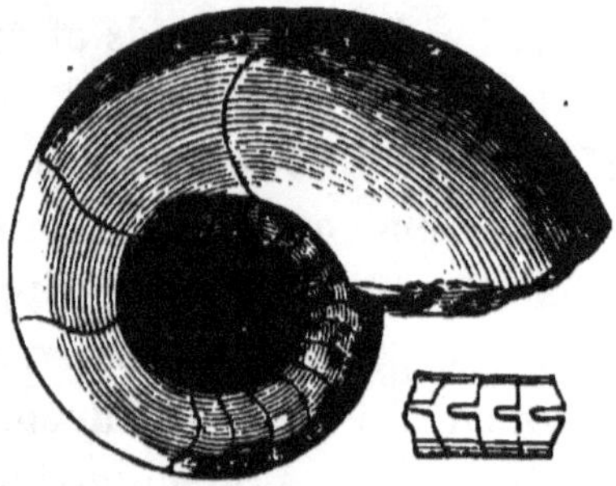

Goniatite.

latter is like the former, but is partly coiled, thus resembling the modern nautilus. The name (*gonia*, an angle), refers to the sinuous form of the partitions which separate the different chambers. The Hamilton Group, in its limestone layers, has fine crinoids and corals, but the predominant fossils are brachiopods and conchifers,—species which flourish in muddy waters. Among the former are many beautiful ones belonging to the family of spirifers. A peculiar coral, commonly styled the *cup coral* (see 1 and 7, Fig. 67) is noticeable. It is horn-shaped, and was occupied by a single polyp, which, when alive, with its tentacles expanded, must have been seven or eight inches in diameter. Fish-bones are common in

DEVONIAN CORALS.

FIG. 67.

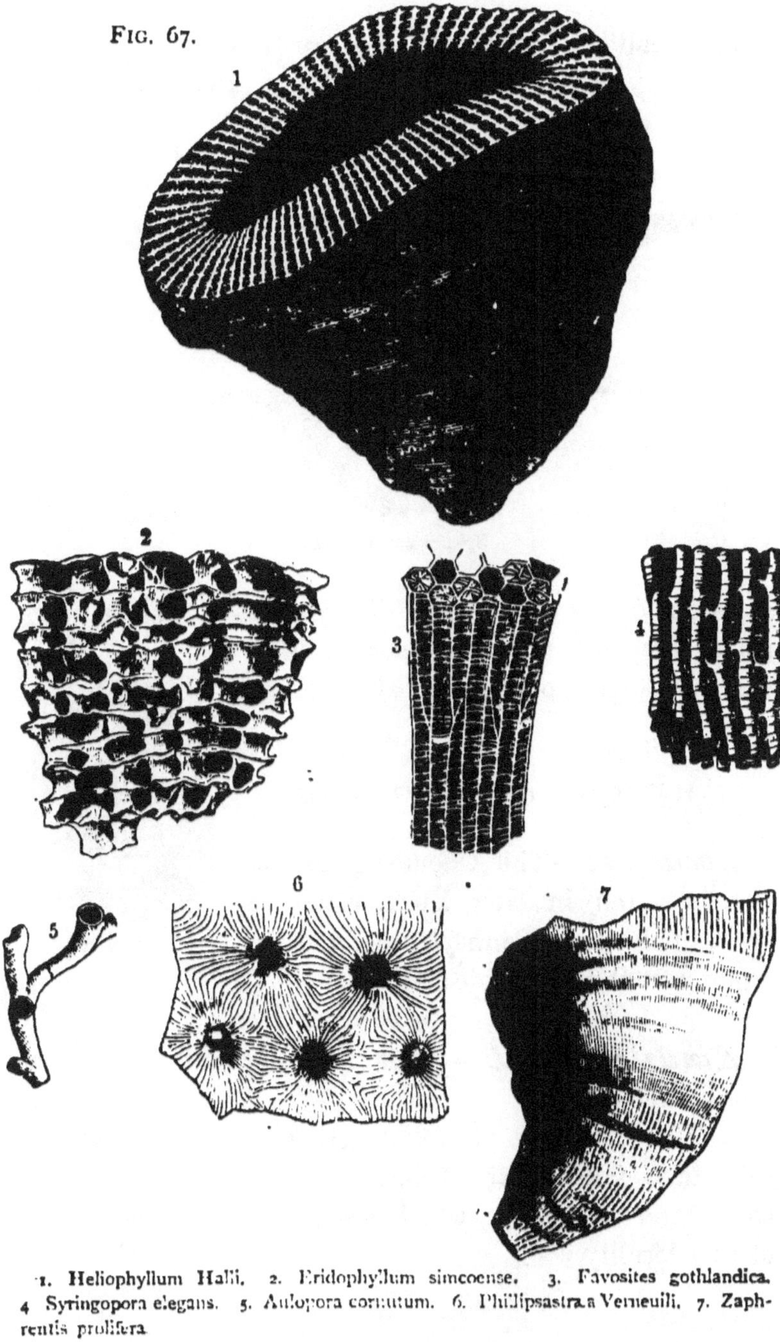

1. Heliophyllum Halli. 2. Eridophyllum simcoense. 3. Favosites gothlandica. 4 Syringopora elegans. 5. Aulopora cornutum. 6. Phillipsastræa Verneuili. 7. Zaphrentis prolifera.

some localities. A small trilobite (*Phacops bufo*, lens-eyed-toad) is conspicuous because of the perfect pre-

FIG. 66.

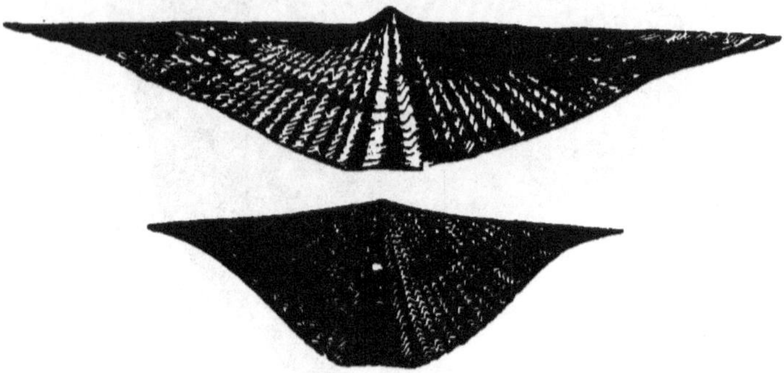

Spirifer mucronatus.

servation of its eye lenses. Terrestrial plants are an interesting feature, since they now first appear in any abundance.

FIG. 68.

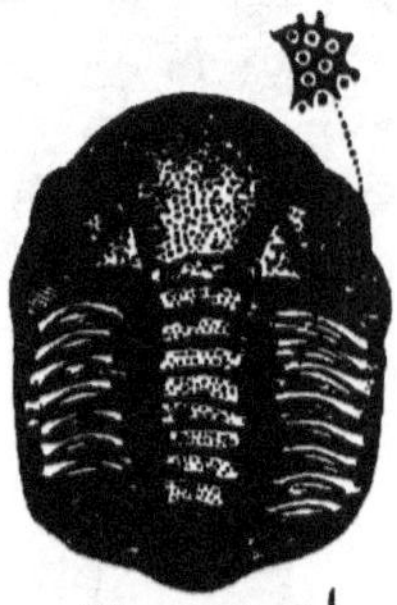

Phacops bufo.

CHEMUNG PERIOD.

Location.—The Chemung formation is found in New York, attains a great thickness in Pennsylvania, and extends west through Ohio.

Kinds of Rock.—This period contains in New York three epochs.

1. THE PORTAGE GROUP receives its name from the celebrated falls in the Genesee River. It consists of shales and sandstones, which are nearly 1,000 feet thick at that locality.

2. The Chemung Group, named from the Narrows in the Chemung * River, is composed of coarse shales and shaly sandstones of an olive or greenish color.

3. The Catskill Group covers the upper range of the Catskill Mountains. It also consists of shales and sandstones, but of a reddish color, and oftentimes gritty character. The harder layers of the sand-rock sometimes weather in a peculiar way, dividing into thin layers resembling a pile of boards. All of the Chemung rocks abound in ripple-marks, mud cracks, and other proofs of broad, low flats, swept by a muddy sea.

Fossils.—The Portage and Catskill Groups contain few fossils. The Chemung, however, in many localities abounds in organic remains. Large slabs are found completely covered with impressions of shells. Brachiopods and conchifers are plentiful, and occasionally a trilobite or an orthoceratite is met. A prominent brachiopod is the broad-winged spirifer, which is commonly known as a "petrified butterfly." It resembles the one shown in Fig. 66. Beautiful fern impressions are also presented—a prophecy of the abundant vegetation of the Carboniferous Age.

Remark.—*Geography.*—The Empire State is now nearly finished, as is also Wisconsin. Interior Michigan is yet an inland sea, while the ocean washes in unrestrained freedom the vast area of the Mississippi valley.

---

* The name Chemung—meaning big horn—was given to it by the Indians because of a mammoth tusk which they found in the bed of the river.

SCENIC DESCRIPTION.—Let us try to picture to ourselves a scene in the Devonian landscape. The air is yet heavy with mist, and we strain our eyes to catch a view of the land, like a voyager before whom, amid the fogs and dews of early twilight, looms an unknown shore. Gleams of light here and there reveal to us hill-sides green with forests of lofty ferns and club mosses of gigantic size. The rivers, fringed with tall, slender rushes and reeds, look almost familiar; but back from the banks no grass carpets the meadows, no moss clings to the rocks, no flowers deck the landscape, no forests cover the mountains.

The sea-shore, however, is stirring with life. Eurypteri crawl over the slimy bottom, and, thrusting out their long, muscular arms, draw into their voracious maws sea-weeds, fish, and other organic remains thrown up by the tide. Innumerable fish, the armor-clad pirates of the Devonian seas, impregnable against attack, dart through the water in eager pursuit of their prey, which they crush between their poniard-like teeth. In the deeper waters the coral tribes are busily at work, clearing the water and building up the continent, while on the shallow, muddy bottoms, shell-fish congregate in myriads, furnishing food for the rapacious monsters of the deep.

Nowhere in the rocky book of Nature do we read a page of quiet, free from pain or death. From the beginning the flesh-eater preyed on the plant-eater, and, as now, the weak succumbed to the strong. The struggle for existence began with its gift, and the reign of death was inaugurated by the enjoyment of life. Thus only can Nature preserve the equipoise between growth and decay, between the means of subsistence and the development of life.

III. THE CARBONIFEROUS AGE.

CARBONIFEROUS AGE.
1. Sub-carboniferous Period.
2. Carboniferous Period.
3. Permian Period.

This age is so named from the abundance of coal formed in its time.

FIG. 69.

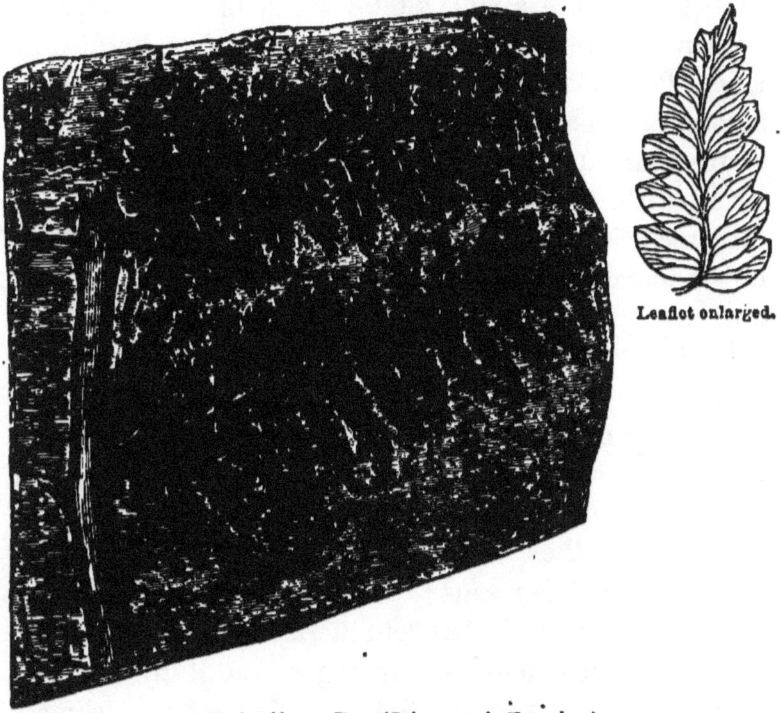

Leaflet enlarged.

A Carboniferous Fern (Sphenopteris Egyptiaca).

General Characteristics.—At the beginning of the age the growing continent had increased by the successive additions of the Silurian and Devonian Ages, so that the shore-line of the Atlantic extended through southern New York, thence west through the southern part of Ohio, across the future Mississippi valley. The Gulf of Mexico reached north to central Iowa. Lake Superior was the only one of the great lakes in existence. The pressure of the waters in the Atlantic and Pacific oceans gradually deepened their beds and produced a corresponding uplift of the future continent, so that after a time the water drained off the site of the present southern and the middle States south of the coast line, against which the warm water of the Gulf had beaten so long. The low muddy tracts, the former sea-bottom, became a wide extended marsh, warmed to a tropical temperature by the internal heat. The atmosphere, dense with moisture, and containing, in the form of carbonic acid, all the carbon now locked up in the coal-beds,* was rich in vegetable food. These favorable conditions rendered the earth a very greenhouse, fit to teem with luxuriant vegetation. This same acid, however, would have been fatal to air-breathing animals. Hence, before they could be introduced, the atmosphere must be prepared for their use. Here came a pause, as it were, in the progress of the animal life of the world. The plant must purify the air for the animal. The All-creative Hand, suiting the means to the end, at once covered the land with a new and abundant flora. Forests of strange form and prodigious size sprang up as if by magic to meet this new demand of Nature. No change of climate

* The atmosphere now contains 1 part in 2,500 of carbonic acid. According to M. Brongniart, it had from 7 to 8 parts in 100 in the Carboniferous Era.

varied the productions of the ground, but everywhere flourished the same tropical growth. The crust of the earth was unsteady, and frequent elevations and depressions alternated. At one time it was lifted up to be covered with vegetation, and at another sunk with the ruins of the forests below the incoming ocean to receive a deposit of sedimentary rocks. The theater of these repeated changes was the whole of the present coal area, and much besides from which the coal has been swept by subsequent denudation. During a season of verdure a vast amount of vegetable débris, such as leaves, limbs, fallen trunks, etc., accumulated, only to be overwhelmed by the flood of sand, pebbles and mud washed in by the rushing waters. The peat-deposit gradually changed to coal, and the sediment hardened to shales, sandstone, or clay. Sometimes the water became deep and clear enough for corals or mollusks to exist, and Nature, suiting the life to the new condition, populated the shallow sea with swarming millions, and there a limestone was interpolated. Perhaps a hundred times in the course of the age this process was repeated, and as many alternate layers chronicled the changes in regular succession. In a Nova Scotia coal-bed Lyell found in a portion 1,400 feet thick no less than sixty-eight levels, showing as many different old soils of forests, one above the other, where the trunks of trees were still furnished with roots.

These characteristics culminated in the Carboniferous Period of the age, being preceded by the Sub-carboniferous and followed by the Permian, in both of which the land of these formations was submerged by the sea, receiving mainly rock deposits.

SUB-CARBONIFEROUS PERIOD.

Location.—This formation is so named because it is the base of the great carboniferous system of the continent. It is found in southern New York, southward along the Appalachian region, and westward through Iowa, Illinois, and Mississippi.

Kinds of Rock.—In New York and in some parts of Pennsylvania, Ohio, Kentucky, and Tennessee, it is a hard conglomerate of quartz pebbles cemented with sand. It is very massive in appearance, and the ledges often separate into huge blocks, with intervening fissures. Where the larger portion has been swept off by subsequent geologic changes, the remains often present a striking resemblance to the streets and blocks of a ruined city. In Pennsylvania and Virginia it is overlaid by a vast deposit of sandstone and shale to a depth of several thousand feet. At the West* it is a compact yellowish or grayish limestone, of great thickness and wide extent.

Fossils.—The limestone abounds in crinoids. Nowhere else are these stone-lilies—the blossoms of the Sub-

---

* The following are the subdivisions in Illinois, given by Worthen:

1. The Chester Group, 500 to 800 feet thick.
2. The St. Louis Group, 50 to 200 feet thick.
3. The Keokuk Group, 100 to 150 feet thick.
4. Burlington Limestone, 25 to 200 feet thick.
5. Kinderhook Group, 100 to 150 feet thick.

The Marshall Group, so named from Marshall, Michigan, is doubtless, in part at least, of this period. It is worked at Cleveland and Waverly, Ohio, furnishes the grindstones of Berea and Huron, and underlies the limestone bluff at Burlington, Iowa. Dana thinks the Kinderhook and Marshall groups are on about the same geologic horizon.

carboniferous sea—found in such profusion and beauty. There are also many brachiopods and fish remains. In England this rock is termed the Mountain Limestone. When the stone is worn away by the elements, the round, hard joints of the crinoids are found lying loose in the soil, and are gathered and strung as beads by the children.*

Remarks.—*1. Caves.*—Many of the most famous caves are in this rock; for example, the Mammoth Cave, the Wyandotte Cave, etc. In many places in Indiana and Kentucky, "sink-holes" are abundant, sometimes so numerous as to interfere with plowing. These are openings in the earth where the soil has been washed down probably into subterranean caves never yet seen by man. The Mammoth Cave is the largest in the World. It has been explored to a distance of over thirty miles. Views of the grandest description are constantly presented. Royal thrones, sparry grottoes, diamond arches, flowers of every zone sparkling with crystalline beauty, reflect the light of the traveler's torch. Stalactite halls decorated with fantastic pillars, and mar-

---

* Thus Sir Walter Scott, in allusion to the popular fable concerning this formation, says:

"But fain St. Hilda's nuns would learn
If on a rock by Lindisferne
St. Cuthbert sits, and toils to frame
The sea-born beads that bear his name:
Such tales had Whitby's fishers told,
And said they might his shape behold,
And hear his anvil sound,—
A deadened clang, a huge, dim form,
Seen but and heard when gathering storm
And night were closing round."

Hugh Miller humorously remarks that if St. Cuthbert made all these beads, he must have been the busiest saint in the calendar.

ble statues draped with crystal mantles, charm with their magical splendor. At one point the River Styx rolls its sad waters beneath dark vaults, the windings of which are indented by a thousand rocks. In its dismal depths gropes a kind of fish—the Cyprinodon—which is blind, as it should be, since of what service are eyes where absolute darkness reigns?

2. *Reptiles.*—In Sub-carboniferous rocks at Pottsville, Pa., the footprints of a reptile, having a stride of thirteen inches, have been found. Later in the age, there appear many advance scouts, as it were, of the reptilian hosts of the succeeding age.

CARBONIFEROUS PERIOD.

Location.—The great coal-beds of the country lie in six detached areas as seen in the Frontispiece. They are styled respectively the Rhode Island, Appalachian, Michigan, Illinois, Missouri, and Texas coal-fields. The Rhode Island is the smallest, and comprises an area of only 1,000 square miles; the Missouri is the largest, and covers 100,000 square miles.

Kinds of Rock.—The Carboniferous Period was inaugurated by the formation of a great conglomerate sandstone known as the Millstone Grit. As it often contains thin seams of coal, it is frequently termed the False Coal Measures. During this era of convulsion, the fishes and ferns of the Devonian Age were buried deep beneath vast accumulations of lifeless sand and gravel. This was interrupted, however, by frequent times of quiet, when, for a brief interval, the land was partially clothed with vegetation. The coal-measures proper present stratified rocks of every kind—sandstone, shales, limestone, etc. They can be distinguished from Silurian or Devonian strata only by the fossils. There is generally about one foot of coal to fifty feet of rock. The thickness of the coal-bed is at some places only that of paper, and at others from thirty to forty feet. The "mammoth vein" exposed to view at Wilkesbarre, and worked at Carbondale, Mauch Chunk, Shamokin, etc., is 29½ feet thick.* The Pittsburg seam is 8 feet thick, and may be traced for a long distance as a conspicuous black band along the high banks of the Monongahela. The miners estimate that a coal-bed gives 1,000,000 tons to the square mile for every foot of thickness. Iron ore is also abundant. Iron pyrites (sulphuret of iron) is distributed either in nodules, often of many pounds weight, or in thin seams, so as to greatly injure the coal. The best quality of coal contains a trace of this impurity, which gives the disagreeable odor of coal-gas.

Fossils.—I. PLANTS are the characteristic fossils of this period. Everywhere the shales bear impress of the deli-

---

* "The amount of vegetable matter in a single coal-seam six inches thick is greater than the most luxuriant vegetation of the present day would furnish in 1,200 years. Boussingault calculates that luxuriant vegetation at the present day takes from the atmosphere about half a ton of carbon per acre annually, or fifty tons per acre in a century. Fifty tons of stone-coal, spread evenly over an acre of surface, would make a layer of less than one-third of an inch. But suppose it to be half an inch, then the time required for the accumulation of a seam of coal three feet thick—the thinnest which can be worked to advantage—would be 7,200 years. If the aggregate thickness of all the seams of coal in any basin amounts to sixty feet, the time required for its accumulation would be 144,000 years. In the coal measures of Nova Scotia are seventy-six seams of coal, of which one is twenty-two feet thick, and another thirty-seven."—*Winchell's Geological Sketches.*

cate tracery of ferns, leaves, stems, depicted with the sharpest outlines.* Trunks of trees, erect or prostrate, appear with their roots yet imbedded in the layer of clay, the very soil in which they grew, underneath the coal. These fossils reveal to us most perfectly the vegetation of the Period. It is the fulfillment of that which scantily appeared in the Devonian Age. It was almost entirely a flowerless growth. The leading forms were tree-ferns, rushes, and club-mosses, which grew to a size unknown in our climate. If we should collect the cryptogams (flowerless plants) of North America to form a forest, it would hardly overtop a man's head, and the ferns would have an undergrowth of toad-stools, mosses, and lichens (Dana).

1. *The Ferns.*—Ferns which to-day creep at our feet, then towered into stately trees, with trunks a foot and a half in diameter. They are abundant fossils, and doubtless contributed most to the formation of coal.

2. *The Calamites* were jointed, rush-like plants. Unlike the "horse-tail" or "scouring rushes" of the present, which are rarely two feet long, their Carboniferous prototypes shot up like a gigantic asparagus, with a woody fiber, to a height of a score or more of feet. The impressions of their huge prostrate stems are frequent.

---

* "The most elaborate imitations of living foliage upon the painted ceilings of Italian palaces, bear no comparison with the beauteous profusion with which the galleries of these instructive coal mines are overhung. The roof is covered as with a canopy of gorgeous tapestry, enriched with festoons of most graceful foliage, flung in wild irregular profusion over every portion of its surface. The effect is heightened by the contrast of the coal-black color of these vegetables with the light ground-work of the rock to which they are attached. The spectator feels himself transported, as if by enchantment, into the forests of another world; he beholds trees of forms and characters now unknown upon the surface of the earth, presented to his senses almost in the beauty and vigor of their primeval life."—*Dr. Buckland.*

3. *The Sigillaria* (seal-marked) is curiously ornamented with vertical ribs, along each of which is a row of seal-like impressions. These are the scars left where the leaves fell off. They wind in a spiral around the trunk. The roots (*stigmariæ*) are also dotted with scars. They are generally found separate, though sometimes combined with the parent tree. The sigillarian tree-trunks frequently occur standing in coal mines. The miners sometimes cut them off below, when their tapering form permits the whole mass to descend upon the workmen beneath. These "coal-pipes," as they are styled, are therefore much dreaded.

4. *The Lepidodendra* (scaly-stems)—the club-mosses of that time—were lofty trees, sixty feet high, with pitted trunks and branches. The scars are arranged diagonally or in a quincunx order.

5. *Conifers*, or cone-bearing trees, were not infrequent, with their boughs laden with fruit. Such was the vegetation which flourished in the Carboniferous Age, and which we now use to warm and light our houses and to drive our engines.

II. Animals.—In a coal mine near the Bay of Fundy, in the stumps of two sigillariæ, there have been found the remains of several small reptiles bearing frog-like and lizard-like forms, a centipede, and the shell of a land snail. These little creatures had probably crept into these hollow trees for shelter, and were overtaken by the convulsions which overwhelmed them. Several larger fossil reptiles have since been identified. Two or three species of insects, with broad gauze wings, like the dragon-fly, have also been discovered. Remains of fishes,

FIG. 70. CARBONIFEROUS FOSSILS.

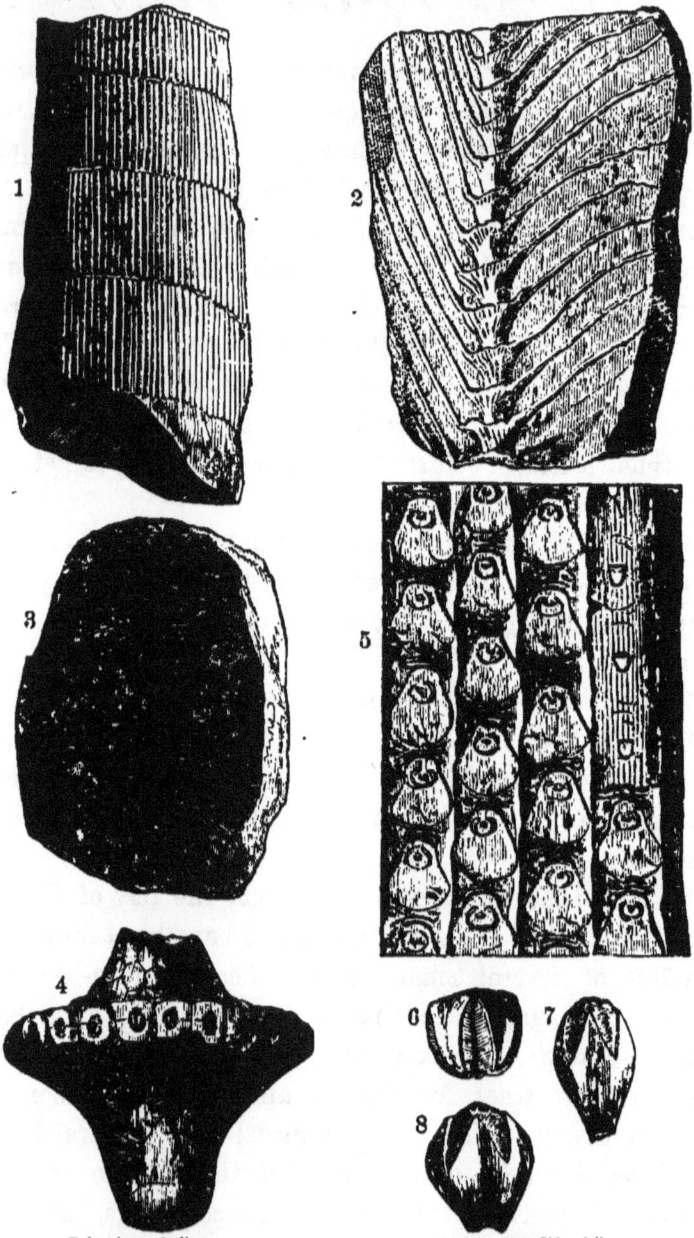

1. Calamites cistii.
2. Archimedes Worthii.
3. Asterophyllites equisetiformis.
4. Actinocrinus chrystii.
5. Sigillaria attenuata.
6. Pentremites Godoni.
7. Pentremites pyriformis.
8. Pentremites Koninckana.

(4, 6, 7 and 8 are varieties of Crinoids.)

FIG. 71.

Ideal Scene in a Carboniferous Forest.

Ada's Trust.

Beth's Promise.

Flemings.

Mad Penitent of Todi

Heiress of Carrigmona

Warp and Woof.

Tangled Paths

3 May Brooke

Palms

Coaina

Stories for Sunday [illegible]

[illegible] of [illegible]

Adrift

Student of Blenheim Forest

Nora Brady's Vow

Mona the Vestal.

brachiopods, crinoids and corals are abundant. (See Fig. 70.)

SCENIC DESCRIPTION.—In Fig. 71 is an attempt to reproduce the characteristic features of a carboniferous landscape. On the right are two naked trunks of a lepidodendron and sigillaria (whose foliage is entirely unknown); between them is a tall tree-fern with its umbrella-like top. At the foot of these great trees are smaller ferns, and, in front, a stigmaria, whose curiously dotted and branching roots reach out into the water. On the extreme left is an asterophyllite, like the calamite, with its gigantic bamboo-like trunk. Next is a conifer, with a few pine-like branches. In front is a sigillaria, and at its foot, prostrate, a sigillaria and a lepidodendron mingled with ferns and vegetable débris. In the centre is a clump of smaller lepidodendra. The background is filled with tall calamites. In the foreground are the asparagus-like buds of young calamites just rising out of the water. At the right several tiny stems of asterophyllites show their pretty, finely-cut branches. In the water float two fishes, and the archegosaurus shows its long-pointed head.

What a strange scene is presented as we stem the muddy current of the sluggish rivers, or thread the mazes of those tropical jungles. It is as if the plants of a wet meadow had shot up into forest trees. The trunks, not gnarled and rough as in modern times, spring up like the sculptured shafts of a medieval temple, graceful in proportion and rich in ornament. Each column is embossed with its varied fluting spirals and ovals of curiously intricate patterns. The tall ferns at every breath of wind wave their feathery crowns like beautiful plumes. The scent of the morning air is hot and damp as that of a greenhouse. The sky, ever somber and veiled, shuts down heavy with oppressive clouds. A wan and dubious light scarcely makes visible the tangled stems of lepidodendra and sigillariæ, and sheds a vague and shadowy hue of horror over the scene. The flowers, few and inconspicuous, fail to enliven the somber tints with a gayer color. No song of bird, and rarely the hum of insect is heard; and, save when the alligator-like bellowings of the archegosaurus wake the echoes of this dismal forest, the awful silence is supreme.

THE PERMIAN PERIOD.

Location.—This formation is named from the ancient kingdom of Permia, in Russia, where it was first recognized. It is wanting in the older States, but is well developed in Kansas, and has been recognized in Nebraska and Texas.

Kinds of Rock.—Limestones predominate, though sandstone, shales, etc., are found. At Manhattan, Kan., a limestone is quarried from this series for architectural purposes, which is so soft that it may be sawed with a hand-saw and planed with a jack-plane, and yet is very durable. It is the cheapest material of which the pioneer can construct his house—cheaper even than it would be to resort to the forest, if such existed, for logs (Foster). Hayden notices the occurrence of a similar limestone, and belonging to the same age, in Nebraska. The best building material in England is the Permian limestone of which the new houses of Parliament are constructed.

Fossils.—The Permian system is more a new rock-formation than a new life-period. Many of its forms are identical with those of the Carboniferous Period. The air has been cleared by the action of the abundant vegetation, and the empire of animal life trembles between the fishes and reptiles. The former are decreasing, while the latter are increasing in size and number. The first definite reptiles are seen, while the old armor-clad fishes disappear. The coal flora has not entirely died, though the coal-making epoch is passed; the low swampy lands seem to have been raised so as to be unfavorable to its growth, and no new vegetation fills the place. It is nearing the close of the great Palæozoic Time. Older forms are dying, and the Creator develops no fresh world-thoughts to mark the dawn of a new era. The coal is stored in the earth, and the continent now moves forward in its preparation for the advent of man, for whom it has been so wonderfully contrived.

Remarks.—*1. Appalachian Revolution.*—The close of the Palæozoic Age was marked by terrific convulsions. Neither animal nor plant survived the catastrophe. The tremendous pressure of the two oceans during the Carboniferous Age, had kept the newly-formed continent continually vibrating to and fro; but at last the tension was too great, and the crust was upheaved in gigantic folds thousands of feet high, extending from Vermont to Alabama. The Appalachians, being nearest the Atlantic force, were thrown up far higher than they are at present, often toppling over from their dizzy heights, while more gentle elevations were made toward the central portion of the continent. Since then many of these folds have been denuded. A striking illustration, occurring near Chambersburg, Pennsylvania, has already been alluded to on page 82. At that point, along a fracture of twenty miles in extent, rocks of the Upper Silurian lie opposite those of the Lower. A man can stand astride the crevice with one foot on Trenton limestone and the other on Hamilton slates, and, in addition, put his hand on some great fragments of Oneida conglomerate, caught as they were falling down the chasm, and held in its earthquake jaws. All the strata between these two extremes, at the time of the Appalachian Revolution, must have formed an immense wall 20,000 feet high and twenty miles in length.

Metamorphic Action.—This fearful earth-storm sweeping over the continent not only twisted and dislocated the horizontal coal-beds, but lifted them above their former level. An evolution of the internal heat accompanied the convulsion, and thus the bituminous coal was metamorphosed into anthracite. This effect, like that seen in the rock strata, was most felt near the Atlantic coast; hence we find anthracite coal in the Appalachian Mountains, next semi-bituminous, and in the western area bituminous coal alone. The same metamorphic force, where greatest, as in the eastern States, produced granite, gneiss, and other crystalline rocks. Nine-tenths of the rocks on the surface of the globe were made prior to this period. Many of these beds during this revolution were crystallized, and also stored with mines of gold, tin, copper, lead, etc., thus fitting them for the purposes of art and commerce.

2. *Progress of Life.*—We have beheld seas—vast watery deserts—become densely populated. We have traced the Creative thought slowly advancing among the ruins of ages. A vast progress has been made in the life of the world. The four types of structure have all been introduced, and all, except the vertebrate, developed to their highest orders. The lower forms have, one by one, given place to the higher. We now pass over a chasm to where the distinctions stand out in bold relief. We take leave of the trilobites, graptolites, orthoceratites, eurypteri and corals of the Silurian seas, of the mail-encased fishes of the Old Red Sandstone, of the sigillariæ, stigmariæ, and lepidodendra of the Carboniferous jungles, and go forward to meet higher forms of life more nearly resembling those of the present age. The Palæozoic types fade away in the world's progress to its brighter future. "As the stars sink, one by one, in the west, and new stars rise in the east, to be succeeded by the dawn and then the day, so through the night of the past sank the old life-forms, to be succeeded by the new, approaching nearer to the dawn of the day in whose morning we live." (Denton.)

The Mesozoic Time.

The Mesozoic or Middle-life of Geologic History comprises but one age, that of reptiles.

The Age of Reptiles.	1. Triassic Period. 2. Jurassic Period. 3. Cretaceous Period.

General Characteristics.—A new cycle now begins. The four grand old types of life remain, but they are presented under new and more familiar features. The four orders of vertebrates are at last complete. The air is purified for land animals. A flora arises capable of supporting a more abundant fauna. Birds, mammals, common or bony fishes, palms and flowering plants appear. The plants of the Palæozoic were mainly *endogens* (in-growers), i. e., plants which grow by increasing within, like the corn, cane, etc. To these are now added *exogens* (out-growers), i. e., plants which grow by external layers of annual increase, like the beech, oak, etc. The endogens have leaves with parallel veins, and the parts of the flowers arranged by *threes;* the exogens have leaves with net-veins, and the parts of the flowers commonly arranged by *fives.* The former expand, and make their development mainly in the sculptured stem; the latter, in the beauty of fruit and flower. The Palæozoic corals had rays or arms arranged in *fours;* the later corals, in *sixes.* The Palæozoic chambered shells had plain and simple divisions; the later shells have intricately-folded ones. The Palæozoic fishes had tails unequally lobed; since then, the equally-lobed or undivided tail has been the usual form. Aside from these general features, the distinguishing characteristic of the Mesozoic Time is the extraordinary development of reptiles. These animals astonish us by their vast number, gigantic size, and unwonted appearance. Through those antique forests enormous lizards, forty to fifty feet in length, dragged their ponderous bodies,—the modern representatives of which are inoffensive little creatures a few inches long, that seek only to hide from our view in the grass.

Geography.—The continent has grown by the addition of the Carboniferous area. The Appalachian region has been uplifted above the sea. The scene of rock-making is pushed to the borders of the Atlantic and the Gulf, and to the slopes of the Rocky Mountains. The accompanying map is an attempt to show some of the outlines of the Mesozoic continent. New England was a peninsula. The beautiful valley of the Connecticut was an arm of the ocean, with broad, flat, muddy shores. The Gulf States were out at sea. The Gulf of Mexico swept along the eastern flank of the Rocky Mountains to the Arctic Ocean, while the Pacific Ocean laved the western flank of the Sierra Nevada. New Jersey, Maryland, Delaware, North and South Carolina, were as yet only half made. (See Fig. 72.)

TRIASSIC AND JURASSIC PERIODS.

These groups are not fully separated in America. The Triassic (triple) takes it name from the fact that, in Germany it is composed of three distinct groups.* It is sometimes termed the New Red Sandstone, to distinguish it from the Old Red Sandstone of the Devonian. The Jurassic is so called because it is extensively developed in the Jura Mountains, Switzerland. The foreign divisions are the *Lias, Oölite,* and *Wealden.*

FIG. 72.

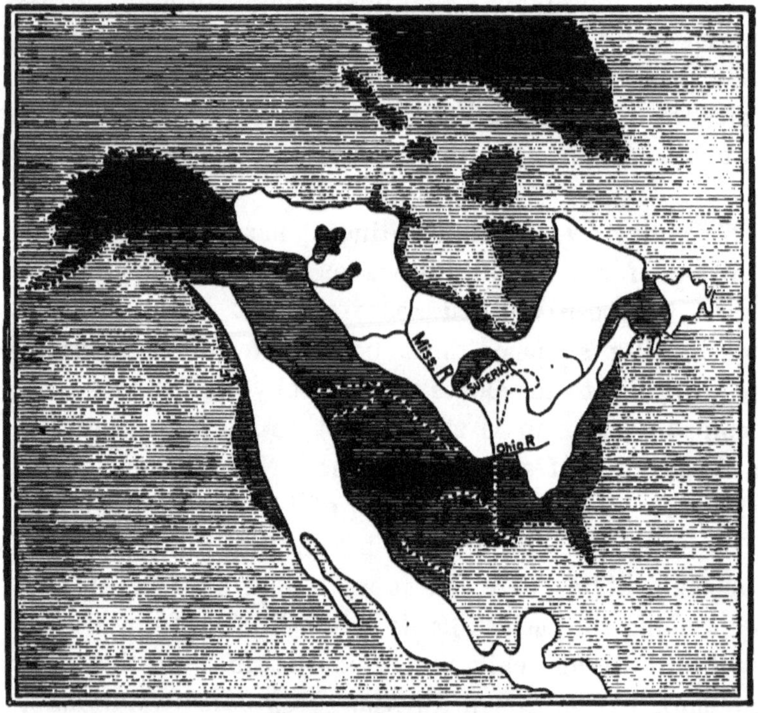

The Mesozoic Continent.

Location.—In the United States the rocks of this period are found along the Connecticut Valley from

* The ***Bunter Sandstein*** or colored sandstone, the ***Muschelkalk*** or mussel chalk, and the ***Keuper***, a miner's term, meaning a group of red and green marls and shells.

Long Island Sound to the northern boundary of Massachusetts; thence they may be traced from the Palisades on the Hudson, in long, narrow, scattered strips through New Jersey, Pennsylvania, Virginia, and North Carolina. (See Frontispiece.) They probably occupy the synclinal valleys running north and south, left between the great folds of the Appalachian Revolution. During that time they were under the water, and formed deep inland bays, receiving the washings from adjacent hills to work into rock formations. The beds are from 3,000 to 6,000 feet thick; hence these valleys must have constantly settled and as steadily filled with the accumulating sediment. The great Pacific Triassic belt extends from Mexico to British Columbia, through a width of perhaps four degrees of longitude (Whitney). The rocks are also found extensively in Colorado and Nevada.

Kinds of Rock.—The rocks of the Connecticut valley are principally sandstones, which are extensively quarried for the "brown-stone fronts" of New York city. The popular "free-stone" of Portland, Conn., and Newark, N. J., is a Triassic rock. Near Richmond, Va., and Deep River, N. C., are valuable coal beds in the rocks of this era. At the west this formation consists of beds of brick-red marl and sandstone. The celebrated Solenhofen limestone, so much used in lithography, is of the Jurassic Period.

Fossils.—The organic remains are of the most varied and wonderful description. They reveal very clearly the plant and animal life of these periods.

I. Plants.—The vegetation included numerous varieties of ferns, conifers, and calamites, which formed graceful forests, as in the Carboniferous Period; but there were no jungles of lepidodendra or sigillariæ. Instead of these, the *Cycad* appeared. This had a short trunk, and at the top a tuft of branching leaves (Fig. 82, left of the center). In shape, the leaves resembled those of the palm, but did not split lengthwise, while they unrolled from a coil, like those of the fern. The structure of the wood and fruit was like that of the conifers. The cycad, combining thus characteristics of three orders of plants—conifers, ferns, and palms—is another illustration of what we have termed a comprehensive type.

II. Animals.—Birds and mammals make their first appearance, completing the last and highest order of animals. Spiders, beetles and other insects have been discovered, and even their tracks in the soft mud have been preserved. Fish remains are plentiful, as at Sun-

Fig. 73.

Ostrea marshii. Middle Oölite.

Fig. 74.

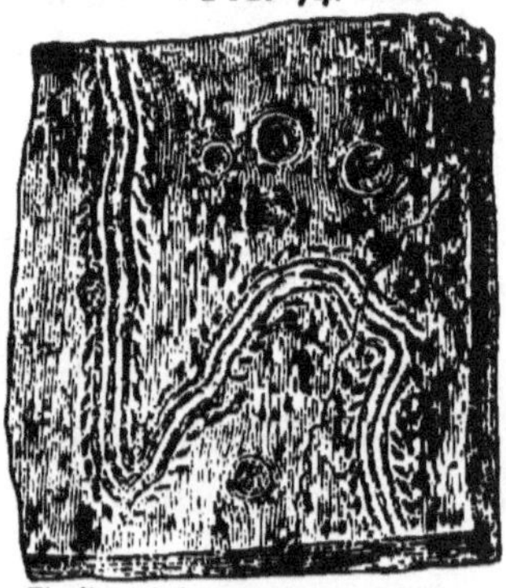

Trails of Insects and Prints of Rain-drops.

derland, Mass. Fig. 73 represents an Oölitic oyster, the progenitor of our modern bivalve. Marine life seems wanting in this country, but the European rocks contain a prolific record of the Mesozoic seas. Crinoids were abundant; one of these, the Lily Encrinite, is especially beautiful (Fig. 75). The cephalopods reached their culmination in the ammonite and belemnite.

FIG. 75.

Encrinite (*krinε*, a lily) moniliformis (from the necklace shape of the stalk).

The *Ammonite* is the fully coiled and perfected orthoceratite of the Silurian seas. It derives its name from its resemblance to the horn which decorated the front of the temple of Jupiter Ammon and the bas-reliefs and statues of that pagan deity. It is found of all sizes, from that of a pin's-head to a cart-wheel. The shell is thin, but strengthened by many sinuous partitions (septa), which add to its beauty and strength.* This curious internal archwork, by its joinings with the external shell,

* The economy of the Ammonite designed it to live mainly at the bottom of deep waters, but to be able to rise at pleasure to the surface. For this purpose the outer chamber (*o o*) (Fig. 76) of the wreathed shell was fitted for the reception of the animal, while the interior chambers (*i i*) were hollow, so as to make the whole structure nearly of the same weight as the element in which it moved. Through all of these chambers an elastic tube passed by means of a pipe or siphuncle (*s s*), the tube being in connection with the cavity of the heart, which, under ordinary circumstances, was filled with a dense fluid. When alarmed, or wishing to descend, the animal withdrew itself within the outer chamber, and the pressure upon the cavity of the heart forced the fluid into the siphuncle, so as to increase the gravity of the shell, by which means it readily sunk to the bottom. On the other hand, when wishing to ascend, it had only to project its arms, and the fluid, being freed from the pressure, returned from the siphuncle to the cavity of the heart, thus restoring the whole structure to its ordinary floating gravity. As the pressure of water at the sea-bottom would break any ordinary shell, we perceive that the septa were essential to the preservation of the little animal, enabling it to resist a weight which would otherwise crush it.

adorns it with graceful figures resembling the most delicate foliage or embroidery. The chambers are often found lined with quartz crystals, making tiny geodes of

FIGS. 76–7.

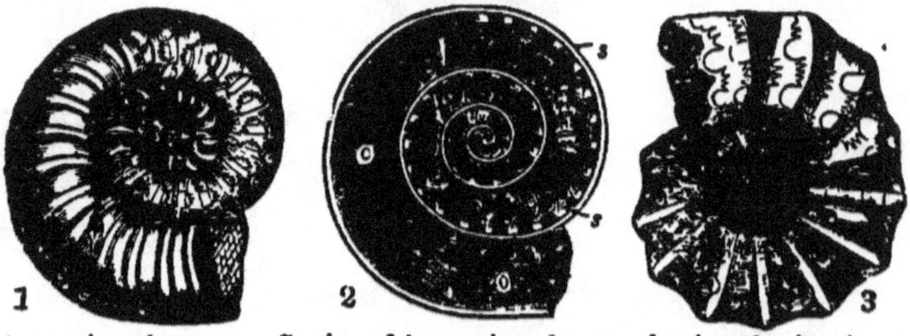

1. Ammonites obtusus; 2. Section of Ammonites obtusus, showing the interior chambers and siphuncle; 3. Ammonites nodosus.

exquisite beauty, while the edges of the partitions, being converted into iron pyrites, form a kind of golden tracery, glittering in the midst of the pellucid spar. The only surviving member of this family is the modern nautilus (*naus*, a ship), the "fairy sailor" of the Indian seas.

The *Belemnite* (*belemnon*, a dart) is so called from the peculiar shape of the fossil (Fig. 78). They have also

FIG. 78.

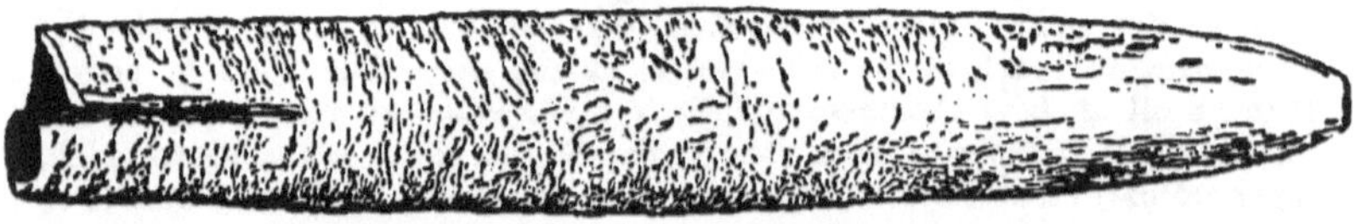

Belemnitella mucronata, Cretaceous Period, N. J.

been vulgarly called "thunder-heads," "lady-fingers," etc. The relics do not give any idea of the animal to which the name was applied. They were merely the terminal bones of the body and were surrounded with flesh. The animal resembled the modern cuttle-fish.* It secreted a kind of ink which it used as a means of defence. In an emergency, it blackened the water in its vicinity, and escaped from sight. These ink-bags have been found so perfectly preserved that their contents have been used in sketching their fossil remains.

FIG. 79.

Belemnite restored; *a*, the Ink-bag in place.

The enormous reptiles are, however, the distinguishing fossils of the age. We shall notice only the more prominent ones.

1. The *Ichthyosaur* (fish-lizard) is a striking illustration of a comprehensive type, having the general contour of a dolphin, the snout of a porpoise, the head of a lizard, the jaws and teeth of a crocodile, the vertebræ of a fish, the sternal arch of the water-mole,† the paddles of a whale, and the trunk and tail of a quadruped. Its habits were doubtless aquatic, while, like the whale, it breathed atmospheric air, and was

* All are familiar with "cuttle-fish bones," so commonly used as food for canary birds. The substance, it is well to observe, is not a "bone," nor derived from a true "fish." It is simply the rudimentary shell of a mollusk. The cuttle-fish of our own shores is a harmless animal, only ten or twelve inches long, but the one frequenting the African seas attains a formidable size. This is the "devil-fish," so graphically described by Victor Hugo. Its staring, glassy eyes strike terror to beholders. It has eight huge, muscular arms, many times the length of its body, with which it holds its prey in a grasp so tenacious that the arms have been severed before they would yield.

† The ornithorhynchus or water-mole of New Holland is a mammalian-furred quadruped with webbed feet and the bill of a duck. In this animal the Creator seems to have repeated the curious contrivance originally provided for the Ichthyosaur.

thus compelled to come frequently to the surface of the water. Its neck was short and thick, its head large, and its body twenty or thirty feet long. Its jaws had an enormous opening, some having been found with 160 teeth, which could be renewed many times, as above each tooth was always the bony germ of a new one. The eyes were often two feet in diameter. Surrounding the pupil of each one was a circular series of thin bony plates. This apparatus, which still exists in the eyes of turtles and lizards, could be used to increase or diminish the curvature of the cornea, and adapt the magnifying power to the wants of the animal. The eye could thus be used as a telescope or a microscope to see its prey far and near, and to descry it in the darkness and depths of the sea. The fossil excrements of the Ichthyosaur are styled *coprolites*, and when polished are sold as jewelry.* They reveal distinctly the food and the internal organism of this Mesozoic saurian. In them have been found the scales and bones of smaller animals of their own species. The quarries of Lyme Regis, in Dorsetshire, England, abound in the remains of the Ichthyosaur.†

* Under the name of "*beetle stones*" coprolites have been also used for artistic purposes. Dr. Buckland, the celebrated English geologist, had a table in his drawing-room that was made entirely of these fossils, and was often much admired by persons who had not the least idea of what they were looking at. "I have seen," says his son, "in actual use, ear-rings made of the polished portions of coprolites (for they are as hard as marble); and while admiring the beauty of the wearer, have made out distinctly the scales and bones of the fish which once formed the dinner of a hideous reptile, but now hung pendulous from the ears of an unconscious belle, who had evidently never read or heard of such productions."—*Buckland's Curiosities of Natural History.*

† In 1811, Mary Anning, a poor country girl, who made her precarious living by picking up fossils, for which the neighborhood was famous, was pursuing her avocation, hammer in hand, when she perceived some bones projecting a little out of the cliff. Finding, on examination, that it was part of a large skele-

Ichthyosaur and Plesiosaur.

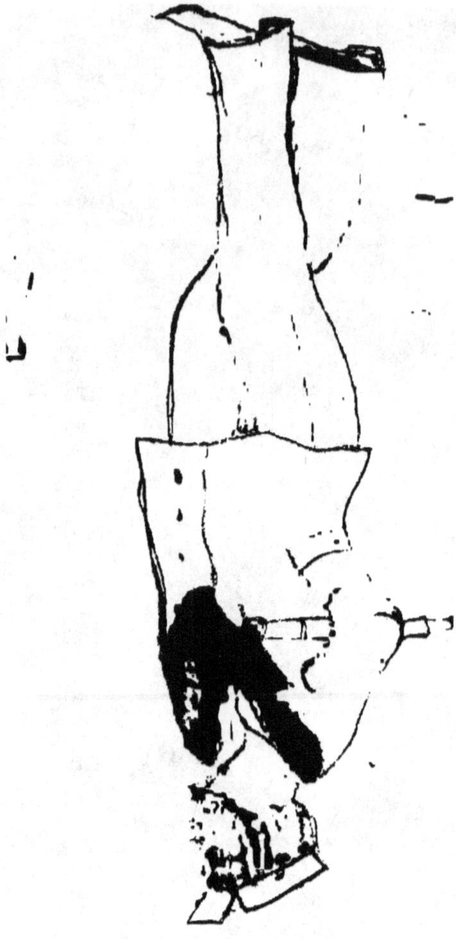

2. The *Plesiosaur* had the head of a lizard, the teeth of a crocodile, the neck of a swan, the trunk and tail of a quadruped, the ribs of a chameleon,* and the paddles of

FIG. 81.

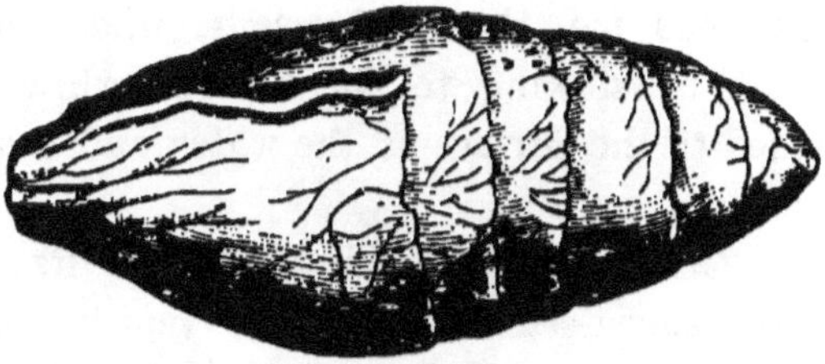

A Coprolite.

---

ton, she cleared away the rubbish, and found the whole creature imbedded in the block of stone. She hired workmen to dig out the block of lias in which it was buried. In this manner was the first of these monsters brought to light; a monster some thirty feet long, with jaws nearly a fathom in length, and huge saucer eyes—which have since been found so perfect that the petrified lenses have been split off and used as magnifiers.

Hugh Miller gives the following graphic description of the lias of Scotland: "It consists of laminæ as thin as sheets of pasteboard, which, of course, shows that there was but little deposited at a time, and pauses between each deposit. Yet never did characters or figures lie closer on a printed page than the organisms on the surfaces of these leaf-like laminæ. We insinuate our lever into a fissure, and turn up a portion of one of the laminæ, whose surface had last seen the light when existing as part of the bottom of the old Liassic sea, when more than half of the formation had still to be deposited. The ground of the tablet is of a deep black, while the colors of the fossils stand out in various shades, from opaque to a silvery white or deep gray. *There*, for instance, is a group of large ammonites, as if drawn in white chalk; there, a cluster of minute bivalve shells, each of which bears its thin film of silvery nacre. We turn over another page. Here are ammonites of various sizes, but all of one species, as if a whole argosy had been wrecked at once and sent to the bottom. And here we open yet another page, which bears a set of extremely slender belemnites. They lie along and athwart, and in every possible angle, like a heap of boarding-pikes thrown carelessly down a vessel's deck on the surrender of her crew. Here, too, is an assemblage of bright, black plates, that shine like pieces of Japan work, the head-plates of some fish of the ganoid order; and here an immense accumulation of minute, glittering scales of a circular form. And so, leaf after leaf, for tens and hundreds of feet together, repeats the same strange story. The great Alexandrian Library, with its unsummed tomes of ancient literature, the accumulation of long ages, was but a poor and meager collection, scarce less puny in bulk than recent in date, when compared with this vast and wondrous library of the lias of Scotland."

* Each pair of ribs surrounded the body with a complete girdle formed of five pieces, thus affording great facility for the expansion and dilation of the lungs.

a whale. Its tail was shorter than that of the ichthyosaur, being only sufficient to act as a rudder in guiding the body. To compensate this loss and assist in propulsion, its paddles were much larger and more powerful. Its appearance presented a striking contrast to that of its more ponderous foe, the ichthyosaur, whose attacks it could escape by sinking to the bottom, while its long neck reached to the surface of the water and maintained respiration.

3. The *Pterodactyle* (wing-fingered), in its apparent monstrosity* surpassed even the two reptiles just mentioned. It was so named because the bone of one finger was greatly expanded in order to support an extended membrane for flying (Fig. 82). It was a true aërial reptile. Its wings resembled those of bats. Its bones were hollow, like those of birds, but it bore no feathers, and had a mouth full of teeth. Remains have been found indicating a spread of wing of not less than sixteen feet; but the usual species of the Liassic did not exceed ten inches in length. Its ordinary position was upon its hind feet, walking uprightly with folded wings, or perched on trees, or climbing along cliffs with its hooked

* The fins of the fishes of the Devonian seas became the paddles of the ichthyosaur and of the plesiosaur; these, in their turn, became the membranous foot of the pterodactyle, and, finally, the wing of the bird. Afterwards came the articulated fore-foot of the terrestrial mammalia, which, after attaining remarkable perfection in the hand of the ape, became, finally, the arm and hand of man, an instrument of wonderful delicacy and power, belonging to an enlightened being gifted with the divine attribute of reason! A careful examination of the fore paddles of the plesiosaur reveals all the essential parts of the human arm—the scapula, humerus, radius and ulna, the bones of the carpus, the metacarpus and the phalanges. Was not this a prophecy of man? "Let us, then, dismiss this idea of monstrosity, which can only mislead us, and not consider antediluvian beings as mistakes or freaks of nature. Let us not regard them with disgust; let us learn, on the contrary, to behold in them with admiration the divine proofs of design which they display, and, in their organization, to see the handiwork of the sublime Creator of all things."

FIG. 82.

Haunts of the Pterodactyle.

claws and feet. The smaller ones lived on insects, but the larger probably pounced on struggling reptiles, or, diving into the water, preyed on fish. More than twenty species of the pterodactyle have been discovered in the old world, but in the new there have been found only a pair of finger-bones, at Phœnixville, Pa. Poets have long pictured to us a flying dragon of the olden time, which played a conspicuous part in pagan mythology. It breathed fire, poisoned the air with its exhalations, and disputed with man the possession of the earth. In the Jurassic times we find the realization of this creature of poetic fancy, but it is only an uncouth reptile, utterly unworthy of those fabled conflicts in which gods and heroes shared.

4. The *Dinosaurs* (terrible lizards) were land reptiles of enormous size that roamed elephant-like over the river-plains, or browsed in the forests of the Oölitic and Wealden Epochs. These included the megalosaur (large lizard), hylæosaur (wood-lizard), iguanodon, etc. (Fig. 83), huge monsters from forty to seventy feet in length. The megalosaur * was carnivorous, having teeth curved backward like a pruning-knife, and with a double edge of enamel so as to cut like a sabre equally on each side. The iguanodon † (ig-wan-o-don) was herbivorous, twigs of cypress having been found fossil in its stomach, and its teeth often being half-worn to the roots.

* A thigh-bone has been found four and a half feet long, indicating a leg eight or nine feet in length, and an animal taller than a man on horseback.

† A party of twenty-one scientific men, at the invitation of Dr. Hawkins, once took dinner within the restored body of this animal. On that occasion Dr. Owen, the celebrated geologist, sat in the head for brains! This model contains 650 bushels of artificial stone, 100 feet of iron hooping, 600 bricks, 20 feet of inch bar iron, 900 plain tiles, and 650 two-inch, half-round drain tiles; while the legs are four iron columns, nine feet long and four inches in diameter. ("Penny Guide to the Crystal Palace at Sydenham.")

FIG. 83.

The Megalosaur and Hylæosaur. Restored by Hawkins.

There is a restoration of a megalosaur in the Crystal Palace at Sydenham, England. This model was constructed under the direction of B. Waterhouse Hawkins. On the back of the animal is a hump like the withers of a horse. (See p. 269.) From the few bones discovered at that time, this celebrated anatomist decided that, to make the huge head effective, a mass of muscle and bone on the fore shoulders was essential. This bunch was thought by other geologists to be a mere monstrosity of his own invention. Subsequently, the entire skeleton being found, the conclusion was proved to be correct.

5. *The Labyrinthodon* was a frog-like quadruped, often attaining the size of an ox. It is so named because the outer coating of its teeth was bent inward in intricate mazy folds. Its head was protected by a helmet, and its body by a scaly armor.

The Ramphorhyncus, the remains of which have been found in the quarries of Solenhofen, is a curious intermediate link between birds and reptiles. Its tail, a singular appendage shown in the figure, was long, reptile-like, and dragged upon the ground, while its foot-

FIG. 84.

Labyrinthodon of the Trias restored, with its foot-prints

prints were bird-like. No wonder that palæontologists hesitate whether to class it with birds or with reptiles.

FIG. 85.

The Ramphorhyncus, with Oölitic Vegetation.

Bird-tracks.—In the red sandstones of the Connecticut valley, numerous foot-prints have been found, described

FIG. 86.

Imprints of Feet, Turner's Falls, Massachusetts.

by Hitchcock as mainly the tracks of birds. The number of these foot-prints is wonderful. Tracks of many different sizes and species often traverse the same slab. The largest tracks are fifteen inches long, and so deep as to hold nearly two quarts of water. They were made by an animal walking erect and having a stride of three feet. Hitchcock estimates that it far exceeded the ostrich in size, being at least twelve feet high, and weighing from 400 to 800 pounds. From the fact that parallel rows of tracks are found, we infer that these strange bipeds frequented in flocks the shores of the Connecticut, and waded into its shallow waters in quest of the fish and mollusks of the Mesozoic types, now long extinct.* Geologists are divided in opinion as to whether any of these tracks were made by birds, and not rather by three-toed reptiles somewhat similar to the ramphorhyncus. (Fig. 85.)

Remarks.—*1. Climate.*—The Gulf Stream, sweeping northward through the center of the continent, combined with the other causes already named to ameliorate the climate so as to permit a sub-tropical growth as far north as latitude 60°. Corals and ammonites, now restricted to torrid seas, then flourished in the

---

* "It is a solemn and impressive thought that the footprints of those dumb and senseless creatures have been preserved in all their perfection for thousands of ages, while so many of the works of man which date but a century back have been obliterated from the records of time. Kings and conquerors have marched at the head of armies across continents, and piled up aggregates of human suffering and experience to the heavens, and all the physical traces of their march have totally disappeared; but the solitary biped which stalked along the margins of a New England inlet before the human race was born, pressed footprints in the soft and shifting sand which the rising and sinking of the continent could not wipe out."—*Winchell.*

valley of the Upper Mississippi, while the prairies of Ohio and Illinois were green with perennial palms and pines.

2. Salt Beds.—The most extensive salt deposits in Europe are of the Triassic Period, and it has hence been sometimes styled the *Saliferous* formation. In Cheshire, England, are two beds of rock salt, each nearly 100 feet thick. At Cordova, Spain, is a mountain of salt several hundred feet high. This salt rock is pure as glass, and is carved into images, cups, etc., for sale to travelers. At the base is a brook, which in rainy seasons swells into a river, and carries down so much salt as to destroy the fish.* The mines of Cracow, Poland, have been worked at a depth of over 1,000 feet in galleries whose total length is 270 miles. At one point is a village with streets and houses, and even a chapel with altar, pulpit, statues, etc., all hewn out of the solid rock. The deposits in the salt beds indicate that the same conditions existed in portions of Europe during the Triassic as in New York during the Salina Period.

3. The Gold-bearing Rocks of California are mainly Jurassic or Triassic metamorphic sandstones, with interstratified quartz containing gold. Where the quartz veins have come to the surface and weathered, the particles of gold have been washed out, and thus formed the auriferous sands. There are frequent dikes of trap and outcrops of granite. On the crests of the Sierra Nevada these masses of granite often assume a dome

---

* This mountain presents a wondrous beauty to the looker-on at sunrise. Aside from its graceful and majestic form, it seems to rise above the river like a mountain of precious gems, displaying the brilliant colors of the rainbow.

shape, and reach a height of 15,000 feet above the sea-level.

4. Disturbances.—Long-continued upheavals and perhaps even terrific convulsions attended the close of this era, whereby such stupendous mountain ranges as the Sierra Nevada, Sierra Madre, etc., were lifted above the interior sea. The trap rocks of Mts. Holyoke and Tom, East and West Rocks near New Haven, Conn., the Palisades on the Hudson, and Bergen Hill in New Jersey, are all illustrations of the wide extent of the igneous action. Everywhere trap dikes and ridges attend this formation. The proofs that the trap was thrown out in a melted state are abundant. The adjacent sandstone has been baked by the heat, the layers uplifted by the escaping steam, and the fissures often filled with crystallized minerals.

CRETACEOUS PERIOD.

Location.—The Cretaceous rocks occur on the Atlantic coast from New York to South Carolina, along the Gulf through Texas, and northward over the slopes of the Rocky Mountains, at a height of 6,000 feet above the sea, through Colorado to the head-water of the Mississippi river. (See Frontispiece).

Kinds of Rock.—The name is derived from the Latin *creta*, chalk. The famous white chalk cliffs of Dover are of this formation. On our continent this group contains no chalk. The beds consist of layers of sand of various colors—white, green, or red, and are often so loose that they may be rubbed to pieces with the hand or dug with a spade. Beds of "*green sand*" are abundant in New Jersey. This is composed of small rounded grains, consisting mostly of silicate of iron and potash. The peculiar shape of these granules is probably due to the fact that they are the casts of microscopic shells. It is termed *marl*, and is extensively used for fertilizing purposes. In western Texas are beds of cream-colored limestone called "Chimney Stone," from its use in building chimneys. When taken from the quarry, it is soft enough to hew with an axe or smooth with a plane. The Cretaceous beds of the west contain many valuable seams of coal, such as the deposits of Mt. Diablo, near San Francisco, of Bellingham Bay, Washington Territory, etc. The quicksilver mines of New Almaden are also referred to this period.

FIG. 87.

A common Fossil of the Green Sand—the Exogyra costata.

Fossils.—CHALK.—If we examine chalk with a powerful microscope, we shall find that it is composed of the remains of numerous zoöphites, of various kinds of minute shells, and above all of rhizopods* (foramenif-

* The imagination fails to conceive the countless millions of these foramenifera in all ages. In Nature nothing is small. She seems to have delighted in achieving the grandest results with the feeblest means. The history of this ani-

era), so tiny that their very smallness seems to have rendered them indestructible. Eighteen hundred of

FIG. 88.

Chalk of Gravesend (Ehrenberg).

these placed in a row would occupy but an inch of space. Schleiden says that the chalk on a visiting card

malcule is a striking illustration of this truth. A handful of sand taken up on the sea-shore is often half composed of these microscopic shells. The Paris chalk contains them so abundantly that D'Orbigny found 58,000 in a cubic inch of the rock. Paris itself is built up of these cast-off abodes of the tiny rhizopod. The species vary in different sections and ages. A curious application of this has lately come to notice. Ehrenberg was requested to assist in tracing the robbery of a case of wine. It had been repacked by the criminal in sand differing from that in the original case. Ehrenberg, by a microscopic analysis, determined that the sand was found only on a certain ancient sea-coast in Germany. On this fact being discovered, the locality of the crime was speedily found and the thief arrested.

is a microscopic cabinet of a hundred thousand shells. Throughout the beds of chalk are scattered nodules of flint, which, being broken, reveal at the center shells, corals, etc., the nuclei around which the flint collected out of the chalk before that had consolidated from the pasty mass in which it first formed on the sea-bottom.

DEEP SEA DREDGINGS.—The soundings made in 1857–8 along the great telegraphic plateau which reaches from Valentia Bay to Newfoundland show that the sea-bottom is covered with a fine calcareous mud. Microscopic examination proved this to consist of shells of rhizopods and other species allied to the Cretaceous Period. These fragile and delicate shells were found to be in a perfect state of preservation. Many similar discoveries have since been made in different parts of the ocean. Depths of the sea so profound that the highest peaks of the Rocky or the Himalaya Mountains could be engulfed within them are believed to be inhabited by organic forms which have undergone little if any change since the Mesozoic Age.

THE AMERICAN FOSSILS are far removed from the microscopic remains of the Old World. While chalk-beds were accumulating on the deep-sea bottom in Europe, the shallow waters on the American shore teemed with as busy and strange a life as swarmed upon the coasts of England, France or Germany during the entire Mesozoic Age. The Cretaceous beds of New Jersey have furnished abundant reptilian remains.*

1. The *Cimoliasaur* and the *Elasmosaur* were huge

* We are indebted to the untiring and skilful labors of Dr. Cope and Dr. Leidy, of Philadelphia, for the following description of these Cretaceous reptiles.

sea-serpents, twenty-five to forty feet long, with bodies larger than an ox, sharp teeth, and flippers like a whale, —the latter having a flattened tail, which it used like an oar for sculling.

2. The *Mosasaur* was a whale-like, carnivorous monster, shorter and stouter than the preceding reptiles. Its ponderous bones are wrecked along the old sea-coast, and may be seen on the Alabama river projecting from the limestone cliffs.

3. *Snapping-turtles*, six feet long and of many varieties, lived in the salt water, as the now living species do in fresh water.

4. *Crocodiles* were exceedingly abundant. Three-fourths of all the bones found in the marl-pits are those of the crocodile. These creatures swarmed along what is now the river-front of Philadelphia, and peopled every pool and lagoon on the ancient shores of Pennsylvania. Most obstinate combats must have taken place between these fierce crocodiles and the great snapping-turtles which inhabited the same waters.

4. The *Dinosaurs* rivaled in size the elephants of our day. Their aspect was strange and portentous; some chiefly squatted, some leaped on their hind limbs like the kangaroo, and some stalked on erect legs like great birds, with small arms hanging uselessly by their sides, as with bony visage they surveyed land and water from their lofty elevation.

5. The *Hadrosaur* was a massive, herbivorous reptile about thirty feet long. The fossil remains have been lately restored by Hawkins, and are set up in the Museum of Natural Sciences, Philadelphia. This monster doubtless walked mainly on its hind legs, its knees

thrown upward and forward, and its huge tail trailing behind. Its expression was that of a perpetual grin, as its open mouth revealed several rows of shiny teeth with which it cut the twigs on which it fed.

6. The *Lælaps* was a powerful, carnivorous animal, and the destructive enemy of the preceding smaller reptiles. A full-grown specimen was probably twenty-three feet in length. Its toes were long and slender like those of a bird of prey. They were armed with flattened, hooked claws, ten to twelve inches long, and adapted to grabbing and tearing. Its teeth were curved, knife-shape, saw-edged, and fitted like scissors for cutting. The tail was long, rounded, and strong, and capable of striking a blow or of throwing an enemy within reach of the kick or grab of the terrible hind leg. It could leap like the kangaroo, and probably captured its prey by a few immense bounds.

SCENIC DESCRIPTION.—Let us picture to ourselves a landscape in this Mesozoic Age. It is an arm of the ocean with broad, flat, muddy shores, at the bottom of which is slowly gathering a sandy rock. The fog has just lifted, and discloses a view of surpassing beauty. On either hand the summits of the hills are crowned with lordly pines, while the sloping land is overgrown with palms and tropical trees. The shore is green with ferns and reeds, whose tufted tassels nod in the gentle breeze. No grass carpets the plain, no flowers embellish the scene, no birds sing in the trees. It is the reign of reptiles. On every hand they swarm—crawling, hopping, stalking by the shore. The water is alive with them—swimming, diving, and filling the air with an indescribable din. All day long enormous lizards crawl through the forests, crushing the reed-like trees before them in their headlong course, or plunge into the sea, leaving behind a broad wake like a steamer; while others, more fearful still, spread their wings and riot in the air. Sailing in and out among the shallow coves and bays of the coast, the plesiosaur, arching its long neck, eagerly watches a shoal of fish swimming near. But with quick sharp strokes of its whale-like paddles, the huge ichthyosaur darts into view, and glares upon its prey with its great bulging eye. Instantly the swan neck disappears under the water, and the plesiosaur is hidden from its rapacious foe—the terror of the Mesozoic seas. Mighty dinosaurs, rivaling the elephant in size, stalk along the shore or squat on the beach stupidly gazing on the scene, save when the lælaps, with fearful bounds, leaps among their frightened herds, and tears them with his eagle-claws. But night draws on apace. In the dim recesses of the woods the pterodactyle—that winged dragon so terrible to behold—sails slowly along on its broad, leathern wings. As the shadows deepen, mighty sea-serpents dart to-and-fro, battling with the rising billows; that huge bloated frog—the labyrinthodon—jumps by with great ungainly hops, while a tiny mammal,* the first of its kind, flies frightened to the shelter of the woods.

* This was the Dromatherium Sylvestre, the jaw-bone of which was discovered by Emmons in North Carolina. It is the only mammal yet known to have existed in America during the Mesozoic Age. In Europe, two or three insignificant ones of the lowest order have been discovered. No true bird remains have been found on this continent, but in the quarries of Solenhofen they have been scantily preserved. One, called the Archæopteryx, and Bird of Solenhofen, is very clearly identified, except the head.

Mesozoic Disturbances.—The Mesozoic Time, like the Palæozoic, was closed by mighty upheavals. As Winchell beautifully says: "The ever-shrinking earth-nucleus necessitated the ever-enlarging wrinkles of the enveloping crust; the furrows must deepen and the folds must rise." The increasing pressure of the Atlantic and Pacific oceans produced another upheaval of the land, and another addition to the growing continent. This was probably not a sudden convulsion, but a long-continued upward movement. By it, however, the conditions of life were changed. All the Mesozoic types disappeared—not a species survived the catastrophe. A few mammals, birds and flowering plants, types prophetic of the Cenozoic Time, had appeared, but they all went down in the shock.—Another cycle of geologic history is finished, another phase of life has swept across the slowly-forming world, culminated and broken on the shore of the past. The reign of reptiles is closed.

V

CENOZOIC TIME.

The Cenozoic or *recent life* of geologic history comprises only one age, that of mammals.

AGE OF MAMMALS. { 1. Tertiary Period.
2. Post-Tertiary Period.

General Characteristics.—The more striking scenes of life hitherto have been confined to the water; they are now transferred to the land. Extensive bodies of fresh water teem with fishes resembling pickerel, perch, eels, etc. Molluscan life takes on the types of modern times—the bivalves increasing and the gasteropods taking the lead. Insects throng every element—earth, air and water. Birds are also found in greater numbers. It is emphatically, however, the age of mammals. Quadrupeds of enormous bulk—many identical with existing species—occupy the land. The herbs, shrubs and trees—the flowers, fruits and grains—all that can gladden the senses or satisfy the wants of man—appear and confirm the harmony that always exists between organic and inorganic nature.

FIG. 89.

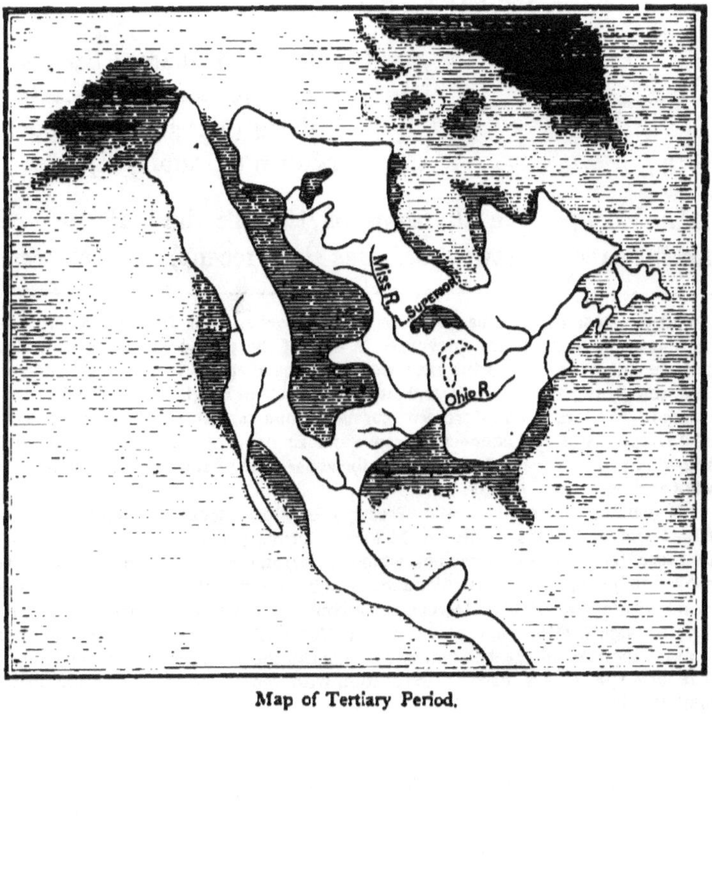

Map of Tertiary Period.

Geography.—The great Mesozoic upheaval burst asunder the Gulf Stream, which had sent the warm waters of the tropics to the Arctic Ocean. On the southwest it retired to nearly its present limits, but a long arm reached up the Mississippi valley to the mouth of the Ohio river (Fig. 89). On the north it broadened into the great Tertiary Sea which extended through Nebraska and the western part of Dacotah.* The Pacific Ocean still held possession of the western coast, while the Atlantic Ocean covered the southeastern border of the continent, and the coral builders were yet at work upon Florida.

TERTIARY PERIOD.

TERTIARY† PERIOD.
1. Claiborne (Alabama) Epoch.
2. Jackson (Mississippi) Epoch.
3. Vicksburg (Mississippi) Epoch.
4. Yorktown (Virginia) Epoch.

In Europe, the divisions of the Tertiary Period are *Eocene* (recent dawn), *Miocene* (less recent), and *Pliocene*

* At the close of the Mesozoic Age, Europe was still far from displaying the configuration which it now presents. A map of the period would represent the great basin of Paris (with the exception of a zone of chalk), the whole of Switzerland, the greater part of Spain and Italy, the whole of Belgium, Holland, Prussia, Hungary, Wallachia, and northern Russia, as one vast sheet of water. A band of Jurassic rocks still connected France and England at Cherbourg. This disappeared at a later period, and caused the separation of the British Islands from what is now France.—*Figuier*.

† The name Tertiary is a relic of early geological science. When introduced, it was preceded in the system of history by Primary and Secondary. The first of these terms was thrown out when the crystalline rocks, so called, were proved to belong to no particular age, though not without an ineffectual attempt to substitute it for Palæozoic; and the second, after use for a while under a restricted signification, has given way to Mesozoic. Tertiary holds its place simply because of the convenience of continuing an accepted name (Dana). The term Quaternary, used in connection with the Post-Tertiary Period, had a similar origin.

(more recent). On this continent these terms do not apply, and an American classification has been adopted. In the Pliocene, most of the species are allied to existing forms; in the Miocene, fewer are thus related; and in the Eocene, we recognize only the dawn of modern forms. The Claiborne, Jackson, and Vicksburg beds have been referred to the Eocene, the Yorktown to the Miocene, and the Sumter and Darlington divisions, recognized by some authorities, to the Pliocene.

Location.—The *Marine* Tertiary beds lie on the Atlantic, Pacific, and Gulf borders,* and extend up the Mississippi valley to the mouth of the Ohio river. *Fresh water* Tertiary beds occur on the eastern slopes of the Rocky Mountains and in the upper Missouri region. There are no great continental strata, as in the Silurian Age, but rather such a diversity as we find in formations now in progress on the sea-coast, where the beds often change in character within small distances. These modern deposits give us the key to the ancient ones. (See pp. 23 and 29.)

---

* "What are known as the Pine Barrens, in the southern States, is a belt of country more than 1,700 miles long, and often 170 miles broad, stretching from Richmond, along the Atlantic and Gulf coasts, to beyond the western line of Louisiana, where the soil, derived from the decomposition of the newest member of the Tertiary series, is sandy, and where the principal arborescent form is the long-leaf pine. It is emphatically the "poor man's region." These forests, while affording a valuable article of lumber, also yield pitch, tar, and turpentine. On the Pacific slope the Tertiary rocks, which are referred to the Miocene Group, appear to be coterminous with the Cretaceous. They enter into the frame-work of the Coast Ranges, stretching from the Columbia to San Louis Bay, and probably to Cape St. Lucas; and throughout the entire extent the strata are upheaved, plicated, and metamorphosed, and, at frequent intervals, invaded by igneous products. They repose in horizontal strata upon the foot-hills of the Sierra, but are in a disturbed position where they fold around Shasta."—*Foster's Mississippi Valley, published by Messrs. S. C. Griggs & Co., Chicago.*

Kinds of Rock.—The Tertiary beds consist of sand, clay, marl, pebbles, etc. There are, however, valuable buhrstones, shell-rocks, limestones, and, near San Francisco, slates and sandstones, hardly distinguishable from more ancient formations.

The Eocene of the old world contains strata of NUMMULITIC (*nummus*, a piece of money) limestone thousands of miles in length and hundreds of feet in thickness. It is so called because it is largely composed of a fossil* having the shape of a coin. The most noted Pyramids are built of this stone, and wagon-loads of the fossils, disintegrated by the weather, lie at their base.

Extensive beds of light bituminous coal (lignite) are found scattered from Pike's Peak to the Arctic Ocean, across the treeless regions west of the Missouri, and thence into Oregon. The wide distribution and convenient locality of these Tertiary coals must exercise a vast influence in facilitating communications over the great deserts of the west, and can but be considered as a providential forecast of the wants of man.

FIG. 90.

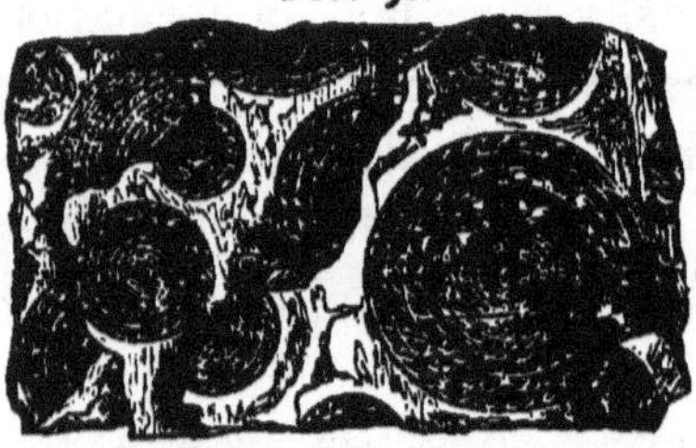

Rhizopods (Nummulites ataica).

Fossils.—I. PLANTS.—The abundance of vegetable remains proves the land to have been covered with an exuberant flora. Leaves of oak, maple, poplar, hickory,

* The nummulite is a rhizopod, being the giant of that family. (See p. 100.)

cinnamon, fig, palm, and pine are abundant.* A leaf of a fan-palm has been found on the Upper Missouri, that, when entire, was probably twelve feet across (Dana). Nuts are common in some localities, as at Brandon, Vt. In the London basin a single collector gathered 25,000 specimens of fossil fruits representing five or six hundred species. Many of them were products of aromatic and spice groves, such as now flourish in Ceylon and the West Indies. The extensive deposits of diatoms at Richmond, Va., and Bilin, Germany, etc., which have been already mentioned (page 48) are of this period.

II. Animals.—Tertiary shells of over 3,000 species have been found in America. They have the look and oftentimes the freshness of modern specimens, as may be seen in the accompanying cuts of Miocene Gasteropods. (See Fig. 91.) In Colorado and Utah are shales containing insects so well preserved that even the microscopic hairs of the wings can be detected (Denton). The first bee made its appearance in the amber † of the Eocene, locked

---

* The earth had already its seasons, its spring and summer, its autumn and winter, its seed-time and harvest, though neither sower nor reaper was there; the forests then, as now, dropped their thick carpet of leaves upon the ground in the autumn, and in many localities they remain where they originally fell, with a layer of soil between the successive layers of leaves—a leafy chronology, as it were, by which we read the passage of the years which divided these deposits from each other. Where the leaves have fallen singly on a clayey soil favorable for receiving such impressions, they have daguerreotyped themselves with the most wonderful accuracy; and the trees of the Tertiaries are as well known to us as are those of our own time.—*Agassiz in Geological Sketches.*

† See Fourteen Weeks in Chemistry, page 195. Amber has been found quite abundant on the shores of the Baltic, washed out of the lignite beds by the waves. Species of coniferous trees existed, from which gum or resin flowed, and becoming fossilized, amber was the result. In flowing down the tree, insects, spiders, small crustaceans, and leaves were covered; and thus we find them preserved in the transparent amber. Over 800 species of insects, and 98 of trees and shrubs have been observed, besides numerous mosses, fungi, and liverwort.—*Denton in Our Planet.*

FIG. 91. GASTEROPODS OF THE MIOCENE.

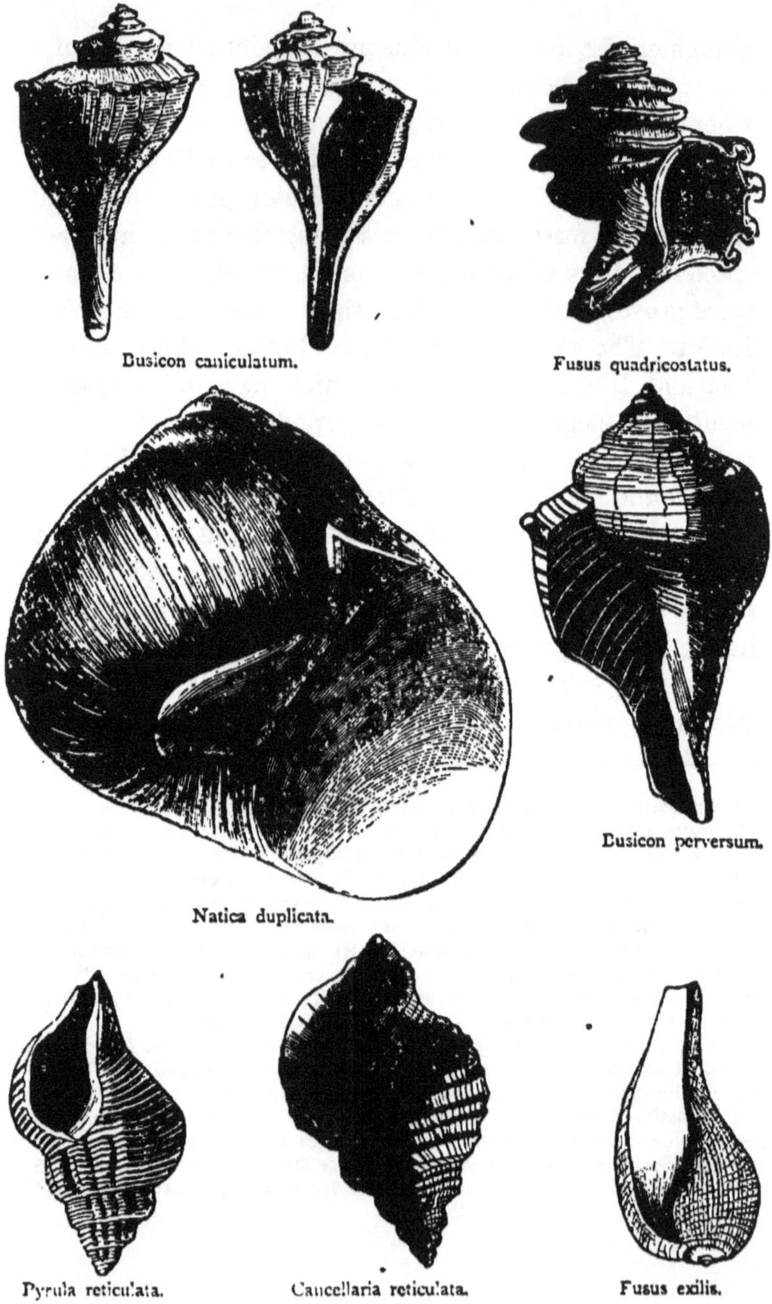

FIG. 92. GASTEROPODS OF THE MIOCENE.

Murex globosa. (Half natural size.)

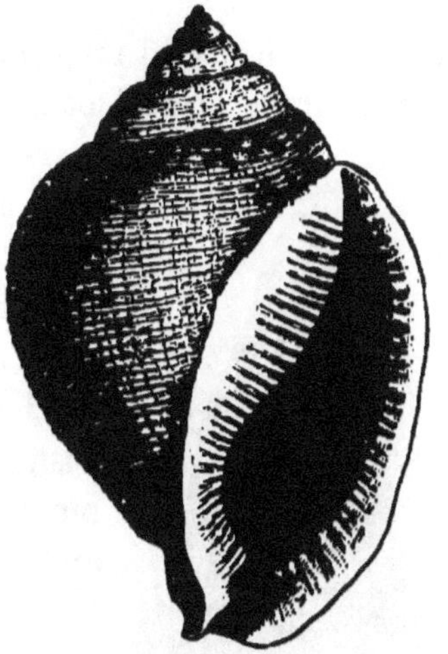

Galeodia Hodgii.

FIG. 93. ECHINODERMS OF THE MIOCENE.

Rosette, beneath.

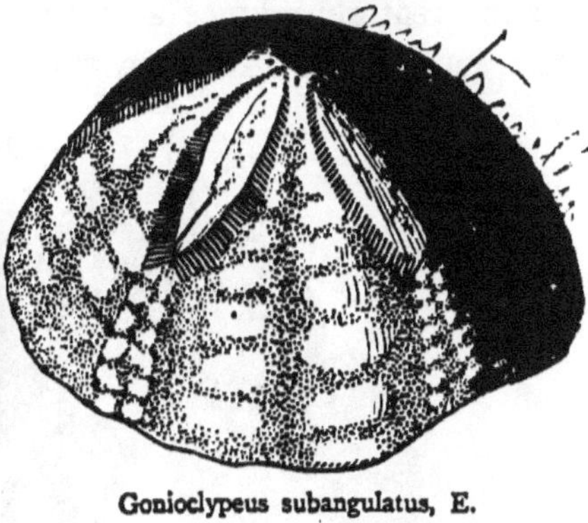

Gonioclypeus subangulatus, E.

FIG. 94.

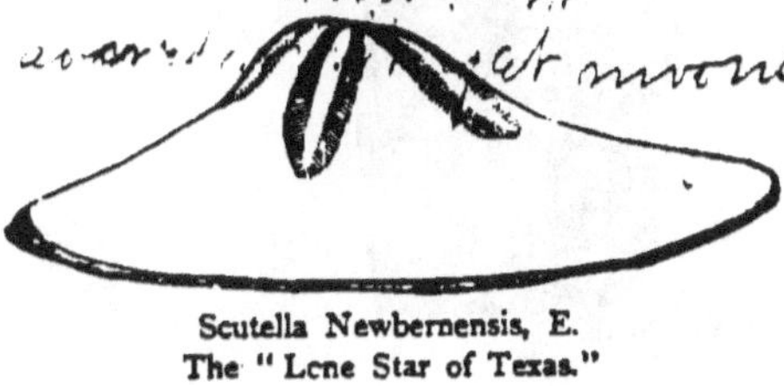

Scutella Newbernensis, E.
The "Lone Star of Texas."

FIG. 95.

Echinus Ruffini.

up hermetically in its gum-like covering—"an embalmed corpse in a crystal coffin," as Hugh Miller quaintly remarks. Broken wings of butterflies also attest the presence of flowers. Ants, crickets, grasshoppers, beetles, and dragon-flies are so numerous that some kinds seem to have afforded food to the first mammals that appeared. Fish existed in great abundance, mostly allied to the modern perch and salmon. Sharks' teeth have been found six inches in length.

FIG. 96.

Oxyrhina Desorii.
Shark's Tooth from N. C.

The bones of a species of whale called the *Zeuglodon* (yoke-tooth), so called from the shape of its teeth, occur in great abundance scattered over the cotton lands of the south. In Alabama they have been laid up in

FIG. 97.

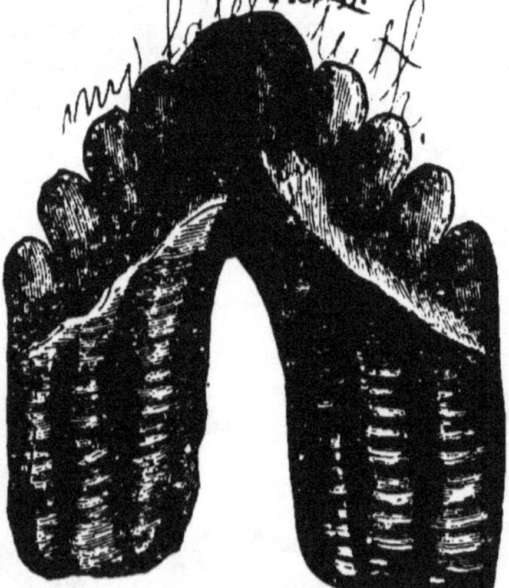

Zeuglodon's Tooth.

walls for fences, or burned for lime. A single vertebra is a load for a man to carry. The animal was about seventy feet long.*

QUADRUPEDS, thick-skinned and ruminating mammals, were the great feature of the Tertiary life.

European Quadrupeds.—Cuvier was the first to bring to light the forms of these long-extinct animals. In the Gypsum quarries, near Paris, bones were dug up in great

Fig. 98.

Scene in Paris Basin.
1. The Paleotherium. 2. The Anoplotherium. 3. The Xiphodon.

numbers, but they were disregarded, as they were thought to be those of existing species, until the attention of this great naturalist was directed to them. He gathered a large quantity in a room, and commenced the work of assorting and re-creating. "At the voice of comparative anatomy every bone and fragment resumed its place."

* The restored skeleton of a Zeuglodon is on exhibition in Wood's Museum, Chicago. It contains 118 vertebræ, and its head is six feet long. Prof. Winchell pronounces it, for the most part, an accurate representation of this alligator-like whale.

(Cuvier.) He restored the animals, assigned them to their classes, and investigated their habits.

The neighborhood seems to have been a gulf of the sea, into which emptied several rivers. Animals inhabiting the banks of these streams were borne down, and de

FIG. 99.

View of the Bad Lands.

posited in the sediment which gathered at the mouth. Among the quadrupeds the most conspicuous was the *Paleotherium* (ancient wild beast), peaceful flocks of which must have inhabited the plateau which environed the ancient basin of Paris. It resembled the South American tapir, but was as large as a horse.

American Quadrupeds.—On this continent similar discoveries have been made in the Mauvaises Terres, or Bad Lands of Dacotah. This region consists of immense beds of clay cut out by rivers into winding channels, leaving thousands of irregular columnar masses often one to two hundred feet in height. So thickly is the surface studded with these natural towers, that the traveler must thread his way through deep, confined labyrinthine passages not unlike the narrow, irregular streets and lanes of some quaint old European town.* The soil is barren and arid. It is a literal Golgotha—a place of bones. At every step in this charnel-house the explorer treads upon the remains of a former age. The clayey walls are built up with broken skeletons. Hundreds of fossil turtles (see Fig. 100) are strewn about, many weighing a ton each. On every side are scattered bones strangely like the familiar forms of to-day, but of unknown species and unwonted combinations. The *Titanotherium* was one of these wonderful animals. It resembled a hornless rhinoceros, but was eighteen or twenty feet long, and nine feet high.

The Origin of this Region was, probably, as follows: The great Tertiary sea was at first salt, but receiv-

---

* These rocky piles, in their endless succession, assume the appearance of massive artificial structures decked out with all the accessories of buttress and turret, arched doorway and clustered shaft, pinnacle and finial and tapering spire. On a nearer approach the illusion vanishes, and all the forms which fancy has conjured are resolved into barren desolation. The bottom of the vale is an earth of chalky whiteness, baked by the sun, and utterly destitute of vegetation. The water which oozes out of the foundation-wall of the prairie is brackish and unpalatable. In winter, the wind and snow rush through the lanes and corridors of this city of the dead in eddying whirls, while the withered grasses and the voiceless and motionless solitude, together with the relentless frost and never-tiring storm, make the place the realization of utter bleakness and desolation. In summer the scorching sun literally bakes the clays which have been kneaded by the frosts and thaws of spring; and the daring explorer of the scene finds no tree nor shrub to shelter him from the fervid rays poured down from above, and reflected from the white walls which tower around him, and the white floor which almost blisters his feet.—*Sketches of Creation*—*Winchell.*

ing fresh water from the drainage of the adjacent land, and having an outlet into the ocean, it gradually became a brackish, and at last a fresh-water sea. As the continent was elevated, this great inland sea was drained in part, and in time probably became broken up into a

FIG. 100.

Testudo Oweni.

chain of fresh-water lakes.* The basin of one of these, now constituting the Bad Lands, is thought by Hayden to have covered an area of 150,000 square miles—five times as great as that of Lake Superior. The shores of these lakes during the Tertiary and Post-Tertiary Periods were inhabited by the rhinoceros, elephant, camel, horse, beaver, wild cat, wolf, and many quadrupeds, whose entire species are now extinct. In these familiar haunts,

* It is not difficult, with the discoveries already made in Colorado, to call up the country as it existed on the eastern side of the mountains about the close of the Miocene Period. A long and wide lake covered the spot where Golden City and Denver now stand, and stretched north and south for an immense distance. Its banks were clad with forests of pines, palms, and gum-bearing trees.—*Denton.*

amid a semi-tropical vegetation, they lived and died. Their remains, sinking in the soft mud, reveal to us to-day the forms of Tertiary life.

POST-TERTIARY PERIOD.

(*Quaternary Epoch.*)

POST-TERTIARY PERIOD.
1. Glacial Epoch.
2. Champlain Epoch.
3. Terrace Epoch.

1. GLACIAL EPOCH.

(*Drift or Bowlder Period.*)

The continent has been steadily growing through the ages until now it has attained its full dimensions. It would seem to be ready for man. It abounds in coal, timber, water, game, and the domestic animals necessary for man's use. We naturally expect his creation next, and, almost unconsciously, look about for traces of his presence. But God's plan is not yet complete. The next period seems one of retrogression, and a superficial view would lead one almost to despair of the result. We must not, however, be impatient, but wait the slow development of Nature's laws. The earth having passed the ordeal by fire and water, now enters upon that by ice. The long summer is over. For ages a tropical climate has prevailed, and on the borders of the Arctic Ocean animals have roamed and plants have flourished which now find a home only beneath the burning sun of the Tropics. Their reign is past. A tedious Arctic winter succeeds. During its rigors life disappears, and half of the continent reverts to its primeval desolation. Let us notice some of the traces of this wonderful change—this apparent check in the world's progress.

Drift.—This includes the loose unstratified* deposits of clay, sand, gravel and stones familiar to all inhabitants of the northern States. It does not extend south of latitude 39°† nor west of the Rocky Mountains (Whitney and Foster). In some places the Drift material forms only a slight covering over the solid rock, while in others it is piled up in hills and ridges.

BOWLDERS.—The stones are of all sizes, from small cobble-stones up to great rock-masses. In Whittingham, Vt., is a bowlder whose length is forty feet, and whose estimated weight is 3,400 tons; another in Bradford weighs over 2,000 tons. Plymouth Rock is a bowlder of syenitic granite, ledges of which are to be seen near Boston. The pedestal of the statue of Peter the Great was hewn from a block of granite weighing 1,500 tons, which was found in a neighboring marsh. Bowlders are sometimes so nicely poised that they can be rocked by the hand, although an immense force would be required to dislodge them.

Bowlders are more or less rounded, as if water-worn, and their structure and mineral composition are different from those of the rocks on which they rest. They have evidently been transported to the places they occupy.

* When the deposit is arranged in layers, it is termed *Modified Drift*. Modified Drift at many places forms knolls of a most picturesque description. On account of their beauty, they are oftentimes chosen for burial places. Mt. Hope at Rochester, and Woodlawn at Elmira, N. Y., Mt. Auburn at Cambridge, and the cemeteries at Plymouth, Newburyport, and North Adams, Mass., are all delightfully located on sites of this formation.

† 39° is about the latitude of Washington, Cincinnati, St. Louis, Kansas City, Pike's Peak, and Sacramento City.

The "parent ledges" from which they were derived can generally be found at the north of the locality—some-

FIG. 101.

View near Gloucester, Mass.

times at a distance of a few rods only, at others of many miles. Long Island and Martha's Vineyard are covered with rocks derived from the main-land. The southern part of Rhode Island is strewn with iron ore from Iron Hill (Cumberland, R. I.). On Hoosic Mountain is a bowlder of 500 tons weight, which has been carried from a ledge across an intervening valley 1,300 feet deep, and at the same time elevated 1,000 feet above its source. Masses of native copper from Lake Superior are scattered over Wisconsin, Michigan, and even Ohio and Indiana. The streets of Cincinnati are paved with stones quarried by the hand of Nature in the region of the Upper Lakes (Winchell). Azoic rocks are found on the western prairies, from 400 to 600 miles distant from their homes. Such bowlders are significantly termed *lost rocks.** A bushel of pebble-stones gathered in any northern State will often represent nearly every geological formation found for hundreds of miles north of that locality.

GLACIAL STRIÆ.—A careful examination of many of these bowlders shows us that they are covered with parallel grooves (*striæ*). These have obviously been caused by the scraping of the bowlders on the solid rock, as if the Drift material had been carried forward by an irresistible force, since the "bed rock" (the rock in place) in the regions covered by the Drift is polished and grooved in a similar manner. These striæ consist of long, straight, parallel lines,—furrows a foot broad and several inches deep, or scratches fine as a pin would make. The surfaces of hard rocks, as quartz, are often polished smooth as glass, while the markings can be seen only with the microscope. The general course is that in which the bowlders have been carried, i. e., from north to south,†

* In New England, oftentimes the surface for many miles is covered with these erratic blocks; on the prairies, however, they are found only occasionally. This may be caused by the different character of the rocks at the east and at the west. While every location shows the intrusion of foreign material, the great mass is made up by the destruction of neighboring rocks. The Silurian and Devonian rocks of the Mississippi valley would naturally produce a soil far different from that of the crystalline and metamorphic rocks of New England. The agent which transported the rocks might have ground the softer class to an impalpable powder, and left the other of a far coarser texture.

† "In general, these striæ do not alter their course for any topographical feature of the country. They cross valleys at every conceivable angle, and even if the striæ run in a valley for some distance, when the valley curves the striæ will leave it, and ascend hills and mountains even thousands of feet high. But these striæ are never found upon the south sides of mountains, unless for a part of the way where the slope is small. Mt. Monadnoc, of New Hampshire, is an illustration of these statements. It is a naked mass of mica schist, 3,250 feet high, rising like a cone out of an undulating country. And from top to bottom it has been scarified on its northern and western sides, indicated by striæ running up the mountain, at first south-easterly, and at the top at S. 10° E. There are deep furrows and other phenomena on the summit, and the striæ extend a short distance up the southern slope of the mountain."—*Hitchcock.*

varying generally not more than 20° east or west. There are frequently two or more sets of striæ, differing a little in direction. At Stony Point, Lake Erie, the limestone

FIG. 102.

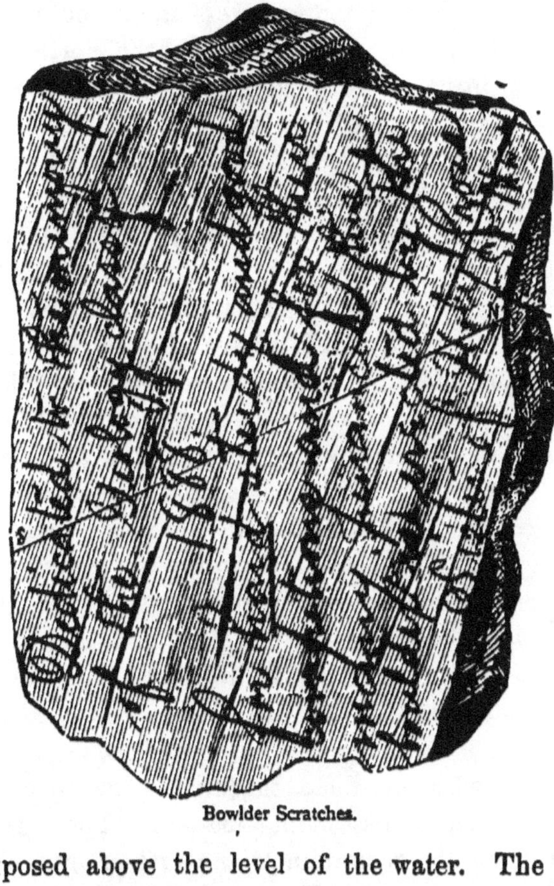

Bowlder Scratches.

lies exposed above the level of the water. The bed is planed down smooth as a floor, and at one place the parallel grooves strikingly resemble the deep ruts produced by a loaded wagon. On the Platte river there is a ledge of limestone so regularly planed that, without further working, it can be used for caps and sills in houses. At Marquette, on Lake Superior, there are surfaces as uniform as if worked to a level and afterward rubbed with sand-paper. Near the sea-shore at Portland, Maine, the striæ run parallel for great distances and then disappear in the water. Everywhere in the northern part of the continent, up to a height of five or six thousand feet above the level of the sea, where the bed-rock is laid bare, it is found covered with these Drift-tracings. We can best understand the cause of the Drift phenomena by noticing similar cases now exhibited in Alpine regions.

Glacial Phenomena.—The snow which falls on the mountains of Switzerland, above the height of 9,000 feet does not melt, but accumulates to a great thickness. By its own weight it generally packs into a solid mass. Thawing superficially by day, tiny streams of water percolate through, and convert it into the beautiful azure-tinted ice, so much admired by tourists. Seas of ice (*mers de glace*) fill the spaces between the summits, while from them, down every valley, pour rivers of ice, glaciers, from 200 to 5,000 feet deep. These ice-streams, fed by the snows above, extend downward until they are melted by the summer sun in the valley below. They sometimes plough irresistibly into the cultivated fields, so that a person can, with one hand, touch the growing corn, and with the other the descending ice-wall. The glacier advances down the mountain at the rate of from eight to twelve inches per day. Frost, rain, hail, and avalanches of snow are continually detaching from the mountain-peaks masses of rock, which roll down upon the glacier. If the ice were stationary these would merely gather in a

FIG. 103.

A Swiss Glacier, with lateral and terminal moraines.

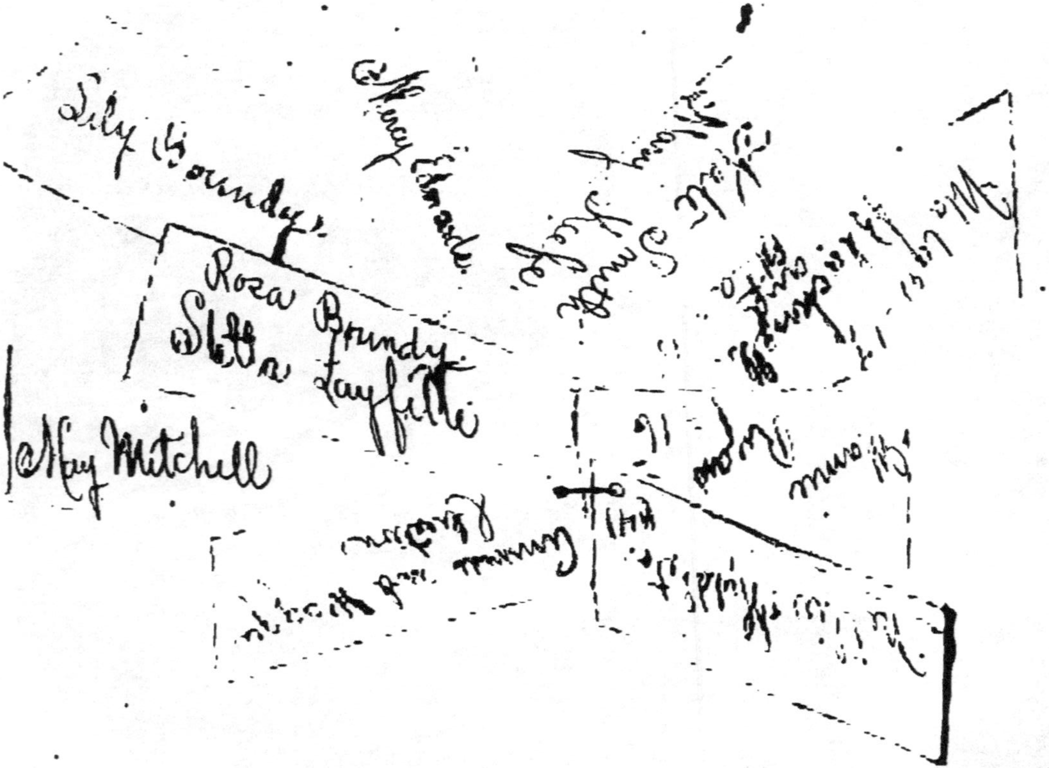
Lily Boundy
Rosa Boundy
Mary Mitchell
Mercy Edwards

confused pile, but owing to the forward movement of the glacier, they form along the outer edge a line of stones which is termed a *Moraine.* When the rocks fall from opposite mountains and on each side of the glacier, they make two parallel trains which are called *Lateral Moraines* (Fig. 103). At the foot of the glacier the débris gathers in ridges, styled *Terminal Moraines.** In this way enormous blocks of stone have been carried many miles. They are often found perched on points of the Alps far above existing glaciers, or dispersed over distant plains. Masses thus conveyed on the surface of the glacier are little worn. Blocks, pebbles, etc., however, which become frozen in the ice, are forced along in the onward progress of the glacier, scoring the rock beneath with parallel lines, and smoothing its surface as emery polishes steel, while they are themselves rounded and scratched in every direction, and even ground into impalpable powder. The glacier thus becomes a gigantic rasp hundreds of feet thick, thousands wide, and miles in length, scouring the rocks between and over which it passes.

---

* "The masses of snow which hang upon the Alps during winter, the rain which infiltrates between their beds during summer, the sudden action of torrents of water, and more slowly, but yet more powerfully, the chemical affinities, degrade, disintegrate, and decompose the hardest rocks. The débris thus produced falls from the summits into the circles occupied by the glaciers with a great crash, accompanied by frightful noises and great clouds of dust. Even in the middle of summer I have seen these avalanches of stone precipitated from the highest ridges of the Schreckhorn, forming upon the immaculate snow a long black train, consisting of enormous blocks and an immense number of smaller fragments. In the spring, a rapid thawing of the winter snows often causes accidental torrents of extreme violence. If the melting is slow, water insinuates itself into the smallest fissures of the rocks, freezes there, and rends asunder the most refractory masses. The blocks detached from the mountains are sometimes of gigantic dimensions; we have found them sixty feet in length, and those measuring thirty feet each way are by no means rare in the Alps."—*Revue des Deux Mondes—Martin.*

Evidences of Former Glaciers.—Moraines, erratic blocks, polished surfaces, striæ, etc., become to the geologist infallible signs of the former existence of glaciers,* and enable him to follow them in their course and fix their origin. One who is familiar with tracing the furrows of this mighty ice-plow will recognize at once where the large bowlders have hollowed out their deeper gashes, where small pebbles have drawn their finer marks, where the stones with angular edges have left their sharp scratches, and where fine sand and gravel have rubbed and smoothed the rocky surface, and left it polished as if it came from the hand of the marble-worker.

Glaciers of Greenland.—Glacial phenomena are displayed on the grandest scale in Greenland. On its western coast is a glacier 1,200 miles long. It presents to the voyager a perpendicular wall of ice 2,000 feet high. A great glacial river, says Kane, seeking outlets at every valley, rolling icy cataracts into the Atlantic and

* Some or all the marks above enumerated are observed in the Alps at great heights above the present glaciers and far below their actual extremities; also in the great valley of Switzerland, fifty miles broad; and almost everywhere on the Jura, a chain which lies to the north of this valley. The average height of the Jura is about one-third that of the Alps, and it is now entirely destitute of glaciers; yet it presents almost everywhere similar moraines, and the same polished and grooved surfaces and water-worn cavities. The erratics, moreover, which cover it present a phenomenon which has astonished and perplexed the geologist for more than half a century. No conclusion can be more incontestable than that these angular blocks of granite, gneiss, and other crystalline formations came from the Alps, and that they have been brought for a distance of fifty miles and upward across one of the widest and deepest valleys in the world; so that they are now lodged on the hills and valleys of a chain composed of limestone and other formations, altogether distinct from those of the Alps. Their great size and angularity, after a journey of so many leagues, have justly excited wonder; for hundreds of them are as large as cottages; and one in particular, composed of gneiss, celebrated under the name of Pierre à Bot, rests on the side of a hill about 900 feet above the Lake of Neufchatel, and is no less than forty feet in diameter.—*Lyell.*

the Greenland seas, and at last reaching the northern limit of the land which has borne it up, pours a mighty frozen torrent into Arctic space. Unlike the Alpine glaciers, which melt in the warm valleys below, this empties into the ocean, and vast masses becoming detached, are floated away, to be dissolved in the milder water of southern seas. Thousands of these icebergs throng the northern ocean, freighted with débris to be deposited on the sea-bottom of lower latitudes.* Could we examine the track of these ice-rafts, we should doubtless find striæ cut in the polished rocks, and blocks deposited in long trains where the bergs had struck, scraped along by their enormous momentum and at last stranded.

We are now prepared to understand the meaning of the Drift phenomena.

Origin of the Drift.—The Arctic regions are elevated.† The climate of the whole continent feels the change. The cold creeps down every valley. Each northern blast brings a frost. The verdure of forest and plain withers and falls. The sun loses a part of its heat. The sea becomes cold. Tertiary life perishes

---

* Describing Cape James Kent, Kane says: "As I looked over this ice-belt, losing itself in the far distance, and covered with millions of tons of rubbish—greenstones, limestones, chlorite slates, rounded and irregular, massive and ground to powder—its importance as a geological agent in the transportation of Drift struck me with great force. Its whole substance was covered with these contributions from the shore; and farther to the south, upon the now frozen waters of Marshall Bay, I could recognize raft after raft from last year's ice-belt, which had been caught up by the winter, each one laden with its heavy freight of foreign material."—*Arctic Expedition.*

† It is proper to remark that, while all geologists agree as to the temperature of this period, all do not accept the theory given above as to the cause of the cold. Many different opinions are advanced. The above is supported by Dana, Winchell, and many prominent geologists. (See note in QUESTIONS, p. 272.)

in this frigid temperature. Arctic vegetation covers the land where tropical flowers have so lately bloomed in beauty. The musk-ox and the reindeer roam the south of Europe where, in modern times, are to grow the olive and the vine.* New species of animals spring into being, clothed with a raiment of wool to protect them from the rigors of the climate, and furnished with teeth of a peculiar complexity, to enable them to browse on the new vegetation. The seas are frozen to their lowest depths. Rivers are stopped and turned to ice. Snow gathers in the wintry air, and wraps in its mantle of white all the desolation that has been wrought. Glaciers, born in the icy north, invade the land. Sullenly they move southward, along every great river valley,† ploughing the rock, paring down acclivities, filling up ancient

* In the Drift are found the musk-ox, the reindeer, the walrus, the seal, and many kinds of shells characteristic of the Arctic regions. The northernmost part of Norway and Sweden is at this day the southern limit of the reindeer in Europe; but their fossil remains are found in large quantities in the Drift about the neighborhood of Paris, and quite recently they have been traced even to the foot of the Pyrenees. Side by side with the remains of the reindeer are found those of the European marmot, whose present home is in the mountains, about 6,000 feet above the level of the sea. The occurrence of these animals in the superficial deposits of the plains of Central Europe, one of which is now confined to the high north, and the other to mountain-heights, certainly indicates an entire change of climatic conditions, since the time of their existence. European shells now confined to the Northern Ocean, are found as fossils in Italy—showing that, while the present Arctic climate prevailed in the Temperate Zone, that of the Temperate Zone extended much farther south to the regions we now call subtropical. In America there is abundant evidence of the same kind; throughout the recent marine deposits of the Temperate Zone, covering the low lands above tide-water on this continent, are found fossil shells, whose present home is on the shores of Greenland. It is not only in the Northern hemisphere that these remains occur, but in Africa and in South America, wherever there has been an opportunity for investigation, the Drift is found to contain the traces of animals whose presence indicates a climate many degrees colder than that now prevailing there.—*Agassiz's Geological Sketches.*

† The Connecticut Valley seems to have had an independent glacier, as the striæ are parallel with the general course of the river; the Mohawk another; the Hudson a third one; and traces of many smaller ones are being discovered.

river-channels,* burying forests under masses of débris, scoring and polishing the surface, grinding up the stones into soil, and strewing rocks, gravel, and sand over southern fields. Reaching the coast of New England, they fringe the ocean with an ice-wall for hundreds of miles. Mighty icebergs, breaking loose, float southward, and, grinding their way through river-channel and strait, deposit their rocky burdens in long trains over the sea-bottom,† or, grounding on its shore, drop them in promiscuous piles.

II. CHAMPLAIN AND TERRACE EPOCHS.

Depression of the Continent (CHAMPLAIN EPOCH).—The epoch of Arctic elevation ceases. The northern regions descend toward their former level. Again the continent feels a change. A geologic spring-

* There is proof of the existence of rivers in different channels from the present. At the Whirlpool, on the west bank of the gorge, three miles below Niagara Falls, there is a deep ravine filled with gravel and sand. This old channel can be traced to Lake Ontario, four miles west of the present mouth of the river, and must have been the ancient bed. During the Glacial Epoch, the mighty ice-plow pared off the ridge, and filled the ravine with Drift materials, so that the river was forced to seek a new route, and since then has worn away the present tremendous gorge between Queenstown and the Falls. In boring for oil, and in excavating for railroads, such ancient river-channels, now filled with Drift, are frequently found.

"In excavating one of the canals for supplying the mills of Lowell, the old channel of the Merrimack was found under the Drift and alluvium, half a mile from the present bed of the river."—*L. S. Burbank.*

† "There is one of these trains in Berkshire county, Mass. The mountains from which the angular blocks of hard talcose slate have been torn off, lies in Canaan, N. Y.; and from thence they lie in trains, running for a few miles. S. 56° E., and then changing to S. 34° E., and extending yet further, making in the whole distance not less than fifteen or twenty miles; at least one of them extends that distance, passing obliquely over mountain ridges some 600 or 800 feet high. Its width is not more than thirty or forty rods. The blocks are of all sizes, from two or three feet in diameter to those containing 16,000 cubic feet, and weighing nearly 1,400 tons, and in some places almost cover the surface of the common Drift, and are not mixed with it."—*Hitchcock.*

time has come. The fetters of winter fall off. The glacier feels the touch of heat, and myriad streams leap gladly

FIG. 104

Stream issuing from a Glacier.

forth. The snow-fields disappear. Torrents of water, hastening to the ocean, deluge the continent. They cover the southern States with fine sediment, the débris of the glacier, and strew pebbles from the Appalachian to the very border of the Gulf* (Winchell). A genial warmth pervades the air. Vegetation springs to life. The depression of the land still continues. The ocean covers a part of Maine. The River St. Lawrence and Lake Champlain become arms of the sea, tenanted by seals and whales. The valleys are filled with broad, deep, majestic rivers, whose waters, flowing to the sea, dig deep channels, open new routes to the ocean, plough through mountain-ridges, sort and sift the Drift débris, arranging it in layers, and forming alluvial deposits of a great thickness. In many parts of the northern States, only the loftiest mountains emerge above the engulfing waters. Billows roll where birds sang and flowers bloomed. The land gained during all these long ages of geological history seems lost again. The ocean triumphs, and once more the Gulf joins its waters with the Arctic Ocean.

Elevation of the Continent (TERRACE EPOCH).—Slowly the continent rises from its last baptism. Before reaching its former level it stops. The rivers dig deeper channels in the soft alluvial deposit of the valleys, and leave their former banks far up on side-hills to mark their submersion during the Champlain Epoch. The lakes retire to smaller limits and form new beaches like the old they have deserted. The ocean yields the seacoast, where it has so recently dashed in eager conquest, and the land it has just reclaimed, and sullenly retreats.

* There are no "cobble-stones" in the southern States. The streams do not seem to have had sufficient force to carry the coarse material of the Drift. Thus the sediment naturally becomes finer toward the south, and coarser north.

There are several pauses of this kind in the upward progress of the continent.* At each stage the retiring waters toy with the sand and gravel, arrange them in beds, spread the alluvial soil upon the muddy bottom, and put the finishing strokes to the work of fitting the continent for man's use.

Proofs of these Oscillations.—Over the entire continent we find in the river valleys, overlying the true Drift, alluvial deposits reaching far above the present

FIG. 105.

Terraces on Connecticut River, south of Hanover, N. H. (Dana).

* The theory given in the text is that generally received. The author, however, does not himself believe in these extreme oscillations of the continent, and its submergence to the extent claimed by many geologists. Some places have doubtless been too hastily accepted as sea-beaches, and the whole subject demands more careful investigation. There is reason to believe, however, that at this period the Great Lakes were filled with salt water and inhabited by Arctic fauna. Their depths are even now, probably, tenanted by life of that type.

river beds. Looking up or down the banks of almost any principal river, one can trace horizontal lines, marking one or more terraces indicating the higher level of the stream in former times.* Many villages owe the beauty of their sites to these natural terraces. At a distance from the present shore of lakes, we find beaches of sand and gravel similar to those now existing on the borders of the lakes, and, in general, parallel with them. There are several of these on the south shore of Lake Erie; one extending for many miles is locally known as the "Ridge Road." At Mackinac there are three of these stair-like ridges, the highest 100 feet above the present water-level.† Remains of whales and seals have been found at Montreal, and the skeleton of a whale has been dug up on the borders of Lake Champlain, sixty feet above its present level. Near Brooklyn a sea-beach exists 100 feet above the ocean. Along the River St. Lawrence, and in the Champlain and Hudson valleys, there are deposits termed "Champlain Clays," containing marine shells. They are found over 500 feet above the ocean. It is evident that

---

* I counted to-day forty-one distinct ledges or shelves of terrace embraced between our water-line and the syenitic ridges through which Mary River forces itself. These shelves, though sometimes merged into each other, presented distinct and recognizable embankments or escarps of elevation. Their surfaces were at a nearly uniform inclination of descent of 5°, and their breadth either 12, 24, 36, or some other multiple of twelve paces. This imposing series of ledges carried you in forty-one gigantic steps to an elevation of 480 feet; and as the first rudiments of these ancient beaches left the granite which had once formed the barrier sea-coast, you could trace the passing from Drift-strewn rocky barricades to clearly-defined and gracefully curved shelves of shingle and pebbles. I have studies of these terraced beaches at various points on the northern coast of Greenland. They are more imposing and on a larger scale than those of Wellington Channel, which are now regarded by geologists as indicative of secular uplift of coast.—*Kane's Arctic Explorations.*

† When the lake stood at this level, it is probable that the water poured in floods down the Illinois River valley, swelling it to a mighty stream. Traces of its former grandeur are abundant far above its present banks.

the banks exhibiting these remains were ancient sea-beaches, and that the ocean level has since sunk and the land risen.*

Fossils of the Post-Tertiary Period.—This is the current era of geologic history. The record no longer lies deep in the solid rock. We find it in the

---

* The most distinct beaches occur below 1,200 feet above the ocean level. A very fine beach, however, is found on the west side of the Green Mountains, in West Hancock, Vt., 2,196 feet high. Others are found in Peru, Mass., 2,022 feet; at the Franconia Notch of the White Mountains, 2,665 feet; and at the Notch of the White Mountains (Gibb's Hotel), 2,020 feet. Upon comparing together the heights of beaches in different parts of New England, we find a number of them having essentially the same elevation; thus showing that they were formed contemporaneously. For example, there are beaches in Ashfield and Shutesbury, Mass.; in Norwich, Corinth, Elmore, Hardwick, and Brownington, Vt., each 1,200 feet above the ocean, and the most remote are nearly 200 miles apart.—*Hitchcock's Elementary Geology.*

Page, in "Chips and Chapters," referring to the raised beaches and submarine forests of Great Britain, remarks substantially as follows: From 120 feet down to the present sea-level we have a series of well-marked shore-lines—120, 63, 40, 25, and 12 feet—marking a succession of uprises, all clearly pre-historic, if we except the last, which indicates no very high antiquity. Every successive uplift, while it increased the dimensions of the British Islands, also decreased the general temperature of the country in the proportion of 1° F. for every 250 feet of uprise or nearly. These raised beaches are not all alike well marked and decided, owing partly to the nature of the rocks into which they have been respectively cut, and partly to the length of time at which the sea stood at these respective levels. The lowest or twelve-feet beach is generally marked by terraces of recent shells and gravel. Though the latest of British-raised beaches, this uprise must have taken place long antecedent to history; and there is not, so far as we are aware, any certain evidence either of upheaval or depression since the time of the Romans, although certain misinterpreted appearances have led some observers to an opposite conclusion. Any remains found in the caves of the twelve-feet beach are savage and pre-Celtic, showing that the uprise had taken place before (perhaps long before) the occupation of these primitive inhabitants. The twenty-five-feet beach is perhaps the most striking—stretching for miles in unbroken continuity, composed in many districts of recent shells and gravel, frequently backed by old caverned cliffs, and forming the level site for most of our modern sea-ports and fashionable watering-places. The sixty-three-feet beach is also well defined on many tracts of the seaboard, but its once overhanging cliffs have been obliterated by the tear and wear of the elements, its shells and exuviæ dissolved and destroyed, and its gravel beds now covered by soil and greensward. Of the higher beaches little is known with precision or accuracy.

marls and sediment of filled-up lakes; in beds of sand and clay; in the alluvial deposits of rivers; in the growth of peat-bogs and morasses; in the deep, muddy accumulations of swamps; in the stalagmites of fissures and caverns, and in the ice of Arctic regions. The plant-remains—willow, hazel, fir, beech, and oak—are familiar to those who now live in the same latitudes. The fresh-water shells are identical with those which throng the neighboring ponds. The marine fossils—oysters, clams, mussels, etc.—cannot be distinguished from those which inhabit the surrounding ocean. When, however, we turn to the land animals, the change, probably through the instrumentality of man, becomes more apparent. The quadrupeds, as in the Tertiary Period, take the precedence, and attract our attention by their enormous bulk. We shall describe the following: the *mammoth, mastodon, megatherium, glyptodon, Irish elk, cave-bear,* and *hyena.*

1. THE MAMMOTH, or *fossil elephant*, was about one-third larger than any known to modern times. A tooth, in the Ward cabinet, Rochester, weighs fourteen pounds. This animal wandered in great herds over England, thence to Siberia, and across Behring's Straits into North America. Its remains are very abundant.* Over 2,000 molar-teeth

* In 1663, Otto von Guericke, the illustrious inventor of the air-pump, witnessed the discovery of the bones of an elephant buried in the shelly limestone, or muschelkalk. Along with it were found its enormous tusks, which should have sufficed to establish its zoölogical origin. Nevertheless they were taken for horns, and the illustrious Leibnitz composed, out of the remains, a strange animal, carrying a horn in the middle of its forehead, and in each jaw a dozen molar-teeth a foot long. Having fabricated this fantastic animal, Leibnitz named it also; he called it the *fossil unicorn*. For over thirty years the unicorn of Leibnitz was universally accepted throughout Germany, and nothing less than the discovery of the entire skeleton of the mammoth could change the

were found in a few years by the fishermen of the little village of Happisburg. The islands in the sea north of

FIG. 106.

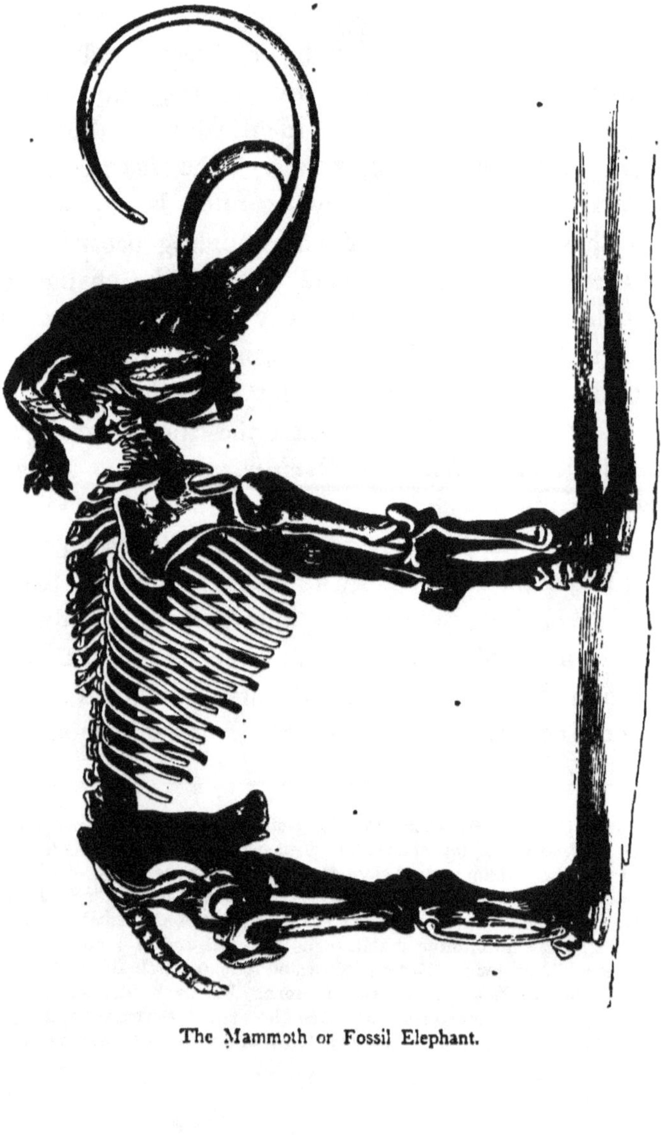

The Mammoth or Fossil Elephant.

Siberia are but conglomerations of sand, ice, and the tusks and teeth of elephants. During every storm, the waves wash loose and cast ashore this fossil ivory, which becomes a profitable article of commerce. Single tusks are found weighing over 200 pounds. In 1844, 16,000 pounds are said to have been sold at St. Petersburg. The ivory thus obtained has been exported to China for five centuries, and yet the supply seems undiminished. The colossal size of these remains has given rise, among the Tartars, to a curious legend. They were believed to belong to an enormous animal—an elephantine mouse—which lived underground, like the mole, and which instantly perished when exposed to the least ray of sun or moon.

In 1799, a fisherman discovered among the icebergs on the banks of the Lena, an odd-shaped block of ice. Two years after, he found the tusks and flank of a mammoth protruding from it, and in five years the entire body became disentangled, and fell upon the sand. He removed the tusks and sold them. Two years subsequent, Mr. Adams, of the St. Petersburg Academy, heard of the discovery, and visited the spot. The people of the neighborhood had cut off pieces of the flesh for their dogs, and wild beasts had mangled it, but the skeleton was nearly entire. The skin yet covered the head; one of the ears, well preserved, was furnished with a tuft of hair; the neck had a flowing mane; and the body retained scat-

popular opinion, and then not without a keen controversy. In 1700, a veritable cemetery of elephants was discovered near the banks of the Necker River, in Wurtemberg. Not less than sixty tusks were exhumed. As a curious instance of the superstition of the times, the fact may be mentioned that the court physician possessed himself of the fragments which were left, to aid him in combating fever and colic! Chinese apothecaries now use similar remedies.

tered tufts of reddish wool and black hair. Mr. Adams collected the bones, repurchased the tusks—which were more than nine feet long—and sold this unique specimen to the Emperor of Russia for $6,000.

2. THE MASTODON resembled the modern elephant, but had, in general, a longer body and more massive limbs.

FIG. 107.

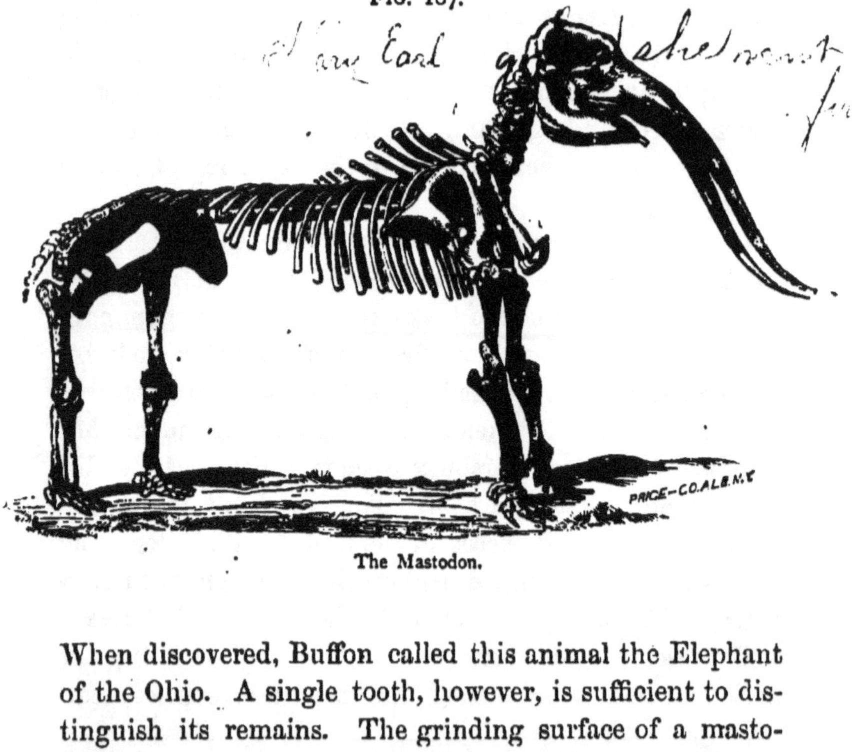

The Mastodon.

When discovered, Buffon called this animal the Elephant of the Ohio. A single tooth, however, is sufficient to distinguish its remains. The grinding surface of a mastodon's tooth is covered with conical projections—whence the name of the animal—while that of the elephant is flat. Teeth have been dug up weighing seventeen pounds each, and tusks fourteen feet in length. Six skeletons were found in Warren county, N. J., by a farmer digging in a bog. Within the ribs of one of them, being evidently the contents of the stomach, were seven bushels of vegetable matter, which, on microscopic examination, proved to consist of cedar twigs, which probably formed the animal's last supper. Similar discoveries, and also the form of the teeth, prove that its food was roots, small branches, leaves, grass, etc. The mastodon was once common in the United States, and probably wandered in herds over all the country west of the Connecticut River.

3. THE MEGATHERIUM * (monstrous beast), at first sight seems the most ill-formed creature we have yet considered. We shall, however, find its structure full of harmony and adaptation. It was simply a huge sloth of the size of an elephant. Like the sloth it fed on leaves, and possibly like the ant-eater, it burrowed deep in the earth. Its fore-feet were each three feet long and a foot broad, and were furnished with gigantic claws. Its tail was two feet in diameter, and must have assisted in supporting its huge body, as it tore down trees for its food, while it constituted also a powerful means of defence. Its massive proportions and clumsy form rendered it extremely slow in its movements, but there was no need of rapid locomotion in an animal that merely burrowed for roots or browsed for leaves in a tropical forest; neither was there necessity for flight, when its most dangerous foe, the crocodile, could be destroyed by a single blow from its gigantic tail. Thus this mighty creature

* The megatherium is shown in Fig. 111, on the right hand; the glyptodon in front at the center, the mylodon just back holding on to a tree, and the mastodon at the left and in the rear.

lived peaceful and respected in spite of its apparently unwieldy structure.*

4. THE GLYPTODON (sculptured tooth) was a mammal clad in the shell of a turtle. This defensive armor measured sometimes eleven feet in length, and weighed 1,000 pounds.

FIG. 108.

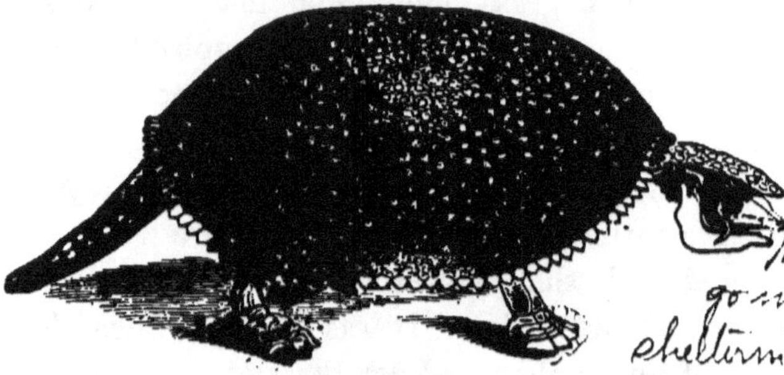

Glyptodon clavipes.

5. THE IRISH ELK was a magnificent and imposing animal. Its antlers were often ten feet long, and spread, from one tip to the other, a distance of three or four yards.

6. THE CAVE BEAR was the most formidable of the ancient flesh-eating animals.

It attained the size of a large horse. Some of the

* During the dry season a hunter discovered, on the banks of the River Salado, S. A., what appeared to be the trunk of a tree. Throwing his lasso over it, with the help of a comrade he drew it upon the bank. It proved to be an enormous bone five feet through; the pelvis of what has since been happily styled the megatherium. To this countryman the bone appeared useless. It did not make half as good a seat as a bullock's skull—the arm-chair of the pampas. Finally this, with other bones, was sent as a curiosity to the owner of the land on which they were discovered. Sir W. Parish found them here, dug out others, and forwarded them to England. From these remains the casts now in Boston, Amherst, etc., were made.—*Denton in "Our Planet."*

skeletons are ten feet long and six feet high. The animal is so named because it dragged its prey into caves, where the remains of a large number of antediluvian repasts are found buried in the stalactites which have

FIG. 109.

The Irish Elk.

since accumulated on the floor. In the celebrated cave at Gaylenreuth, portions of the skeletons of 800 cave-bears have been identified.

7. THE HYENA was very abundant in England. The bones of seventy-five have been discovered in a single cavern. The cave at Kirkdale, England,* is noted as an

FIG. 110.

Cave Bear and Hyena.

* In the summer of 1821, some workmen employed in quarrying stone upon the slope of a limestone hill at Kirkdale, in Yorkshire, came accidentally upon the mouth of a cavern. Overgrown with grass and bushes, the mouth of this cave in the hill-side had been effectually closed against all intruders, and

FIG. III.

Ideal Scene in the Post-Tertiary Period. (See description, bottom of page 229.)

ancient haunt of these animals. "The stalagmitic deposit in this cavern, with its projecting bones," says Buckland, "looks like a pigeon-pie with pigeon's legs sticking through the crust."

In Fig. 110, a cave-bear is seen sitting at the mouth of its den, watching the bones of an elephant, while, above, a hyena waits the proper moment to dispute possession with its formidable rival.

---

its existence had never been suspected. The hole was just large enough to admit a man on his hands and knees, and led into a low broad cavern, with branches opening out from it—some of which have not yet been explored. The whole floor was strewn with hundreds of bones, like a huge dog-kennel. The workmen wondered a little at their discovery, but, remembering that there had been a murrain among the cattle in that region some years before, concluded that these must be the bones of cattle which then died in great numbers; and having thus satisfactorily settled the matter, threw out the bones on the road with the limestone. A gentleman, living near, preserved them; and in a few months, Dr. Buckland, the great English geologist, visited Kirkdale, and examined its strange contents, which proved indeed stranger than any one had imagined; for many of these remains belonged to animals never before found in England. The bones of hyenas, tigers, elephants, rhinoceroses, and hippopotamuses were mingled with those of deer, bears, wolves, foxes, and many smaller creatures. The bones were gnawed, and many were broken, evidently not by natural decay, but as if snapped violently apart. After a complete investigation, Dr. B. convinced himself, and proved to the satisfaction of all scientific men, that the cave had been a den of hyenas at a time when these animals, as well as tigers, elephants, etc., existed in England in as great numbers as they now do in the wildest parts of tropical Asia or Africa. The narrow entrance to the cave still retains the marks of grease and hair, such as are seen on the bars of a cage in a menagerie, against which the imprisoned animals constantly rub themselves, and there were similar marks on the floor and walls. The hyenas were evidently the lords of this ancient cavern, and the other animals their unwilling guests; for the remains of the latter had been most gnawed, broken, and mangled; and the head of an enormous hyena, with gigantic fangs complete, testified to their great size and power. Some of the animals, such as the elephants, rhinoceroses, etc., could not have been brought into the cave without being first killed and torn to pieces. But their gnawed and broken bones attest that they were devoured like the rest; and probably the hyenas then had the same propensity which characterizes those of our own time—to tear in pieces the body of any dead animal, and carry it to their den to feed upon it apart. (Agassiz.)—A detailed account of this investigation, etc., may be found in "Reliquiæ Diluvianæ," by Dr. Buckland.

Remarks.—*1. Glacial Epoch on the Pacific Coast.*—California shows no traces of northern Drift.* The Rocky Mountains probably constituted a sufficient barrier against the advancing glacier that overwhelmed so large a portion of the continent. Yet no section exhibits more frequent signs of glacial action. The glaciers were, however, confined to the elevated regions of the mountains, as the conspicuous moraines, striæ, etc., abundantly prove. Swift torrents sweeping down the slopes of the mountain ranges denuded extensive regions and

FIG. 112.

Cañon of Grand River.

deposited vast quantities of Drift-material. This erosive action doubtless broke up the auriferous rocks and as-

* Whitney in Proc. Cal. Acad. Nat. Sci. Foster says the same remark holds true throughout Oregon.

sorted the materials of the rich gold-fields of California. The great cañons (can-yōnes) of the Colorado and other western rivers are believed by Newberry to have been worn out during this period. They are gorges cut in the solid rock, sometimes to the depth of a mile. For days the adventurer may travel along the brink of such a gulf, unable to cross or to descend to the water which winds along so far below, at the bottom of the appalling chasm.

2. *The Loëss* (Lō-ess, from the German *lösz*, loam). —The alluvial deposits along the banks of rivers are generally composed of coarse materials at the lowest portions, and fine loam (silt) in the higher. Where the current is strongest, coarse gravel is borne along, and where weakest, only sand or mud. A thin film of this fine sediment is spread during floods over wide areas on either bank of the stream. The well-known deposits of the River Nile, to which Egypt owes its fertility, are of this character. The aggregate during a century is said rarely to exceed five inches, though in all it has attained a vast thickness.

Along the valley of the Rhine similar deposits of loam have taken place to a depth of many hundred feet. The color is of a yellowish gray, the structure very homogeneous, and the composition like that of the Nile. Shells most perfectly preserved, whose fragility is too great to endure the rushing of a stream of water, are quite abundant.

3. *Bluff Formation.*—This Loëss or "Bluff Formation" (Swallow) extends to a great distance along the lower Missouri, and often lines its branching rivers. It is

very conspicuous at Sioux City, Council Bluffs, etc. On the Mississippi it reaches from the junction of the Missouri to the delta, forming in the State of Mississippi a belt ten or fifteen miles wide, and often seventy feet deep (Hilgard). The color is a buff, and its composition a siliceous loam. The shells belong to existing species, while the remains of mammoth, horse, lion, musk-ox, etc., are of extinct species. We thence conclude that the physical changes which resulted in the destruction of the land animals did not extend to the inhabitants of fresh water. Foster thinks that the formation is a lacustrian one, and that when it was deposited, the land was depressed a couple of hundred feet below its present level.

4. *Sand Dunes** are hills of sand heaped up along the shore. They are formed by sand drifted inland by the wind, as snow is piled in drifts. The sand is driven with such force as to smooth the surface even of quartz rocks, and to wear holes in window-glass. The sand-dunes of Cape Cod, Long Island shore, Lake Michigan, etc., are conspicuous features of the landscape. Sometimes long, narrow sand-ridges, or Osars, extend back from the shore for miles.

5. *The Mosaic Account* states that on the fifth day the waters brought forth abundantly the moving

* On the east side of Cape Cod, clearly marked in many places on the beach between Provincetown and Truro, the *former shore-line of the west side* may be distinctly traced. The whole mass of sand forming that part of the cape has been carried over westward into the bay. This movement is still going on, and threatens to destroy the harbor of Provincetown. Parties of men have therefore been employed by the United States government to set out beach-grass along the coast. This, by the extension and interlacing of its fibrous roots, tends to hold the sand in place.—*Burbank*.

creature that hath life, the fowl that flies above the earth, and great whales. The sixth day was characterized by two works—the creation of mammals, and lastly of man, to be the lord of all created things.

Geology gives us the same general outline. In the Palæozoic Age, the seas swarmed with life. In the Mesozoic Age, birds appeared, while reptiles (styled, in popular language, great whales or sea-monsters, as the word may be translated) became the dominant life. In the dawn of the Cenozoic, mammals of enormous size and in prodigious numbers covered the earth; while at the close, Man appeared to crown the creative work.

SCENIC DESCRIPTION.—This glimpse of Tertiary times presents a scene of sylvan beauty. Before us is a broad meadow carpeted with grass and blooming flowers, while behind are mountains clad in forests of familiar trees. In the foreground is a lake stretching away in the distance far as the eye can reach, its waves sparkling in the noontide sun. Snipes make their retreat among the reeds which line the low marshy shore; sea-gulls skim the water; owls hide themselves in the trunks of old cavernous trees; gigantic buzzards hover threateningly in the air, poised for prey; great turtles crawl up the bank; heavy crocodiles drag their unwieldy bodies through the high marshy grass; and a huge rhinoceros wallows, grunting, in the mud. Over the plain gallops a troop of wild horses; foxes scamper through the bushes; and flocks of birds sing in the branches of the willows that border a neighboring brook. Everywhere wander great, unwieldy quadrupeds. Here is a solitary megatherium—a gigantic sloth—standing on his massive hind-legs, and propped up by his huge tail, which makes a secure tripod support. See, he slowly reaches out his muscular arms, draws down branches and young trees, and lazily feeds on their tender foliage. Yonder is a herd of mammoths with long curved tusks, broad flapping leathern ears, large as a blacksmith's apron, and legs like fleshy pillars. Now they feed along the bank, now they trumpet shrilly to their companions in the forest, whose responses sound like distant thunder, and now they go crashing through the woods, tearing down trees for sport, and leaving the limbs strewn over the ground, as if a hurricane had passed. Fierce beasts abound. A drove of wild oxen of colossal strength, maned and shaggy, feed over the meadow, and troops of hyenas prowl about, waging relentless war on all weaker tribes. Hark! the yelping of dogs! A pack of hounds out on a hunt. The herd of wild horses catch the dreaded sound, snort with fear, toss their manes, and go flying off like the wind, with their gaunt pursuers in full chase. Scarcely have they disappeared than a drove of camels stalk deliberately down to the water's edge, and while they drink (as only camels can), a troop of monkeys, chattering in the branches overhead, with solemn grimaces, mock the gravity of their slow, awkward movements.

That she planted long ago
In the churchyard on the hillside
For a baby's grave to grow.
But she said he loved the flowers
So well know that they are here
now

The Era of Mind.

Geology, which is the story of the rocks, finds its climax in History, which is the story of Man.

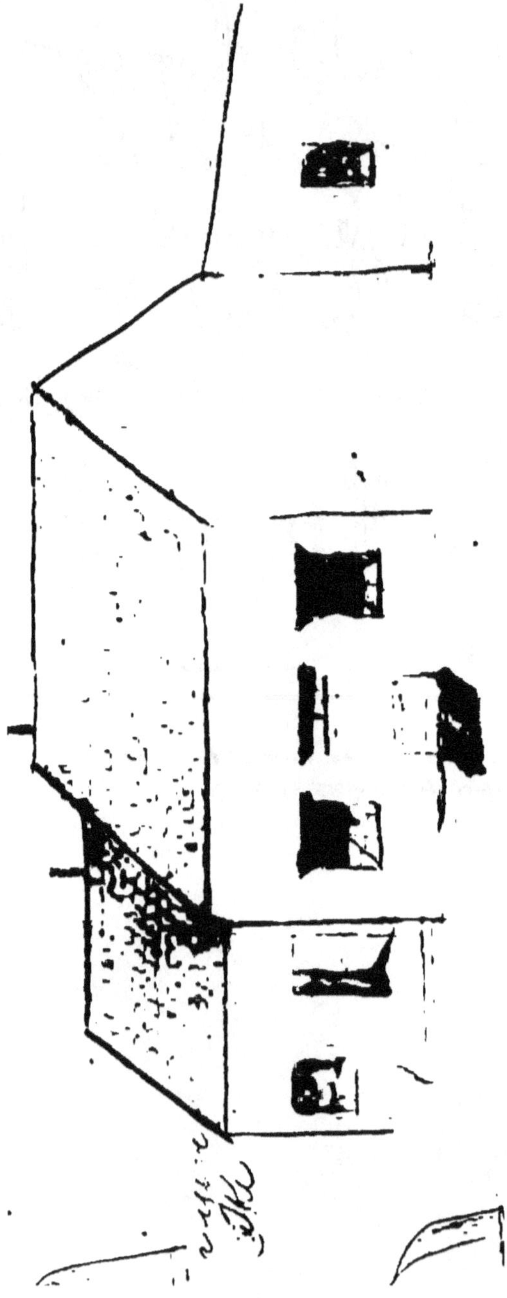

The Age of Man.

The Coming of Man.—We have no means of deciding the exact time when the human race first appeared on the earth. The most scientific man is unable to name centuries or years with any degree of accuracy in connection with any geological event. In the loam (Loess), peat-bog and cave-earth of the Post-Tertiary Period we first find rude stone implements, tree canoes, and the embers of the fire which man alone can kindle or sustain. Side by side with these are the remains of the mammoth,* cave-bear, rhinoceros, Irish elk, etc. It would seem that about the time of the glacial epoch, probably just as the great ice-floats began to melt away, man suddenly appeared among the mighty quadrupeds which then covered the earth, to contest the supremacy.

The Primeval Man.—The life of the pre-historic man has been classified according to the character of the

* In the valley of the River Somme, near Abbeville, flint implements, associated with remains of the mammoth, elephant, hippopotamus, rhinoceros, etc., were found by M. Boucher de Perthes. Near Amiens, in the same valley, another deposit of gravel was discovered, containing flint hatchets, poniards, knives, etc., nearly 400 in number, accompanied also by bones of the above animals.

fossil remains in the following manner. (Saint-Germain, Vogt, and others.)

I. THE STONE AGE.	1. Epoch of extinct animals, mammoth, cave-bear, etc.
	2. Epoch of migrated existing animals, or Reindeer Epoch.
	3. Epoch of domesticated animals, or Polished Stone Epoch.
II. THE METAL AGE.	1. The Bronze Epoch.
	2. The Iron Epoch.

These terms indicate the successive progress of the ancient races. Every nation seems to have had some such stages in its advance. The Indians have hardly passed out of their stone age. The Sandwich Islanders, when discovered, were in that age, while the nations of Asia emerged from it long before the Christian era. Some of these ages may have been contemporaneous in different nations.

THE STONE AGE.

Epoch of Extinct Animals.—The primeval man during this epoch dwelt in caves, dressed in skins, and made weapons chipped out of the rough flint (Fig. 113), by means of which he fought the cave-bear, hunted the Irish elk, and speared the mammoth. He was rude and barbarous, perhaps a cannibal,

FIG. 113.

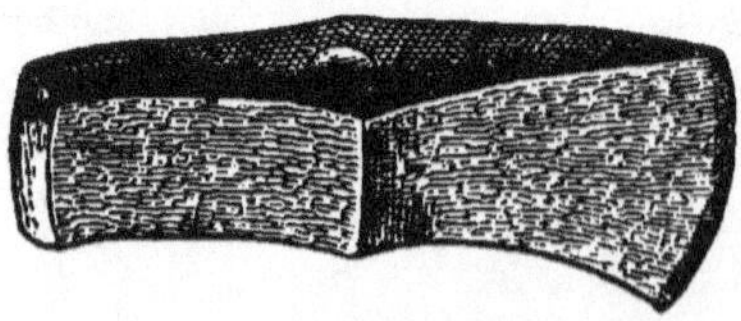

A Danish Axe-hammer.

yet he made fire, instruments of offence and defence, articles of pottery-ware for domestic use (Fig. 114), sewed skins into garments, adorned his person with strings of rudely-carved shells, wrought out images emblematic of his political or religious views, and buried his dead in caves with religious rites and ceremonies.*

FIG. 114.

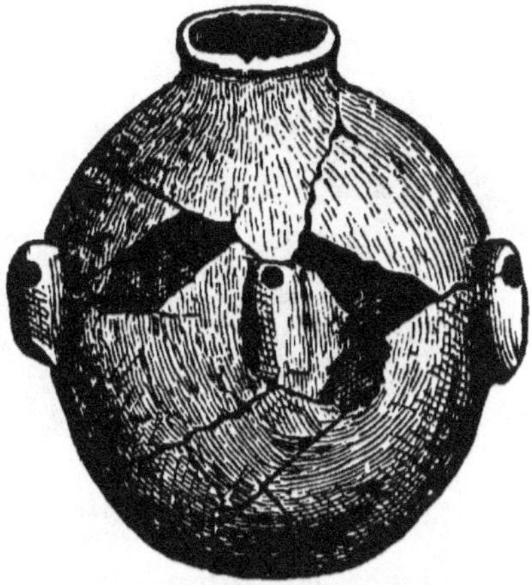

Earthen Vase found in Cave of Furfooz (Belgium).

Reindeer Epoch.—In this epoch man advanced in knowledge, learned to work in bone, ivory,

* In 1842, on the slope of a hill near Aurignac, an excavator, named Bonnemaison, discovered a great vertical slab of limestone covering an arched opening. In the cave thus closed up he found the remains of seventeen human skeletons. These were removed to the village cemetery, and thus lost to science forever. In 1860, M. Lartet, having heard of the event, visited the spot, which, during a long course of centuries, had entirely escaped the notice of the inhabitants. The entrance to the cave was concealed by masses of earth, which, having been brought down from the top of the hill by the action of water, had accumulated in front, hiding a flat terrace, on which many vestiges of prehistoric times were found. As no disturbance of the ground had taken place in this spot subsequent to the date of the burial, this gradual accumulation had protected the traces of these primeval men. The investigations of M. Lartet were attended with the following results:—

He found on the floor of the cave a bed of "made ground" two feet thick. In this were some human remains which had escaped the first investigations; also bones of mammals well preserved, and exhibiting no fractures or teeth-marks, wrought flint-knives, carved reindeer horns, and eighteen small sea-shells pierced in the center, and doubtless intended to be strung together in a necklace or bracelet. He found also a quantity of the bones of the cave-bear, the bison, the reindeer, the horse, etc. The perfect state of preservation of these bones shows that they were neither broken to furnish food for man nor torn by carnivorous animals, as is seen in many cases. It must be concluded,

and reindeer-antlers (Fig. 115); to catch fish; to make saws, knives, and other tools; to form amulets and charms of bone; to ornament the instruments of the chase; and in his leisure to sketch on ivory the outlines of the animals he pursued (Fig. 116).

FIG. 115.

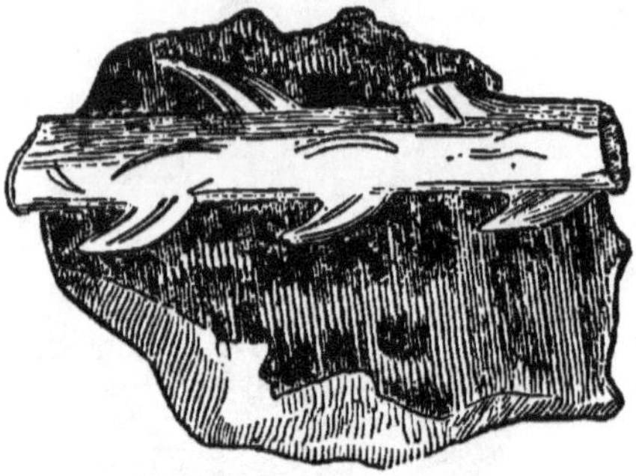

Bone pierced by an Arrow of Reindeer-horn.

Polished Stone Epoch.—The next epoch witnessed a still higher condition. Skiffs were made in which the primitive man ventured out on the sea, and caught the fish of deeper waters.* He made nets for fishing near the

then, that the stone which closed the entrance to the cavern was moved away for every interment, and carefully put back immediately afterward. In explaining the presence of so many foreign objects in the burial-cave, we must admit as probable that the customs which now exist among savage tribes—such as placing near to the dead body the weapons, hunting-trophies, and ornaments belonging to the deceased—existed among the men of the great bear and mammoth epoch. In front of the cave was also found the site of an ancient fire-hearth, where evidently the *funeral banquet* was held. In this bed of ashes and charcoal an immense quantity of the most interesting relics were discovered—a large number of teeth and broken bones of herbivorous animals; a hundred flint-knives; two chipped flints, which are believed to be sling projectiles; several implements made of reindeer's horn, etc., etc. Some of the bones were partly carbonized, others only scorched, but the greater number had been untouched by fire. All the marrow bones were broken lengthwise, showing that they had been used at a feast where the marrow from animal bones furnished a delicious viand. Traces of the hyena were found at this spot. From all these signs we infer that after the death of one of these primitive men, his friends accompanied him to his last resting-place, after which they assembled together to partake of a feast in front of his tomb; then every one took his departure, leaving the scene of the banquet free to the hyenas, which came to devour the remains of the meal.

* Along the coast of Denmark, in Cornwall and Devonshire, England, in Scotland, and even in France, have been discovered what have received the

shore. He domesticated the dog. He attempted agri-

FIG. 116.

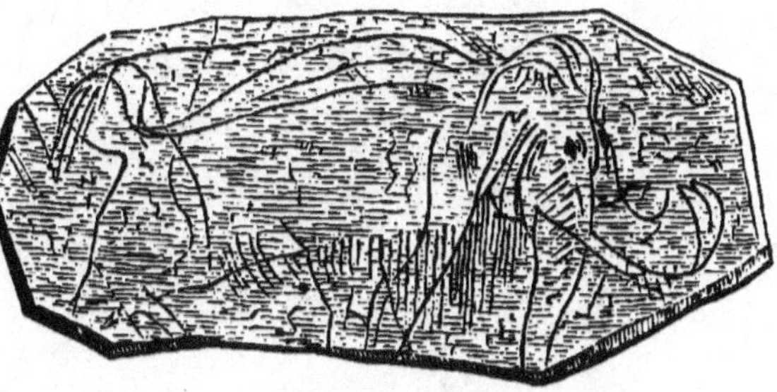

Sketch of a Mammoth graven on a Slab of Ivory.

culture; raised corn, ground it, and thus became less dependent on the chances of the chase. He interred his dead in vaults, and erected monuments to mark their last resting-place. (See Fig. 117).

---

name of "kitchen-middens." They are immense accumulations of shells from 3 to 10 feet in thickness, and from 100 to 200 feet in width; their length is sometimes as much as 1,000 feet, with a width of 250 feet. At first seeming, one would think them banks of fossil shells which had been submerged, and afterward volcanically brought to light. But it has been discovered that these shells belong to four different species which are never found together, and consequently must have been brought there by man. Nearly all the shells are those of full-grown animals. Also traces of fire—remains of hearths—were found in these heaps, which, with the other facts, lead to one conclusion. Tribes once existed there who lived on the products of hunting and fishing, throwing out round their cabins the remains of their meals, especially the débris of shell-fish. Hence the name, which signifies "kitchen heaps of refuse." Nearly all these kitchen-middens are found on the coast, along the *fiords*, where the action of the waves is not much felt. Some have been found inland; but this proves that the sea once occupied those localities from which it has now retired. These refuse deposits consist mostly of various shells of mollusks—such as the oyster, the cockle, the mussel, and the periwinkle. Fishes' bones, in great abundance, are also found. They belong to the cod, herring, dab, and eel. From this we may infer that the primitive inhabitants ventured far out to sea, as the herring and cod can only be caught at some distance from shore. The remains also of the stag, the roe, the boar, and various other mammals are discovered, with some traces of birds—mostly aquatic species. All the long bones are found split to extract the marrow.

FIG. 117.

Row of Menhirs or Monuments set up on Tombs at Carnac, Brittany.

THE METAL AGE.

This age indicates a great advance in civilization. Thenard asserted that we may judge of the civilization of any nation by the degree of perfection it has attained in working iron. We may safely say that, without a knowledge of the metals, man would have remained a barbarian. Iron ores do not readily attract attention, and their reduction is a very difficult process. The method whereby iron becomes utilized in the arts, requires extensive chemical knowledge and high progress in science. Gold, however, is found native, and by its glitter attracts the eye even of the savage. Copper occurs pure, and its ores are rather widely diffused, as are also those of tin. It is strange that bronze (brass), which is an alloy of copper and tin, should have been the first metal used. We can hardly understand the cause of this, since the metals must have been known before the alloy could be manufactured.

Bronze Epoch.—Tools of a better character were now made, and life wore an improved aspect. Extensive villages were built on piles* driven deep in the lake-

* The discovery of the remains of lake-dwellings in Switzerland, and their connection with the bronze epoch—as first asserted by Dr. Keller, of Zurich, and since agreed to by all archæologists—reveal to us many very interesting facts in regard to the pre-historic natives of that country. When, in the dry, cold winter of 1853-1854, the waters of the lakes in Switzerland fell so far below their ordinary level, the inhabitants of Meilen, on the banks of Lake Zurich, thus gaining from the lake a tract of ground, set to work to raise it and surround it with banks. In carrying out this work they found in the mud at the bottom of the lake a number of piles, some thrown down and some still upright, fragments of rough pottery, bone and stone instruments, and various other relics similar to those found in the Danish peat-bogs. Previous to this, various instruments and strange utensils had been obtained from the mud of some of the Swiss lakes, and piles had often been noticed standing up in the water, but no one had thought of attributing any great antiquity to these objects, or, indeed, made much attempt to explain them. The fishermen had for some time been acquainted with the sites of some of these lake settlements, in consequence of having often torn their nets on the piles sticking up in the mud. Thus, guides were at hand to aid in searching out the mystery of these lake abodes. More than 200 settlements are already known, and every year fresh ones are being found. The builders of these lacustrine dwellings seem to have proceeded on two different systems of construction: either they buried the piles very deeply in the bed of the lake, and on them placed the platform which was to support their huts, or they artificially raised the bed of the lake by means of heaps of stones, fixing in them large stakes to make a firm and compact body. Sometimes these are so high as to rise above the water, and form artificial islands; and some of them are still inhabited.

We may reasonably suppose that need for security prompted the ancient people to thus construct their dwellings over the water. Encompassed by vast marshes and impenetrable forests, no means could so effectually secure them from the attacks of wild beasts as to surround themselves with water. In later

bottom, looms were erected, cloth was woven and made into garments (Fig. 118). The horse, ass, ox, sheep and goat were domesticated in great numbers. Hatchets, reaping-hooks, mills, pendants, rings, hair-pins, barbed fish-hooks, and numerous articles of ornament were manufactured (Fig. 119). The clothing became more graceful, and the hair was adorned with the most elaborate taste.

FIG. 118.

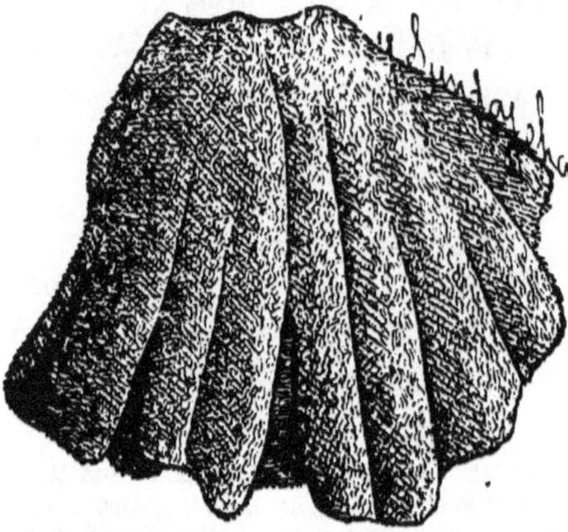

Woolen Shawl found in a Tomb in Denmark.

Wheat, barley and oats were cultivated. The baker's art was established. Glass was discovered. Mats of bark and cord were made. Apples, pears, berries, and other fruits were stored for winter's use.

Iron Epoch.—With the discovery of iron, civilization rapidly advanced. This metal marked the latest period of primeval development. The art of metallurgy

---

times it served to protect them from sudden surprises by their enemies of other clans. The number of piles used in these constructions is surprising. They were often sixteen or twenty feet long, and in the stone-heaps were sometimes ten or twelve inches in diameter. The mind is almost confused when it endeavors to sum up the amount of energy and strong will which, without the aid of iron implements, must have been bestowed in constructing these settlements. One of the largest, that of Morges, in Lake Geneva, is 71,000 square yards in area. The huts themselves seem to have been formed of trunks of trees placed upright side by side, and bound together by interwoven branches. A coating of earth covered this wattling. Some of these huts having been partially destroyed by fire, among the charred débris various articles have been perfectly preserved, such as fishing-nets, basket-work, corn, etc.

had made great progress during the bronze epoch, but now assumed new importance. Extensive smelting works were erected.* The potter's wheel was invented. Better tools were made (Fig. 120). Silver and lead were discovered. Coined money was introduced and commerce flourished (Fig. 121). Agriculture was practiced on a large scale. Fruit trees were cultivated. Civilization was fairly established. At this point the written records and oral traditions take up the story of the past, and the naturalist's labors cease as the historian's begin.

FIG. 119.

Bronze Vase from the Tomb of Hallstadt.

FIG. 120.

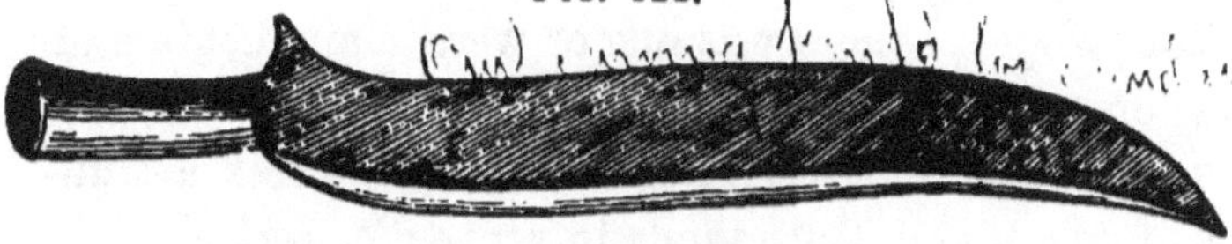

Knife from the Lacustrine Settlements of Switzerland.

The Development Theory.—This primeval man shows no sign of a development from the higher tribes of animals. He is not a perfected monkey. "No gorilla ever took out a patent." No ape ever made any improvement on the condition in which he was born. Man, on the other hand, never stays where he starts. He

FIG. 121.

Bronze Coin from the Lake of Neuchâtel.

* Four hundred iron furnaces have been discovered by M. Quiquerez in the Bernese Jura.

continually progresses. The very names given to the various ages and epochs of his primeval history in Europe indicate this fact. He appears among those huge quadrupeds whose figures stalk like mighty shadows across the scenes of the Post-Tertiary Period, and is at once their lord and master. He uses the bow and spear. He becomes a builder and inventor. He makes tools, subdues the earth, hews down the forest, bridges the river, builds houses, tames wild animals and converts their strength to his purposes, while from every element of Nature he gathers material for use and beauty. Lastly and best of all, he buries his dead with religious ceremonies, in carefully constructed tombs, and deposits in their graves arms and food for their journey to the spirit-land. (Vogt.) His thought reaches out into the life beyond, and he betrays at once the longings of an immortal soul.

Geology gives us no means of answering that oft-asked question, whether there was one or were many centers of man's creation. As far as the facts go, however, the sameness of the remains, wherever found, evinces a similarity of ideas, and thus tends to prove a common origin for the race. Those who, disregarding the unity of language, of mental constitution, and of the religious sentiment of the human race, desire to show that the Mosaic account is only a partial and inaccurate one, must look for arguments elsewhere than in the records of geology.

Geological Theories.—Many of the geological theories we have discussed may be set aside by future discoveries, and be proved to have been vain assumptions. They will yet, however, have served a purpose. The mind instinctively demands order. Each theory is a cord on which to string facts that otherwise might be lost. Theories are generalizations of truth. They give consistency and interest to a science that otherwise would be only a mass of discordant and uninviting detail. Our theories may yet be thrown away, but our facts never, and we can but be grateful for the former in that they have helped us to retain the latter.

The World Unfinished.—Creation is continually going on around us. Astronomy teaches that the stars are changing—new ones flashing out in the sky and others fading away into darkness. Geology did not cease when history began. Since the coming of man, vast physical changes have taken place. The mastodon and Irish elk vanished with his first appearance. The dodo of Mauritius is known only by tradition. The animals of the present—the ostrich, beaver, etc.—are hastening to extinction. The mud and sands of our sea-shore will be the rocks of future hills, and the rocks of our hills the ocean sediment of another age. Rivers have deserted their old channels; the ocean has encroached on the land;* lakes and marshes have disappeared; volcanoes

* There is abundant evidence to show a slow subsidence of the whole eastern coast of the United States, which has been going on for several years past. The movement is one of alternate elevation and depression within the limits of perhaps twenty feet. A map of Cape May, dated 1694, shows Egg Island as containing 200 acres; it now contains less than an acre at ebb tide, and is entirely submerged at high tide. The light-house at the Cape has been moved considerably inland on account of the wear. The shore in front of the boarding-houses at Cape Island must have worn away nearly a mile since the Revolution. During the war of that period, a militia artillery company had its practicing ground here. Their gun was placed near a house which stood just outside the present shore-line, and their target was set up at the outer side of a corn-field, three-quarters of a mile east. Beyond this there were sand-beaches for nearly or quite a quarter of a mile, and then the sea-shore. The whole of this ground is now gone, and one of the boarding-houses has been moved back twice. Sandy Hook has extended out to the northeast a mile since the Revolution. The spot where

have thrown out rivers of lava, and earthquakes have cracked the earth's crust.

> "There rolls the deep where grew the tree;
> O earth, what changes hast thou seen!
> There, where the long street roars, hath been
> The stillness of the central sea."—*Tennyson.*

The Origin of Man.—Was man created directly by God's fiat, or by some intermediate process of secondary causes? "Alas for the impotence of science and the scope of our finite intelligence!" We bring the subtlest agencies to the accomplishment of our designs—Heat, Light, Electricity—but when we seek to develop from them even the intangible forces which clothe the decaying rock with verdure, or mantle the stagnant pool with slime, failure inevitably waits upon us. In vain do we seek to associate vital manifestation with electrical action; we may resolve the vital organism into cells and granules and nuclei, but the *life* eludes our proudest philosophy. If, under certain conditions, inorganic matter assumes organic form, those conditions and the laws which gov-

---

the first boarding-house was erected at Long Branch, together with the road behind it, is now all worn away. The loss is sometimes twelve feet in a year. Where seventy years ago were cultivated fields is now the ship-channel. At several points in New Jersey an enormous quantity of white cedar is found buried in the salt marshes. This indicates extensive forests on land now too low and wet for the growth of trees. Trunks are found sunk at all depths down to the underlying gravel, and so thick that in many places a number of trials must be made before a sounding-rod can be thrust down without striking against them. Tree after tree from one to two thousand years of age lies crossed above each other in every conceivable direction. These cedar logs are *mined* and split into shingles, and thus is carried on a very extensive business. Submarine forests exist on the shore of Martha's Vineyard and also at Rye Beach. All along the sea-coast, from South Carolina to Florida, similar phenomena are to be found which seem to indicate a subsidence of the land.—*See Cook's Geology of New Jersey, pp.* 343-373.

ern them are alike unknown to us. And so we pause on the threshold of created life, and, standing reverently aside, lay humbly down our little wisdom as we recognize the unfathomable greatness of the ONE ALL-WISE CREATOR.

> "We have but faith: we cannot know;
> For knowledge is of things we see;
> And yet we trust it comes from Thee,
> A beam in darkness: let it grow."

CONCLUSION.

We have traced in the dim light of the past the history of our earth and its inhabitants. Everywhere we have found a Divine Hand shaping and moulding to accomplish a Divine ideal. "IN THE BEGINNING GOD." We can add nothing to the old Hebrew declaration. We have gone back to the origin of man, and there too we have rested on that sublime truth, "IN THE BEGINNING GOD." We have winged our imagination backward to the time when our earth was "without form and void," and here again we have felt the force of that same statement—"IN THE BEGINNING GOD." The study of science ought never to lead one astray from this great fundamental thought. God has assuredly never written anything in Nature contradictory of Himself! Science and religion alike are His offspring. Both will ultimately vindicate Him and His attributes. During this transitional period they may oftentimes seem to clash, but they will ultimately come into perfect accord. He who, even now, from an elevated point surveys the contending hosts on this fiercely-fought field, will see that the scientists and the religionists are fast setting out, if not even now moving upon converging lines of thought. By-and-by they will meet. Forgetting, then, the rancor and bitterness of the past in the joy of newly-found truth, they will clasp hands, and together cast the crowns of their triumphs—the triumphs of Science and Christianity—at the feet of their common Author, and God shall be proclaimed LORD OF ALL!

Questions.

FIRST PART.

[*The figures refer to the pages of the book.*]

INTRODUCTION.—State the origin of the earth according to the nebular hypothesis. Why did the earth assume a globular form? Describe the appearance of the first crust. The first rain. Why was the water hot? What was the effect of the rain? Describe the conflict between fire and water.

19. Where do Astronomy and Geology meet? Meaning of the term "day" in the Scriptures? Give the parallel between the Mosaic and the geologic account.

20. Give some idea of the appearance of the earth at that time. Define Geology.

21. How thick is the earth's crust? How deep has it been examined? Condition of the interior? Name the six reasons given to prove that the interior is a melted mass. At what rate does the temperature increase as we descend? Illustrate. Name some artesian wells that furnish warm water.

22. Name some geysers that throw up hot water. Cause of this difference in temperature? Is the earth's crust steady? What does this oscillation show? What are volcanoes? How many are active? Give an illustration of the amount of lava they throw out at an eruption. Cause of volcanoes?

23. How many earthquakes have been recorded in the last half of a century? Cause of earthquakes?* State in what respects the earth is a microcosm. In what way is the present to the geologist the key to the past?

24-5. By what course of reasoning does the geologist infer that certain kinds of rocks were formed by water? Are rocks now being made in this way? What does the geologist call such rocks? How does the ocean record the history of the land?

26. Where does the geologist find the history of the past written? Has the ocean always been where it is now? By what course of reasoning does the geologist conclude that certain rocks have been thrown up in a melted state from the interior of the earth?

27. What name does he apply to such rocks? Can he be mistaken in the principle? Define fossils. Give some illustrations of the mistakes the ancients made concerning them. Plater's blunder. What view was generally held at a later day?

28. Describe the process of fossilization. Are fossils now being made? When we find a fossil bone, what conclusion do we draw? How can a geologist restore the form of an ancient animal, determine its habits, etc.? †

---

* In the text the theory of earthquakes is given as that of "billowy pulsations" in the crust resting on the waves of a lava-ocean. Dana holds that they are produced by the folding up of the rocks in the slow process of cooling and consequent contraction. An earthquake wave consists, as in all wave-motion, of a progressive vibration as well as a vertical oscillation (Phil., p. 128). The upward vibration seldom exceeds two feet in height. The forward movement has a rate of twenty to thirty miles per minute, depending on the character of the crust through which it passes; in the "undisturbed beds of the Mississippi valley the rate being greater than among the contorted strata of Europe." Orton says that no familiarity with earthquakes enables one to laugh during the shock, or even at the subterranean thunders, which sound like the clanking of chains in the realm of Pluto. All animated nature is terror-stricken. The horse trembles in his stall. The cow moans a low, melancholy tune. The dog sends forth an unearthly yell. Sparrows drop from the trees as if dead. Crocodiles leave the trembling bed of the river and run with loud cries into the forest. When the earth rocks beneath our feet, we feel something beside giddiness. "A moment," says Humboldt, "destroys the illusion of a whole life." We realize an utter insignificance in the presence of that mysterious Power that guides the forces of Nature.

† "Such is the unity and persistence of plan which runs through the different classes of the animal kingdom, that a single tooth, whether of a living or extinct species, will often suffice to enable the expert to disclose all the zoölogical relationships of the animal to which it belonged, to delineate its form, and size, and habits of life; as the architect from a single capital rescued from a ruined edifice

29. Illustrate. Why does a geologist think a fossil shell was once inhabited? What does the shell show? What proof is there that an Arctic climate once existed in England and France? Is this good reasoning?

30. What reasons has the geologist for thinking that certain regions were once covered with glaciers or icebergs?

31. How does he know that a race of cave-dwelling men once lived in Europe? That they were contemporaneous with the hyena? Describe the discoveries that could be made in digging through an old lake-bottom.

32. Give the history of the lake as deduced from such data. Can we judge of the antiquity of the lake? State what has been found in draining old Scottish lake-bottoms. The history indicated by these remains.

SECOND PART.

Lithological Geology.—Define. Name the three classes into which it is divided. Define the term "rock."

40. What common minerals compose the larger part of the earth's crust? Properties of quartz? Its tests?

42. Why are quartz pebbles, etc., so abundant? Size, clearness, etc., of quartz crystals? What is rock crystal? Why so called?

---

can declare not only the general style of the entire architecture, but can reproduce the size and proportions of the temple whose spirit and method it embodies. Not less sublime than the work of the astronomer, who sits in his observatory, and, by the use of a few figures, determines the existence and position in space of some far-off, unknown orb, is that of the palæontologist—the astronomer of time-worlds—who, from the tooth of a reptile, or the bony scale of a fish found thirty feet deep in the solid rock, declares the existence, ages ago, of an animal form which human eyes never beheld—a form that passed totally out of being uncounted centuries before the first intelligent creature was placed upon our planet—and by laws as unerring and uniform as those of the mathematics, proceeds to give us the length and breadth of the extinct form; to tell us whether it lived upon dry land, in marshes, or in the sea; whether a breather of air or water, and whether subsisting upon vegetable or animal food. It is this unity of the laws of animal life and organization running through the whole chain of existence, whether past or present, whether extinct or recent, that constitutes the sublime philosophy of palæontological studies, and assures us that one enduring and infinite Intelligence has planned and executed every part of creation."—*Winchell's Sketches of Creation, p. 175.*

Its uses? Illustrate the great variety of forms which quartz assumes. Describe rose quartz.

43. Smoky quartz. Milky quartz. Granular quartz. Its uses. Amethyst. Why so called? Chalcedony. Carnelian. Sard. Chrysoprase. Agate. Name the different varieties of agate.*

44. What is a cameo? Describe some celebrated antique cameos. The process for preparing agates for the market.

45. Describe jasper. Cause of its color? Name and describe the different varieties of jasper. What is opal? Its appearance?

46. For what is hydrophane noted? How is this explained? What gives the color to quartz pebbles, sand, etc.? Show that iron is Nature's universal dye! Describe flint. Its tests. Hornstone. Buhrstone.

47. Cause of its cellular structure? Origin of quartz? What are diatoms? How do they form rocks?

48. What is tripoli? Fossil farina? Infusorial earth? Noted localities? Appearance of flint, etc., under the microscope? What conclusion is drawn from these facts? Describe alumina. Its tests.

49. Sapphire. Corundum. Emery. Composition of limestone. Tests. Lime. Calcite. Iceland spar. Its test. Chalk. Calcareous tufa. The Tiber stone.

50. What are stalactites? Stalagmites? Appearance of Oölite? What is marl? Its uses? Dolomite? Its test? Marble?

51. Describe the Parian marble. Name some works of art wrought from this stone. How is the quality of marble often injured? What is verde-antique? Describe the process of sawing marble. Wherein is this stone especially designed for man's use?

52. Illustrate the abundance of limestone. What was the origin of limestone? Of chalk? What does the abundance of limestone prove? What is gypsum? Its tests? Plaster? Its uses?

53. Forms of crystallized gypsum? A noted locality? What is plaster of Paris? What are silicates? Name the six prominent ones. Tests of feldspar. Three varieties of feldspar. Their tests. What is clinkstone? Common clay?

---

* The peculiar form assumed by the oxyd of iron in the moss-agate is said by microscopists to be due to the presence of tiny fossil sponges in the stone.

54. Kaolin? Why are bricks red and tobacco-pipes white? Common name for mica? Its tests? Its uses? In what forms is it found? Describe hornblende. Why so called? Asbestos. Its uses.

55. Augite. How distinguished from hornblende?* Talc.† Its tests. What is French chalk? Soapstone? Uses?

56. What is serpentine? Its tests? Why so called? Its uses? What is chlorite? Garnet? Its tests? Ancient name? Tourmaline?

57. Name the three general classes of rocks. Define sedimentary rocks. Name the four divisions of sedimentary rocks. What is sandstone? Conglomerate? A siliceous sandstone? An argillaceous one?

58. Name the three kinds of conglomerate. What is a pudding-stone? A breccia? A shale? A sedimentary limestone? What are the characteristics of the landscape in a sandy region?

59. Define igneous rocks. By what other name are they known? Into what two classes are they divided? Describe trap-rocks. Why so called? Their uses? Name the four varieties of trap-rocks. What is basalt? Chrysolite? Greenstone? Common name?

60. Describe porphyry. Why so called? What is a porphyritic rock? An amygdaloid?

61. What form does trap assume in crystallizing? Causes of this? Noted trappean scenery?

---

* The soft, light-colored pencils in common use are made from a soap-stone rock found at Castleton, Vt. It is a silicate, technically known as argillite. This is the only deposit fit for pencils as yet discovered in the world. The rock is blasted, and is worked immediately, as it soon becomes hard and brittle, and hence useless. The stone is first split into slabs about an inch thick, and then sawn into blocks about seven inches long and five wide. These are carried to the "splitting table," where workmen, with a hammer and a bit of steel like the blade of a knife, split them into little plates about one-third of an inch thick. The squares are now of a tolerably uniform size, about an inch wide, one-third of an inch thick, and seven inches long, but are very rough. They are next passed through a planing-machine, which smooths them, and a rounding-machine, which cuts off the corners, and then are sawed to the proper length. Each pencil is afterward sharpened separately on a grindstone. The waste is very great, as not more than one-hundredth of the original stone appears in the form of pencils. This refuse is ground three grades finer than superfine flour, and used to mix with paper pulp to give it body, as it is termed, and a satin finish.

† Talc is found as a compact rock in North Carolina. It is largely used as a black-board crayon.

62. Characteristic features of the landscape in a trappean region? Proof of the igneous origin of basalt?

64. Curious relation between the civil and geologic history of trappean countries? Name the three varieties of volcanic rocks. Describe trachyte? Noted peak of trachyte?* What is lava?

65. Scoria? Its uses? Pumice? Its uses? What are the characteristic features of the landscape in a volcanic region? Define metamorphic rocks.

66. What effect would melted lava have on sedimentary rocks? Illustrate. Cause of fossils in certain kinds of marble? Imperfections in marble? Composition of granite? How may its constituents be distinguished?

67. What is graphic granite? Is the structure of granite uniform? Its value for various uses? Its location in the earth's crust? Process of quarrying granite?

68–9. Estimate of granite by the ancients? Is granite a primitive rock? Has the original crust of the earth been preserved unchanged? State what changes it has probably undergone. Could granite crystallize directly out from lava? State the theory of the formation of granite. If granite be not an igneous rock, how do you explain the fact that it has been thrown up in a melted state? What are the various aspects which granite assumes in a landscape?

71. What is the general appearance of a granitic region? What effect has the purity and sublimity of nature upon the inhabitants? Difference between granite and gneiss?

72. Origin of gneiss? Its use? Appearance of gneiss hills?

73. What is mica schist? Character of a mica schist landscape? What noted scenery is of this description? What is syenite? Why so called? Was this name correctly applied? Is "Quincy granite" a true granite?

---

* Chimborazo is a trachytic dome, which is a characteristic feature of the mountain scenery among the Andes, as sharp granitic pinnacles are of the Alps. (See page 69.) It is a majestic pile of snow, white as if cut out of spotless marble. Yet it once gleamed with volcanic fires. Its ancient name, Chimpurazu, meant mountain of snow. It is a little singular to notice how many lofty peaks in the world are thus named—Himalaya, Mont Blanc, Hœmus, Sierra Nevada, Ben Nevis, Snowdon, Lebanon, White Mountains, Chimborazo, and Illimani.—*Orton's "Andes and the Amazon."*

74. What is quartzite? Repeat the effects of metamorphic action on limestone. Cause of colored veins in marble? How are rocks classified according to their structure?

75. Which class is the more abundant on the exterior of the earth's crust? On the interior? Which is of the greater value in geologic study? Does the crust remain of the same thickness? How are igneous rocks worked over into stratified rocks? How are stratified rocks generally deposited?

76. Show how igneous action has disturbed this uniform arrangement. Value of this disturbance in geologic study? Define outcropping.

77. Define stratum, formation, group, and lamina. Name and define the various terms used to indicate the position of strata.

78. When are strata conformable? What is diverse stratification? Distinguish between lamination and stratification. State the circumstances under which different kinds of lamination are produced.

79. Define a fault. A jointed structure. Illustrate.

80. Value to the quarrymen? Cause of these seams? What are folds? How produced?

81. What is a decapitated fold? Effect in apparently displacing strata? Illustrate.

82. What is a concretion? The nucleus? A septarium?

83. A claystone? A geode? A beetle-stone?

84. A slate structure? How produced? How do the unstratified rocks occur?

85. What is a vein? A dike? Meaning of the term?

86. State Hugh Miller's beautiful comparison.

87. How can the relative age of veins or dikes be estimated? What proof is there that some veins have been filled from below with melted matter?

88. Describe the various ways in which Nature mends her rock-rents.

90. How have metallic veins been formed? What is a lode?

THIRD PART.

HISTORICAL GEOLOGY.—Define historical geology. Name some of the difficulties the geologist finds in reading this history. Value of fossils? Why does the identification of a fossil identify a formation? Are the geologic ages clearly separated? What terms are used to designate the lesser divisions?

96. Name and define the four different Times of geologic history. On what are these divisions based?

THE AZOIC TIME.—Location of the Azoic rocks? Is America the "new world?"*

100. Name the kinds of Azoic rocks. How formed? What ores do they contain? Was there ever a true Azoic time? Is it definitely fixed? State the history of the Eozoön Canadense. What are rhizopods? (See further account on page 188.) What other name do these fossils have?

101. Is the Eozoön accepted universally as a fossil? What effect would its admission have? How are the relative ages of mountains indicated? The oldest mountains in the world?

102. Describe the effect of the metamorphic action on the Azoic rocks.

103. Divisions of the Azoic rocks in Canada. State the probability that life existed at that early day, and that vegetable life had the precedence.

104. Show how the frame-work of the continent was developed in the Azoic Time. The parallel which exists between the Mosaic and geologic accounts.

---

* The oldest land in South America is in Guiana. Its granite peak rose above the ocean an island where now expands a continent. Its Azoic rocks, together with those of Brazil, which afterward appeared as a cluster of islands, were for ages the only dry land south of the Canada Hills. While the Creator was building up a continent at the north, the south seems to have been left for a later age to develop. Carboniferous vegetation mantled the coal regions with a gorgeous flora, monstrous saurians paddled the waters of the upper Atlantic coast, and huge dinotheria wallowed in the mire where now stand the palaces of Paris, London, and Vienna, but as yet only the broad table-land of Guiana and Brazil appeared above the waste of the Palæozoic Sea.—*See Orton's "Andes and the Amazon."*

[If the chapter on Natural History be learned, the questions will readily suggest themselves.]

THE PALÆOZOIC TIME.—Name the ages of the Palæozoic Time.

THE SILURIAN AGE.—Why is the age so called? Name the periods of the Silurian Age. Why is the New York survey taken as the basis of the Silurian and Devonian Ages.*

110. State the method by which the continent grew. The general characteristics of the Silurian Age.

111. Location of the Potsdam rocks? Kinds of rocks?

112. Describe the lingula. The trilobite.

114. The atmosphere of the Potsdam Period.† The early Silurian beach. What sub-kingdoms of animals were represented? Was there any vegetation? Any distinction of zones?

115. Reasons for this uniformity? Show how changes in the sea produced corresponding changes in the life and the rock. What geologic events occurred in the Lake Superior region?

---

* This system has been established by the genius and the indefatigible perseverance of James Hall, LL.D., State Geologist. To his labor the world is indebted for a palæontological work on the rocks of New York, the compeer of Murchison's on the Silurian of Europe.

† Nature does nothing by halves. She does not stop at fractions of enterprises. She never forsakes a part until it becomes a whole. Her works are often a process; often is the process long, but provision is always made for finishing up in a congruous manner whatever she has undertaken. Many human works are finally forsaken at various stages of incompleteness—machines, edifices, books. Nature is no Michael Angelo, leaving piles of unfinished productions. All her parts bid us look for wholes. Did you ever find a fraction whose integer is not come or coming? When you see the crescent moon, be sure that the rest of the sphere is by its side, though for the present unillumined. Look more closely; perhaps you may discern the old moon in the new moon's arms. Look more closely; perhaps you may discover over against yonder organic need in Nature a full supply for that need which Nature has provided. But whether you discover it or not, make sure that the supply exists. Nature does not waste herself. She has no fondness for throwing herself away either wholly or in parts. If you find one of her reservoirs, make sure that there is something to put in it, and as much as it will hold. If you find one of her tools, be certain that it has something to do, and as much as it can do well. A good and careful provider is she, and never to be reckoned as an infidel who does not care for his own! Cuvier finds a bone, and he at once reconstructs the whole animal to which it belongs. How? On the observed fact that whatever is needed to complement a full mechanism in Nature exists or has existed—that wherever shines a Castor of a demand, over against it shines also the twin Pollux of a supply.—*Pater Mundi*, *pp.* 233-5.

116. Draw the parallel between the Mosaic and geologic accounts.

117. Location of Trenton rocks? Principal kinds of rocks? Name the epochs.

118. Scenery of the Galena limestone. Fossils of the Chazy.

119. Characteristic fossils of Bird's Eye and Black River limestones. Describe the orthoceratite.

120. What is the siphuncle? Were species constant? Did animals die as now?

122. What sub-kingdoms of animals existed? Any terrestrial plants? What mountains were elevated at the close of the period? How is this known? Location of Hudson rocks? By what other name is the formation known? Kinds of rock? Does it contain any coal?

123. Describe the graptolite. Geography of the Hudson Period.

124. Location of Niagara rocks? Why so called? Name the epochs.

125. What is Niagara limestone called in Chicago? Minerals at Lockport? Appearance at the west? What abundant and interesting fossil? Describe the fucoids.

126. The crinoids? What common name has the crinoid? What is crinoidal (encrinital) limestone?

127. Condition of the Appalachian region during this period? Location of Salina rocks?

129. Kinds of rock? Why is it so destitute of fossils? Explain the Salt Springs. The gypsum beds.

130. Location of the Lower Helderberg rocks? Kind of rock? Name of the lower beds? What is said of the abundance of fossils? Describe the eurypterus.

131. The tentaculites. Geography of this period.

132. The climate. What animals took the lead? What classes were yet wanting to complete the scheme of life? Illustrate the uniformity of Nature in all ages. The changes which took place in the life at various times.

THE DEVONIAN AGE.—Why so called? What name has it in England? Is it a red sandstone in America? Name its periods. Describe the general characteristics of the age. What is the prominent feature?

135. What is a ganoid? Name and describe the five principal kinds of fish—the coccosteus, the pterichthys, the cephalaspis, the holoptychius, and the osteolepis.

137. Illustrate their singular union of reptilian and fishy traits. What is a comprehensive type? A prophetic and a retrospective one?

139. Location of Oriskany rocks? Kind of rock?

140. Its characteristic fossils? Condition of the sea along the old Appalachian beach?

141. Location of the Upper Helderberg rocks? What other name is applied to them? Why? Name the epochs. Which stone is most valuable for building purposes? What is "chert"?

142. Characteristic fossil? Location of the Hamilton rocks?

143. Name the epochs and describe the different rocks. Physical features of districts underlaid by Hamilton rocks.

144. By what name is the Genesee slate known at the west? Describe the goniatite. The cup coral.

146. For what is the phacops bufo distinguished? When did terrestrial plants first appear? Location of Chemung rocks? Name the epochs. Under what circumstances were the Chemung rocks deposited? What are its prominent fossils? Its geography?

THE CARBONIFEROUS AGE.—Why so called? Name the periods. The general characteristics of the age? Its geography? The conditions favorable to the growth of vegetation? The formation of coal? The frequent oscillations of the land?

152. Location of the Sub-Carboniferous rocks? Kinds of rock? Curious appearance which they sometimes present?* Prominent fossils? Describe the "sink holes" found in this formation. The caves.

154. Peculiarity of the fish found in the Mammoth Cave? What animals appeared, as it were, before their time? Location of Carboniferous rocks? Name the six great coal-fields of the United States. What are the False Coal Measures?

155. Kinds of rock? State some facts with regard to coal

* These remains are popularly styled rock-cities. Several are found in the south-western part of New York.

seams. The effect of pyrites. What are the characteristic fossils?

156. Describe the Carboniferous vegetation. The ferns. The calamites.

157. The sigillariæ. The lepidodendra. The stigmariæ. The conifers. Reptilian remains. Insects. Fishes.

162. Location of Permian Period. Why so called? Kinds of rock? Curious kind of limestone found near Manhattan, Kansas?

163. Describe the character of the Permian fossils. The Appalachian revolution.

164-5. Illustration of the subsequent denudation seen at Chambersburg, Penn. The metamorphic action. Beneficent effects of this upheaval and metamorphism. The progress of life.

THE MESOZOIC TIME.—Name the periods of the Mesozoic Time. The general characteristics of the Age of Reptiles.

167. Grand characteristic? The geography? Origin of the terms Triassic and Jurassic?

168. What name is sometimes given to the Triassic rocks in Europe? What are the European divisions of the Jurassic rocks?

169. Location of the Triassic and Jurassic rocks in the United States? Describe the formation of the rocks. Kinds of rock. Is coal found?

170. What change took place in the character of the vegetation? Describe the cycad. Show that it is a comprehensive type. What classes now make their appearance? Had birds or mammals been known before? Describe the various kinds of fossils—insects, fishes, oysters, crinoids, etc.

171. In what families did the class of cephalopods culminate? Describe the ammonite.

172. How did the ammonite sink? Describe the belemnite.

173. Common names? What is said of the cuttle-fish? The ichthyosaur?

174. Coprolites? Beetle-stones?

177. Tell the story of Mary Anning.

178. Describe the plesiosaur. The pterodactyle. How were the fins of the Devonian fishes a prophecy of man?

181. Describe the dinosaurs. What are the names of the principal of these land reptiles?

182. Describe the megalosaur. The iguanodon. The restoration of the latter animal. What striking illustration of the mutual adaptation of the various parts of the animal occurred in the restoration of the megalosaur?* What naturalist discovered this principle in comparative anatomy (p. 203)?

183. Describe the labyrinthodon. The ramphorhyncus.

184-5. The "bird-tracks" of the Connecticut valley. What is said of the animal by which they were made? What was the climate at that time?

186. Describe the Triassic salt-beds of Europe. The Triassic gold-bearing rocks of California. What was the origin of the gold placers?

---

* The following is an extract from a letter on this subject received from Dr. Hawkins too late for insertion in its proper place, but which is too valuable to be omitted:

"In the first instance, I was much affected toward it by reading that admirable work, The Bridgewater Treatise on Geology, written by the Rev. Dr. Buckland, in which he describes the teeth of that gigantic saurian, and so graphically compares them to the combination of knife, saw and scimeter, which, with the fossil fragment of the jaw in my hand, could not fail to impress me with a precise idea of the manner in which this creature devoured its prey. He did not snap and swallow like an alligator, but did, with tooth and claw, cut off and tear the flesh of his victim, like the lion or tiger. The fragment of the jaw also gave a definite conception of the dimensions of the head, and explained the necessity for the animal to have an active power over the formidable weapons with which he conquered and devoured his prey. To do this successfully, it was necessary for the strong tendon attached to the back of the head to be also firmly anchored at its other extremity to the long spines of the nerve-arches at the junction of the neck and back, as in the horse, stag, elephant, tiger, and all animals having an active use for a large and heavy head. This theoretical reasoning and conviction I embodied in a preliminary sketch with the elevated ridge on the fore part of the back, to submit to the learned savans whom I had the privilege of consulting at that time, and by whom it was condemned as exceptional in the case of reptiles. My convictions, however, were too strong to allow me to yield to their decision. I therefore commenced this gigantic model in the spring of the year 1854, and completed it the 10th June of the same year.

The supposititious hump-like ridge continued to excite various criticisms as to its probability. At the end of the same year I had the pleasure of receiving a visit from Prof. Richard Owen to congratulate me on the discovery in the Wealden sandstone, Sussex, of the bones which justified the exceptional form which I had predicated."

187. Describe the disturbances that marked the close of the Jurassic Period. What noted scenery is of this era? Location of the cretaceous rocks? Kinds of rock?

188-9. Describe the "green-sand" of New Jersey. What is said of the cretaceous coal-beds? Appearance of chalk under the microscope? What is said of rhizopods? Curious story told of Ehrenberg?

190. What is said of the deep-sea dredgings? Are we not now living, in a certain sense, in the Cretaceous Period? Are the American fossils of this period different from the English? Why?

191-4. Describe the cimoliasaur. The mosasaur. The snapping-turtles. The crocodiles. The dinosaurs. The hadrosaur. The lælaps.

Describe the great disturbances which took place at the close of the Mesozoic Age. Cause.

CENOZOIC TIME.—Name its periods. Its general characteristics.

196. Its geography. The epochs of the Tertiary Period. Origin of the term "Tertiary." Geological condition of Europe. European divisions of the Tertiary.

197. Location of the Tertiary rocks. How do we determine the way in which its deposits were formed? Describe the "pine barrens." Extent of Tertiary rocks on the Pacific coast.

198. Kinds of rock. What is nummulitic limestone? Where found? The Tertiary coal-beds? Is coal found *below* the Carboniferous rocks? Above? What is said of the abundant vegetation?

199-202. What peculiar kinds of plants, not belonging to those regions at present, are found fossil? What do they teach? How many species of Tertiary shells? Their appearance? Name the various kinds of animal remains. What is said of the insects found?* Describe the zeuglodon.

---

* The story that these beds tell seems to be this: A large fresh-water or brackish lake existed, covering a considerable portion of western Colorado and eastern Utah. Streams carried down fine sediment and free petroleum, from numerous springs in the surrounding country, for ages; the petroleum increased in flow until the sediment of the lake became thoroughly charged with it, and the cannelite was the result. A change in the level of the country and the course of the streams is indicated by the overlying sandstones and conglomerates, nearly destitute of petroleum, and at least one thousand feet in thickness. During the time that this immense amount of sediment was being deposited, willows, maples,

203. Give an account of the discoveries made by Cuvier in the Paris basin.

204. What was probably the character of this region at that time? Describe the paleotherium. How do we know that flowers existed in the Tertiary Period?

205. What is said of the Bad Lands? Where are they? What fossils do they contain? What animals, since domesticated by man, inhabited the shores of that Tertiary sea?* Describe the titanotherium.

206. What was the probable origin of this region? Were there probably more than one of those great fresh-water lakes in the Tertiary Period?

207. Name the epochs of the Post-Tertiary. Condition of the continent at this time. What change ensues?

208. What is the Drift? Its extent? What is said of bowlders—their size and appearance?

209. From what direction did they come? Illustrate.

210. What are lost rocks? Why are bowlders more abundant at the east than at the west? What are glacial striæ? Describe their appearance. What is their general direction? On which side of mountains are they found?

212. How high do they extend? Describe the formation of glaciers in Alpine valleys.

215. Define the different kinds of moraines. Tell how blocks are conveyed to a distance. How striæ are cut.

---

oaks, and many strange trees grew on the land, palæotheres and turtles swam in the waters, and clouds of insects sported over its surface. The bitumen seems to have flowed from the shales as petroleum after their upheaval, and to have hardened in time into its present form. The character of the ancient vegetation is shown by the fossil wood found in great abundance.—*Proc. Boston Soc. of Nat. History*, 1866.

* "It is a marvelous fact in the history of mammalia that in South America a native horse should have lived and disappeared, to be succeeded in after years by countless herds descended from the few introduced by the Spanish colonists." (Darwin.) These domestic animals, which were then native in America, were not of exactly the same species as those now used by man. The fossil remains of a horse have been found at the west, which, when alive, could not have been three feet high. Horses had entirely disappeared from the continent when the Spaniards landed, and the Indians supposed man and beast to be one animal.

216. Name the evidences of former glaciers. Describe the great glacier on the coast of Greenland.

217–18. How are icebergs formed? What effect do they have in the transportation of rock and formation of striæ? Describe the origin of the glaciers of the Drift epoch. Cause of the cold.* The effects.

219. What change occurred in the Champlain Epoch? Its effect? What proof have we that river-channels were filled by these glaciers?

220–21. Effect of the glacier-streams? How does the coarseness of the Drift vary? Effects of this change? Describe the continental elevation which took place at the beginning of the Terrace Epoch. Its effect? Was the elevation uniform and steady?

222. What are the proofs of these oscillations?

223–4. How were terraces formed? Which were made in the Champlain Epoch? The Terrace? What are ancient sea-beaches? How are they known? How high are they found?

225–6. Localities of Post-Tertiary fossils? Do they resemble modern species? What animals led the life of the period? Name the principal quadrupeds. Describe the mammoth.

---

* There is a growing conviction that the cause of this glacial cold must be sought among astronomical phenomena. It has been suggested, 1. That we are now moving through a comparatively starless, and hence cheerless, region of space; and that as the earth passes from densely to thinly-clustered portions, and *vice versa*, the heat received and consequent temperature must vary; 2. That the axis of the earth may not have always pointed in the same direction or at the same angle as now, and that any variation would have produced a change of climate; 3. That during the Great Year of the astronomers, about 21,000 common years, each hemisphere has two seasons (see Astronomy, page 121, *et seq.*). During half of this time the northern hemisphere has its summer in aphelion, and winter in perihelion; while in the other half this is reversed. When the Great Winter prevails at the north pole, there is an accumulation of ice and snow. This changes the center of gravity of the earth. The water will flow thither to adjust the equilibrium, and thus overflow a part of the northern hemisphere. These Great Summers and Winters, with their accumulations of snow and ice, and consequent submergence of the land, have occurred, it is thought, alternately at either pole at intervals of about 10,500 years through all the past. In the year 1250 (see Astronomy, p. 129) the Great Winter terminated at the south pole, where for 12,500 years these accumulations had been gathering. In the same year the Great Northern Summer culminated. The hemisphere which has its winter in aphelion is not only further from the sun, but has a winter of eight days

227. The locality of fossil ivory in Siberia? What curious legend have the Tartars? Describe the discovery of a mammoth preserved in ice.

228. The mastodon. How can mastodon remains be distinguished from those of the elephant?

229. What was the mastodon's food? How is this known? Describe the megatherium. What was its food? Uses of its tail? Was its structure adapted to its life?

230–4. Describe the glyptodon. The Irish elk. The cave-bear. Why so named? The hyena. Discovery of the Kirkdale cave.

236. What is said by Whitney of the Glacial Epoch in California? Is any Drift found in Oregon?

237. Origin of cañons. What is the Loëss of the Nile? The Rhine? The Mississippi valley?

238. Its location and appearance? Its fossils? What are sand-dunes? Where found? How formed?

THE ERA OF MIND.—Does Geology tell when man appeared? Where are his remains found?

244–7. Name the classifications of these primeval remains. What do these terms indicate? Were these ages coeval? Describe the man of the Stone Age in the first epoch. The second epoch. The third epoch.

248–9. Influence of the metals in advancing civilization? What metals were first used?

250. Describe man's progress in the Bronze epoch. The Iron epoch.

---

longer duration (Astronomy, p. 118). M. Adhémar has worked out this theory very fully. He claims, however, that owing to the movement in the Earth's orbit (Astronomy, p. 128), the Great Year is only 21,000 years long; each hemisphere having a summer of 10,500 years and a winter of equal length. The Great Summer of the northern hemisphere culminated, according to his calculations, 1248 B.C. Since that date our Great Winter has been in progress. Our pole, in its turn, goes on getting cooler continually; ice is being heaped upon snow, and snow upon ice, and in seven thousand three hundred and eighty-eight years the center of gravity of the earth will return to its normal position, which is the geometrical center of the spheroid. Following the immutable laws of central attraction, the southern waters accruing from the melted ice and snow of the south pole will return to invade and overwhelm once more the continents of the northern hemisphere, giving rise to new continents, in all probability, in the southern hemisphere.

A TRIASSIC FISH.

1. Eurinotus ceratocephalus.

Glossary.

Acaleph, *Ak'-a-lef.*
Agate, *Ag'-ate.*
Albite, *Al'-bīte.*
Alumina, *A-lū'-me-na.*
Aluminium, *Al-ū-min'-e-um.*
Amethyst, *Am'-e-thyst.*
Amygdaloid, *A-mig'-da-loid.*
Anoplotherium, *An-o-plo-the'-re-um.*
Argillaceous, *Ar-jil-a'-shus.*
Asbestos, *As-bes'-tus.*
Asterophyllite, *As-ter-off'-e-lite.*
Augite, *Aw'-jīte.*

Basalt, *Ba-sawlt'.*
Belemnite, *Be-lem'-nīte.*
Brachiopod, *Brack'-e-o-pod.*
Bryozoan, *Brī-o-zo'-an.*

Calamite, *Kal'-ă-mite.*
Cephalaspis, *Sef-a-las'-pis.*
Cephalopod, *Sef'-ăl-o-pod.*
Chalcedony, *Kal-sĕd'-o-ny.*
Chrysoprase, *Krys'-o-prase.*
Coccosteus, *Koc-cos'-te-us.*
Conchoidal, *Kon-koi'-dal.*
Conglomerate, *Kon-glom'-e-rate.*
Conifer, *Kō'-ni-fer.*
Coral, *Kor'-al.*
Cretaceous, *Kre-ta'-shus.*
Crinoid, *Krī-noid.*
Crustacean, *Krus-tā'-she-an.*
Cycad, *Sy'-kad.*

Devonian, *De-vō'-ne-an.*
Dinosaur, *Dī'-no-sawr.*
Dinotherium, *Dī'-no-the'-re-um.*
Dodecahedron, *Do-dec-ă-he'-dron.*
Dolomite, *Dol'-o-mite*; (Dolomien, a French geologist.)
Dolerite, *Dol'-e-rite.*

Echinoderm, *E-kin'-o-derm.*
Echinoids, *Ek-i-noids.*
Encrinite, *En'-kre-nite.*
Endogen, *En'-do-jen.*
Eurypterus, *Eu-ryp'-te-rus.*
Eocene, *E'-ō-seen.*
Equisetaceæ, *E-que-se-tā'-she-e.*
Equisetum, *Eq-ue-se'-tum.*
Exogen, *Ex'-o-jen.*
Eozoön, *E-o-zo'-on.*

Fauna, *Fawn'-a.*
Feldspar, *Feld'-spar.*
Foramenifera, *Fō-ram-in-if'-er-a.*

Ganoid, *Ga'-noid.*
Gasteropod, *Gas'-ter-o-pod.*
Geode, *Je'-ōde.*
Glacier, *Glā-seer.*
Gneiss, *Nīce.*
Goniatite, *Gō'-ni-a-tite.*
Granite, *Gran'-it.*
Graptolite, *Grap'-to-līte.*
Gypsum, *Jip'-sum.*

Hadrosaur, *Ha'-dro-sawr.*
Hippopotamus, *Hip-po-pŏt'-ă-mus.*
Holoptychius, *Hol-op-tik'-e-us.*
Hornblende, *Horn-blende.*
Hylæosaur, *Hy'-le-o-sawr.*

Ichthyosaur, *Ich'-the-o-sawr.*
Igneous, *Ig'-ne-us.*

Iguanodon, *Ig-wăn'-o-don.*
Infusoria, *In-fu-zo'-re-a.*

Lamellibranchiate, *Lă-mel-e-brank'-e-ate.*
Lepidodendron, *Lep-e-do-den'-dron.*
Lias, *Li'-as.*
Lignite, *Lig-nīte.*

Mastodon, *Mas'-to-don.*
Megalosaur, *Meg'-a-lo-sawr.*
Megatherium, *Meg-a-the'-re-um.*
Metamorphic, *Met-a-mor'-phic.*
Miocene, *Mī'-o-seen.*
Mollusca, *Mol-lus'-ca.*
Moraine, *Mō-rain'.*
Mosasaur, *Mo'-sa-sawr.*

Nodule, *Nod'-ule.*
Nummulite, *Num'-mu-līte.*

Onyx, *O'-nix.*
Oölite, *O'-o-līte.*
Orthoceratite, *Or-tho-cĕr-a-tīte.*

Paleontology, *Pal-e-on-tol'-o-gy.*
Paleotherium, *Pal-e-o-the'-re-um.*
Palæozoic, *Pal'-e-o-zo-ic.*
Plesiosaur, *Plē'-sē-o-sawr.*
Pliocene, *Plī'-o-seen.*
Porphyry, *Por'-fe-ry.*
Protozoan, *Pro-to-zo'-an.*
Pterichthys, *Ter-ik'-thys.*
Pterodactyle, *Ter-ro-dac'-tyl.*
Pteropod, *Ter'-ro-pod.*
Pyrites, *Py-rī'-teez.*
Pyroxene, *Pir-ox'-een.*

Quartz, *Kwôrts.*

Rhizopod, *Rīz'-o-pod.*
Ramphorhyncus, *Ram-for hin'-kus.*

Saurian, *Säw'-ri-an.*
Selenite, *Sĕl'-en-ite.*
Serpentine, *Ser'-pen-tīne*
Sigillaria, *Sig'-il-lā'-re-a.*
Silurian, *Si-lū'-re-an.*
Siphuncle, *Sī-funk-kl.*
Stalactite, *Stă-lac'-tīte.*
Stalagmite, *Stă-lăg'-mīte.*
Steatite, *Ste'-a-tite.*
Stigmaria, *Stig-mā'-re-a.*
Stria, *Strī-a.*
Syenite, *Sī'-en-ite.*

Talc, *Tălc.*
Tentaculites, *Ten'-tac-u-lites.*
Tourmaline, *Toor'-mă-līn.*
Trachyte, *Trā'-kite.*
Trilobite, *Trī'-lo-bīte.*
Tufa, *Tū'-fa.*

Verd-antique, *Verd-an-teek'.*
Vertebræ, *Ver'-te-bre.*

Wealden, *Weeld'-n.*

Zoophyte, *Zo'-o-fīte.*

The Autumn sun was setting o'er the hills [illegible]
Lighting up the [illegible] landscape [illegible]
It touched the forms of lad and maiden [illegible]
He with deep brown eyes, she with auburn [illegible]
As her lover stood beside her
But never does it matter [illegible]
The [illegible] beside [illegible]
[illegible]

As R— and M— was walking along
Says R— to M— 'your dress is too long
Just give me [illegible] and I'll fix it up
[illegible] go walking [illegible]

Acalephs, 107.
Agate, 43.
Alabaster, 53.
Albite, 53.
Alluvial Deposits, 237.
Alumina, 48.
Amethyst, 43.
Ammonite, 171.
Amygdaloid, 60.
Anoplotherium, 203.
Appalachian Beach, 140.
Appalachian Metamorphism, 164.
Appalachian Mountains, 110.
Appalachian Revolution, 163.
Artesian Wells, 21.
Articulates, 106.
Asbestos, 54.
Athens Marble, 125.
Augite, 55.
Azoic Time, 98.

Bad Lands, 204.
Basalt, 59.
Basaltic Pillars, 63.
Beetle Stones, 84.
Belemnite, 172.
Bird's Eye Limestone, 117.
Bird Tracks, 184.
Black River Limestone, 117.
Black Slate, 144.
Bloodstone, 45.
Blue Limestone, 119.
Bowlders, 208.
Brachiopods, 107.
Breccia, 58.
Bronze Epoch, 249.
Bryozoans, 107.
Buhrstone, 46.

Calamites, 156.
Calc Spar, 49.
Calcite, 49.
Cameo, 44.
Camel, 240.
Canadian Divisions, 108.
Calciferous Epoch, 112.
Cañon, 236.
Canda Galli Grit, 141.
Carbuncle, 56.
Carboniferous Age, 140.
Carboniferous Period, 154.
Carnelian, 43.
Caves, 153.
Cave Bear, 230.
Cenozoic Time, 194.
Cephalaspis, 137.
Cephalopods, 107.
Chalcedony, 43.
Chalk, 49, 189.
Chazy Group, 117.
Champlain Epoch, 219.
Chlorite, 56, 75.
Chemung Period, 146.
Chert, 125, 141.
Chronology, 30.
Chrysoprase, 43.
Chrysolite, 59.
Cimoliasaur, 190.
Cincinnati Limestone, 122.
Clay, 53.
Clay Stones, 83.
Cleavage, 41.
Cliff Limestone, 143.
Clinton Group, 124.
Clinkstone, 53.
Coal, 155.
Coccosteus, 135.

Comprehensive Type, 137.
Conchifers, 107.
Concretions, 83.
Conglomerate, 57.
Conifers, 157.
Continent, Outlines of, 104, 110.
Coprolites, 174.
Coral, 108.
Corniferous Period, 141.
Corundum, 49.
Cretaceous Period, 187.
Crinoids, 108, 125.
Crocodiles, 191.
Crust of Earth, 21.
Crustaceans, 106.
Cycad, 170.

Denudation, 82.
Deep-Sea Dredgings, 190.
Development Hypothesis, 251.
Devonian Age, 134.
Diatoms, 47.
Dikes, 86.
Dinosaur, 181, 191.
Diorite, 60.
Dip, 78.
Diverse Stratification, 78.
Dislocations of Strata, 76.
Dolomite, 51.
Dolerite, 59.
Drift Epoch, 207.

Earthquakes, 23.
Echinoids, 108.
Echinoderms, 108.
Elasmosaur, 190.
Elephant, 227.
Emery, 49.
Eocene, 196.
Escarpment, 78.
Eurypterus, 130.
Eozoön Canadense, 101.

Faults, 80.
Feldspar, 53.
Fingal's Cave, 61.
Flint, 46.
Folds, 81.
Fossil, 27.
Fossil Farina, 48.
Fucoids, 125.

Galena Limestone, 118.
Ganoids, 106.
Garnet, 56.
Gasteropods, 107.
Genesee Slate, 143.
Geodes, 83.
Geology, Definition of, 20.
Geysers, 22.
Glacial Epoch, 207.
Glacial Striæ, 210.
Glaciers, 29, 212.
Glyptodon, 230.
Gneiss, 72.
Gold Rocks, 186.
Goniatite, 144.
Granite, 67.
Graptolite, 123.
Green Mountains, 122, 131.
Greenstone, 59.
Gypsum, 52, 129.

Hadrosaur, 191.
Hamilton Period, 142.
Helderberg Period, 130.
Holoptychius, 137.
Hornstone, 46.
Hornblende, 54.
Horse, 240, 250, 271.
Hot Springs, 22.
Hyena, 232.
Hudson Period, 122.
Hudson River, 123.

Iceberg, 217.
Ichthyosaur, 173.
Iguanodon, 181.
Igneous Rocks, 26, 59.
Infusoria, 105.
Infusorial Earth, 48.
Iron Epoch, 250.
Ironstone, 59.
Irish Elk, 231.
Isinglass, 54.

Jasper, 45.
Jointed Structure, 81.
Jurassic, 167.

Kaolin, 54.
Kitchen Middens, 247.

Labradorite, 53.
Labyrinthodon, 183.
Lælaps, 192.
Lake Bottom, 31.

Lake Dwellings, 249.
Lake Superior, 115.
Lamellibranch, 107.
Lamina, 78.
Lava, 65.
Lepidodendron, 157.
Lias, 168.
Limestone, 49, 58.
Lingula, 112.
Lithological Geology, 35.
Loëss, 237.

Man, Coming of, 243.
Mammoth Cave, 153.
Mammoth, 225.
Map of Azoic Time, 99.
Map of Mesozoic Time, 168.
Map of Cenozoic Time, 195.
Marble, 51, 75.
Marble, Carrara, 67.
Marl, 50.
Marcellus Shale, 143.
Mastodon, 228.
Medina Group, 124.
Megalosaur, 182.
Megatherium, 229.
Metal Age, 248.
Metamorphism, 66, 88, 164.
Metamorphic Rocks, 65.
Mesozoic Time, 166.
Methods of Geological Study, 23.
Mica, 54.
Mica Schist, 74.
Millstone Grit, 154.
Miocene, 196.
Mound Limestone, 125.
Mountains, 101.
Mollusks, 106.
Mosaic Account, 19, 104, 116, 238.

Nature, Uniformity of, 23.
Natural History, 105.
Nebular Hypothesis, 17.
Niagara Limestone, 124.
Nummulitic Limestone, 198.

Obsidian, 66.
Offsets, 80.
Old Red Sandstone, 134.
Oneida Epoch, 124.
Onondaga Group, 141.
Onyx, 44.
Oölite, 50, 168.

Opal, 45.
Oriskany Period, 139.
Orthoceratite, 119.
Ostrea Marshii, 170.
Outcrop, 77.
Oyster, 170.

Palæozoic Time, 108.
Paleotherium, 203.
Pentamerus, 130.
Permian, 162.
Phacops bufo, 146.
Pine Barrens, 197.
Plaster, 52.
Plesiosaur, 177.
Pliocene, 196.
Polyps, 107.
Porphyry, 60.
Post-Tertiary, 207.
Potsdam, 111.
Portage Group, 146.
Primeval Man, 243.
Protozoans, 105.
Pterodactyle, 178.
Pterichthys, 135.
Pteropods, 107.
Pudding-stone, 58.
Pumice, 66.
Pyroxene, 55.

Quartz, 40.
Quartzite, 75.
Quaternary Epoch, 207.
Quincy Granite, 74.

Ramphorhynchus, 183.
Reindeer Epoch, 245.
Rhizopods, 100, 188.
Rhinoceros, 239.
Rocky Mountains, 124.
Rocks, Classification of, 57.
Rocks, Composition of, 40.
Rocks, Metamorphic, 66.
Rocks, Sedimentary, 57.
Rocks, Structure of, 75.
Rocks, Stratified, 57, 78.
Rocks, Trap, 59.
Rocks, Unstratified, 59, 85.
Rocks, Volcanic, 65.

Sand Dunes, 238.
Salina Period, 127.
Salt Springs, 129.

Salt Beds, 186.
Sand, 46.
Sandstone, 57.
Sapphire, 49.
Sard, 43.
Satin Spar, 53.
Scenic Description, 20, 58, 60, 66, 70, 73, 74, 132, 148, 161, 192, 239.
Schoharie Grit, 141.
Scoria, 66.
Sculptured Rocks, 115.
Sea-weeds, 119, 125.
Sea-pens, 123.
Sedimentary Rocks, 24, 57.
Selenite, 53.
Selachians, 106.
Septaria, 83.
Serpentine, 56.
Shale, 58.
Sigillaria, 157.
Silica, 40.
Silicates, 53.
Silurian Age, 109.
Sink-holes, 153.
Siphuncle, 120.
Slate, 75, 85.
Solenhofen Limestone, 169.
Soapstone, 54.
Spirifer arenosus, 139.
Spirifer mucronatus, 146.
Stalactites, 50.
Stalagmites, 50.
Steatite, 55.
Stone River Group, 117.
St. Lawrence River, 123.
St. Peter's Sandstone, 112.
Stone Age, 244.
Stratified Rocks, 57.
Stratum, 78.
Sub-Carboniferous Period, 152.
Syenite, 74.

Talc, 55.
Talcose Schist, 75.
Teliosts, 106.
Tentaculite, 131.
Tertiary Period, 196.
Terrace Epoch, 221.
Theory, Value of a, 252.
Titanotherium, 205.
Touchstone, 45.
Tourmaline, 56.
Tully Limestone, 143.
Turtles, 191.
Trap-rock, 59.
Trachyte, 65.
Travertine, 49.
Trenton Period, 117.
Trilobite, 112.
Triassic Period, 167.
Tufa, 49.

Uniformity of Nature, 23, 132.
Upper Helderberg Period, 141.

Verd-antique, 51.
Veins, 86.
Vertebrates, 106.

Water Lime Group, 130.
Wealden, 168.

Xiphodon, 203.

Zeuglodon, 202.
Zoöphite, 110.

DRAWING.

Chapman's American Drawing Book, . . . *$6 00

The standard American text-book and authority in all branches of art. A compilation of art principles. A manual for the amateur, and basis of study for the professional artist. Adapted for schools and private instruction.

CONTENTS.—"Any one who can Learn to Write can Learn to Draw."—Primary Instruction in Drawing.—Rudiments of Drawing the Human Head.—Rudiments in Drawing the Human Figure.—Rudiments of Drawing.—The Elements of Geometry.—Perspective.—Of Studying and Sketching from Nature.—Of Painting.—Etching and Engraving.—Of Modeling.—Of Composition —Advice to the American Art-Student.

The work is of course magnificently illustrated with all the original designs.

Chapman's Elementary Drawing Book, . . 1 50

A Progressive Course of Practical Exercises, or a text-book for the training of the eye and hand. It contains the elements from the larger work, and a copy should be in the hands of every pupil; while a copy of the "American Drawing Book," named above, should be at hand for reference by the class.

The Little Artist's Portfolio, ... *50

25 Drawing Cards (progressive patterns), 25 Blanks, and a fine Artist's Pencil, all in one neat envelope.

Clark's Elements of Drawing, ... *1 00

A complete course in this graceful art, from the first rudiments of outline to the finished sketches of landscape and scenery.

Fowle's Linear and Perspective Drawing, . *60

For the cultivation of the eye and hand, with copious illustrations and directions for the guidance of the unskilled teacher.

Monk's Drawing Books—Six Numbers, per set, *2 25

Each book contains *eleven* large patterns, with opposing blanks. No. 1. Elementary Studies. No. 2. Studies of Foliage. No. 3. Landscapes. No. 4. Animals, I. No. 5. Animals, II. No. 6. Marine Views, etc.

Allen's Map-Drawing, ... 25 cts.; Scale, 25

This method introduces a new era in Map-Drawing, for the following reasons:—1. It is a system. This is its greatest merit.—2. It is easily understood and taught.—3. The eye is trained to exact measurement by the use of a scale.—4. By no special effort of the memory, distance and comparative size are fixed in the mind.—5. It discards useless construction of lines.—6. It can be taught by any teacher, even though there may have been no previous practice in Map-Drawing.—7. Any pupil old enough to study Geography can learn by this System, in a short time, to draw accurate maps.—8. The System is not the result of theory, but comes directly from the school-room. It has been thoroughly and successfully tested there, with all grades of pupils.—9. It is economical, as it requires no mapping plates. It gives the pupil the ability of rapidly drawing accurate maps.

Ripley's Map-Drawing, ... 1 25

Based on the Circle. One of the most efficient aids to the acquirement of a knowledge of Geography is the practice of map-drawing. It is useful for the same reason that the best exercise in orthography is the *writing* of difficult words. Sight comes to the aid of hearing, and a double impression is produced upon the memory. Knowledge becomes less mechanical and more intuitive. The student who has sketched the outlines of a country, and dotted the important places, is little likely to forget either. The impression produced may be compared to that of a traveller who has been over the ground, while more comprehensive and accurate in detail.

BOOK-KEEPING.

Folsom's Logical Book-keeping, ... $2 00
Folsom's Blanks to Book-keeping, ... *4 50

This treatise embraces the interesting and important discoveries of Prof. Folsom (of the Albany "Bryant & Stratton College"), the partial enunciation of which in lectures and otherwise has attracted so much attention in circles interested in commercial education.

After studying business phenomena for many years, he has arrived at the positive laws and principles that underlie the whole subject of Accounts; finds that the science is based in *Value* as a generic term; that value divides into *two classes* with varied species; that all the exchanges of values are reducible to nine equations; and that all the results of all these exchanges are limited to *thirteen* in number.

As accounts have been universally taught hitherto, without setting out from a radical analysis or definition of values, the science has been kept in great obscurity, and been made as difficult to impart as to acquire. On the new theory, however, these obstacles are chiefly removed. In reading over the first part of it, in which the governing laws and principles are discussed, a person with ordinary intelligence will obtain a fair conception of the *double entry* process of accounts. But when he comes to study thoroughly these laws and principles as there enunciated, and works out the examples and memoranda which elucidate the *thirteen results* of business, the student will neither fail in readily acquiring the science as it is, nor in becoming able intelligently to apply it in the interpretation of business.

Smith & Martin's Book-keeping, ... 1 25
Smith & Martin's Blanks, ... *60

This work is by a practical teacher and a practical book-keeper. It is of a thoroughly popular class, and will be welcomed by every one who loves to see theory and practice combined in an easy, concise, and methodical form.

The Single Entry portion is well adapted to supply a want felt in nearly all other treatises, which seem to be prepared mainly for the use of wholesale merchants, leaving retailers, mechanics, farmers, etc., who transact the greater portion of the business of the country, without a guide. The work is also commended, on this account, for general use in Young Ladies' Seminaries, where a thorough grounding in the simpler form of accounts will be invaluable to the future housekeepers of the nation.

The treatise on Double Entry Book-keeping combines all the advantages of the most recent methods, with the utmost simplicity of application, thus affording the pupil all the advantages of actual experience in the counting-house, and giving a clear comprehension of the entire subject through a judicious course of mercantile transactions.

The shape of the book is such that the transactions can be presented as in actual practice; and the simplified form of Blanks—three in number—adds greatly to the ease experienced in acquiring the science.

NATURAL SCIENCE.

FAMILIAR SCIENCE.

Norton & Porter's First Book of Science, . $1 75

By eminent Professors of Yale College. Contains the principles of Natural Philosophy, Astronomy, Chemistry, Physiology, and Geology. Arranged on the Catechetical plan for primary classes and beginners.

Chambers' Treasury of Knowledge, ... 1 25

Progressive lessons upon—*first*, common things which lie most immediately around us, and first attract the attention of the young mind; *second*, common objects from the Mineral, Animal, and Vegetable kingdoms, manufactured articles, and miscellaneous substances; *third*, a systematic view of Nature under the various sciences. May be used as a Reader or Text-book.

NATURAL PHILOSOPHY.

Norton's First Book in Natural Philosophy, 1 00

By Prof. NORTON, of Yale College. Designed for beginners. Profusely illustrated, and arranged on the Catechetical plan.

Peck's Ganot's Course of Nat. Philosophy, . 1 75

The standard text-book of France, Americanized and popularized by Prof. PECK, of Columbia College. The most magnificent system of illustration ever adopted in an American school-book is here found. For intermediate classes.

Peck's Elements of Mechanics, ... 2 00

A suitable introduction to Bartlett's higher treatises on Mechanical Philosophy, and adequate in itself for a complete academical course.

Bartlett's SYNTHETIC, AND ANALYTIC, Mechanics, . each 5 00

Bartlett's Acoustics and Optics, ... 3 50

A system of Collegiate Philosophy, by Prof. BARTLETT, of West Point Military Academy.

Steele's 14 Weeks Course in Philos. (see p. 34) **1 50**

Steele's Philosophical Apparatus, ... *125 00

Adequate to performing the experiments in the ordinary text-books. The articles will be sold separately, if desired. See special circular for details.

GEOLOGY.

Page's Elements of Geology, ... 1 25

A volume of Chambers' Educational Course. Practical, simple, and eminently calculated to make the study interesting.

Emmons' Manual of Geology, ... 1 25

The first Geologist of the country has here produced a work worthy of his reputation.

Steele's 14 Weeks Course (see p. 34) **. 1 50**

Steele's Geological Cabinet, ... *40 00

Containing 125 carefully selected specimens. In four parts. Sold separately, if desired. See circular for details.

NATURAL SCIENCE—Continued.

CHEMISTRY.

Porter's First Book of Chemistry, ... $1 00

Porter's Principles of Chemistry, ... 2 00

The above are widely known as the productions of one of the most eminent scientific men of America. The extreme simplicity in the method of presenting the science, while exhaustively treated, has excited universal commendation.

Darby's Text-Book of Chemistry, ... 1 75

Purely a Chemistry, divesting the subject of matters comparatively foreign to it (such as heat, light, electricity, etc.), but usually allowed to engross too much attention in ordinary school-books.

Gregory's Organic Chemistry, ... 2 50

Gregory's Inorganic Chemistry, ... 2 50

The science exhaustively treated. For colleges and medical students.

Steele's Fourteen Weeks Course, ... 1 50

A successful effort to reduce the study to the limits of a *single term*, thereby making feasible its general introduction in institutions of every character. The author's felicity of style and success in making the science pre-eminently *interesting* are peculiarly noticeable features. (See page 34.)

Steele's Chemical Apparatus, ... *20 00

Adequate to the performance of all the important experiments.

BOTANY.

Thinker's First Lessons in Botany, ... 40

For children. The technical terms are largely dispensed with in favor of an easy and familiar style adapted to the smallest learner.

Wood's Object-Lessons in Botany, ... 1 50

Wood's American Botanist and Florist, . . . 2 50

Wood's New Class-Book of Botany, ... 3 50

The standard text-books of the United States in this department. In style they are simple, popular, and lively; in arrangement, easy and natural; in description, graphic and strictly exact. The Tables for Analysis are reduced to a perfect system. More are annually sold than of all others combined.

Wood's Plant Record, ... *75

A simple form of Blanks for recording observations in the field.

Wood's Botanical Apparatus, ... *8 00

A portable Trunk, containing Drying Press, Knife, Trowel, Microscope, and Tweezers, and a copy of Wood's Plant Record—composing a complete outfit for the collector.

Young's Familiar Lessons, ... 2 00

Darby's Southern Botany, ... 2 00

Embracing general Structural and Physiological Botany, with vegetable products, and descriptions of Southern plants, and a complete Flora of the Southern States.

NATURAL SCIENCE—Continued.

PHYSIOLOGY.

Jarvis' Elements of Physiology, ...$ 75

Jarvis' Physiology and Laws of Health, . 1 65

The only books extant which approach this subject with a proper view of the true object of teaching Physiology in schools, viz., that scholars may know how to take care of their own health. In bold contrast with the abstract *Anatomies*, which children learn as they would Greek or Latin (and forget as soon), to *discipline the mind*, are these text-books, using the *science* as a secondary consideration, and only so far as is necessary for the comprehension of the *laws of health*.

Hamilton's Vegetable & Animal Physiology, 1 25

The two branches of the science combined in one volume lead the student to a proper comprehension of the Analogies of Nature.

Steele's Fourteen Weeks Course (see p. 34), . 1 50

ASTRONOMY.

Steele's Fourteen Weeks' Course, ... 1 50

Reduced to a single term, and better adapted to school use than any work heretofore published. Not written for the information of scientific men, but for the inspiration of youth, the pages are not burdened with a multitude of figures which no memory could possibly retain. The whole subject is presented in a clear and concise form. (See p. 34.)

Willard's School Astronomy, ... 1 00

By means of clear and attractive illustrations, addressing the eye in many cases by analogies, careful definitions of all necessary technical terms, a careful avoidance of verbiage and unimportant matter, particular attention to analysis, and a general adoption of the simplest methods, Mrs. Willard has made the best and most attractive *elementary* Astronomy extant.

McIntyre's Astronomy and the Globes, . . 1 50

A complete treatise for intermediate classes. Highly approved.

Bartlett's Spherical Astronomy, ... 5 00

The West Point course, for advanced classes, with applications to the current wants of Navigation, Geography, and Chronology.

NATURAL HISTORY.

Carll's Child's Book of Natural History, . . 0 50

Illustrating the Animal, Vegetable, and Mineral Kingdoms, with application to the Arts. For beginners. Beautifully and copiously illustrated.

ZOOLOGY.

Chambers' Elements of Zoology, ... 1 50

A complete and comprehensive system of Zoology, adapted for academic instruction, presenting a systematic view of the Animal Kingdom as a portion of external Nature.

LITERATURE.

Cleveland's Compendiums . . . . each, $*2 50

ENGLISH LITERATURE. AMERICAN LITERATURE.
ENGLISH LITERATURE OF THE XIXTH CENTURY.

In these volumes are gathered the cream of the literature of the English speaking people for the school-room and the general reader. Their reputation is national. More than 125,000 copies have been sold.

Boyd's English Classics . . . . . each, *1 25

MILTON'S PARADISE LOST. THOMSON'S SEASONS.
YOUNG'S NIGHT THOUGHTS. POLLOK'S COURSE OF TIME.
COWPER'S TASK, TABLE TALK, &c. LORD BACON'S ESSAYS.

This series of annotated editions of great English writers, in prose and poetry, is designed for critical reading and parsing in schools. Prof. J. R. Boyd proves himself an editor of high capacity, and the works themselves need no encomium. As auxiliary to the study of Belles Lettres, etc., these works have no equal.

Pope's Essay on Man *20

Pope's Homer's Iliad *80

The metrical translation of the great poet of antiquity, and the matchless "Essay on the Nature and State of Man," by ALEXANDER POPE, afford superior exercise in literature and parsing.

AESTHETICS.

Huntington's Manual of the Fine Arts . *1 75

A view of the rise and progress of Art in different countries, a brief account of the most eminent masters of Art, and an analysis of the principles of Art. It is complete in itself, or may precede to advantage the critical work of Lord Kames.

Boyd's Kames' Elements of Criticism . *1 75

The best edition of this standard work; without the study of which none may be considered proficient in the science of the Perceptions. No other study can be pursued with so marked an effect upon the taste and refinement of the pupil.

POLITICAL ECONOMY.

Champlin's Lessons on Political Economy 1 25

An improvement on previous treatises, being shorter, yet containing every thing essential, with a view of recent questions in finance, etc., which is not elsewhere found.

GERMAN.

A COMPLETE COURSE IN THE GERMAN.

By JAMES H. WORMAN, A. M.

Worman's Elementary German Grammar . $1 50

Worman's Complete German Grammar . 2 00

These volumes are designed for intermediate and advanced classes respectively. Though following the same general method with "Otto" (that of 'Gaspey'), our author differs essentially in its application. He is more practical, more systematic, more accurate, and besides introduces a number of invaluable features which have never before been combined in a German grammar.

Among other things, it may be claimed for Prof. Worman that he has been *the first* to introduce in an American text-book for learning German, a system of analogy and comparison with other languages. Our best teachers are also enthusiastic about his methods of inculcating the art of speaking, of understanding the spoken language, of correct pronunciation; the sensible and convenient original classification of nouns (in four declensions), and of irregular verbs, also deserves much praise. We also note the use of heavy type to indicate etymological changes in the paradigms, and, in the exercises, the parts which specially illustrate preceding rules.

Worman's Elementary German Reader . . 1 25

Worman's Collegiate German Reader . . . 2 00

The finest and most judicious compilation of classical and standard German Literature. These works embrace, progressively arranged, selections from the masterpieces of Goethe, Schiller, Korner, Seume, Uhland, Freiligrath, Heine, Schlegel, Holty, Lenau, Wieland, Herder, Lessing, Kant, Fichte, Schelling, Winkelmann, Humboldt, Ranke, Raumer, Menzel, Gervinus, &c., and contains complete Goethe's "Iphigenie," Schiller's "Jungfrau;" also, for instruction in modern conversational German, Benedix's "Eigensinn."

There are besides, Biographical Sketches of each author contributing, Notes, explanatory and philological (after the text), Grammatical References to all leading grammars, as well as the editor's own, and an adequate Vocabulary.

Worman's German Echo 1 25

Consists of exercises in colloquial style entirely in the German, with an adequate vocabulary, not only of words but of idioms. The object of the system developed in this work (and its companion volume in the French) is to break up the laborious and tedious habit of *translating the thoughts*, which is the student's most effectual bar to fluent conversation, and to lead him to *think in the language in which he speaks*. As the exercises illustrate scenes in actual life, a considerable knowledge of the manners and customs of the German people is also acquired from the use of this manual.

Worman's German Copy-Books, 3 Numbers, each 15

On the same plan as the most approved systems for English penmanship, with progressive copies.

CHARTS.

McKenzie's Elocutionary Chart, ... $3 50

Baade's Reading Case, ... *10 00

This remarkable piece of school-room furniture is a receptacle containing a number of primary cards. By an arrangement of slides on the front, one sentence at a time is shown to the class. Twenty-eight thousand transpositions may be made, affording a variety of progressive exercises which no other piece of apparatus offers. One of its best features is, that it is so exceedingly simple as not to get out of order, while it may be operated with one finger.

Marcy's Eureka Tablet, ... *1 50

A new system for the Alphabet, by which it may be taught without fail in nine lessons.

Scofield's School Tablets, ... *8 00

On Five Cards, exhibiting Ten Surfaces. These Tablets teach Orthography, Reading, Object-Lessons, Color, Form, etc.

Watson's Phonetic Tablets, ... *8 00

Four Cards, and Eight Surfaces; teaching Pronunciation and Elocution phonetically—for class exercises.

Page's Normal Chart, ... *3 75

The whole science of Elementary Sounds tabulated. By the author of Page's Theory and Practice of Teaching.

Clark's Grammatical Chart, ... *3 75

Exhibits the whole Science of Language in one comprehensive diagram.

Davies' Mathematical Chart, ... *75

Mathematics made simple to the eye.

Monteith's Reference Maps (School Series), . . .*20 00

Eight Numbers. Mounted on Rollers. Names all laid down in small type, so that to the pupil at a short distance they are Outline Maps, while they serve as *their own key* to the teacher.

Willard's Chronographers, ... Each, *2 00

Historical. Four Numbers. Ancient Chronographer; English Chronographer; American Chronographer; Temple of Time (general). Dates and Events represented to the eye.

APPARATUS.

Harrington's Geometrical Blocks, ...*$10 00

These patented blocks are *hinged*, so that each form can be dissected.

Harrington's Fractional Blocks, ... *8 00

Steele's Chemical Apparatus, . . *20 00

Steele's Philosophical Apparatus, (see p.28) *125 00

Steele's Geological Cabinet, (see p.28) . . . *40 00

Wood's Botanical Apparatus, (see p.30) . . *8 00

Bock's Physiological Apparatus, ... 175 00

www.ingramcontent.com/pod-product-compliance
Lightning Source LLC
Chambersburg PA
CBHW031338230426
43670CB00006B/375
9783744692144